p. 149

DRUGS IN AMERICA

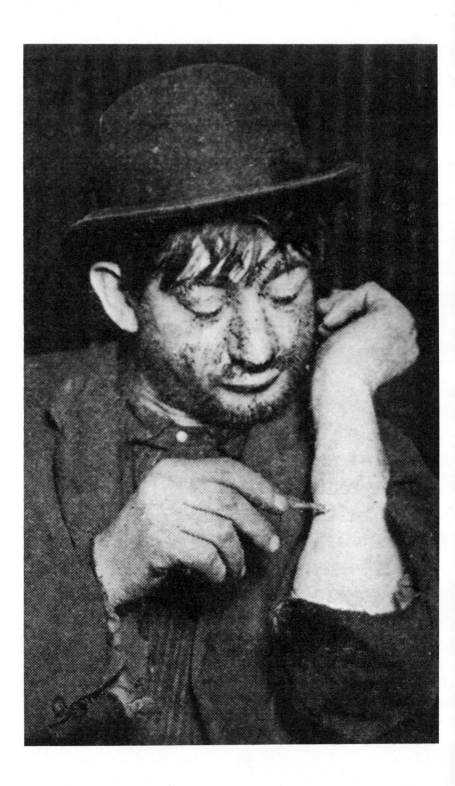

DRUGS IN AMERICA
A Social History,
1800-1980

H. WAYNE MORGAN

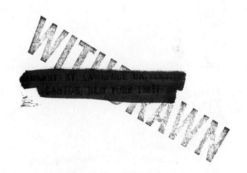

SYRACUSE UNIVERSITY PRESS   1981

H. Wayne Morgan is George Lynn Cross Research Professor of History at the University of Oklahoma, and author of numerous books, including *William McKinley and his America* and *New Muses: Art and American Culture, 1865– 1920,* and editor of *The Gilded Age* and *Industrial America: Readings in the Environment and Social Problems, 1865–1914.*

Library of Congress Cataloging in Publication Data

Morgan, H. Wayne (Howard Wayne)
  Drugs in America.

  Bibliography: p.
  Includes index.
  1. Drug abuse—United States—History. I. Title.
[DNLM: 1. Substance abuse—History—United States.
2. Substance dependence—History—United States.
3. Narcotics—History—United States.   4. Social
problems—History—United States.   WM 11 AA1 M8d]
HV5825.M669   362.2'93'0973   81-14613
ISBN 0-8156-2252-X   AACR2

Manufactured in the United States of America

CONTENTS

Illustrations

PREFACE

THIS BOOK DEVELOPED out of my general interest in the late nineteenth century. While reading through the popular press in connection with another project, I discovered a great deal of comment on the "opium problem," and on drug use in general. I unearthed several addict memoirs and other unusual sources, and the medical literature proved a gold mine of information. After further research, it seemed to me that a brief general survey of the question with some depth and fresh information was in order, and this book is the result.

This work is directed to the general reader rather than the expert, though I hope it will be of use to American historians in general. The subject of drug use is very complex, and I have tried to focus this chronological analytical narrative on the theme of the relationship between the drug user and the perceived drug experience, and society's apparent reactions. I have tried throughout to give a sense of what people at given times thought about the problem, and to let the parties involved tell their own stories wherever possible. My views, and those of others, are clear at appropriate places.

The history of drug use is attracting historians, and scholarly works on various aspects of the subject appear fairly regularly, which was not the case when I started my research. I have decided, therefore, to summarize the aspects of the subject for which there are good secondary sources. I have not recounted in detail the drive for regulation, which is well told in David F. Musto, *The American Disease* (1974). Nor have I retold the story in Arnold H. Taylor's *American Diplomacy and the Narcotics Traffic, 1900–1939* (1969). The same is true of the fine monograph by Richard J. Bonnie and Charles H. Whitebread II, *The Marihuana Conviction* (1974).

My main focus is on opiates, but with some attention to chloral hydrate, cannabis, and cocaine, as well as the procession of chemicals that have so enlivened the drug debate in the twentieth century. I do not cover alcohol, except tangentially in some comparisons, because its history seems separate from that of other drugs, however parallel the stories are in many respects. Nor do I discuss caffeine, tobacco, or tea, what might be called the habits of the home and office, against which there was considerable criticism throughout the larger debate on alcohol and drugs such as opiates and cocaine. Their story merits telling but seems outside my purposes.

A word on sources is also in order. The notes are copious but represent only a fraction of the material I reviewed. In most cases, especially for the nineteenth century, I have cited numerous sources in the notes in chronological order so that the interested reader who pursues them can see the development of the points indicated. I have also often cited material from several geographic parts of the country in order to show how this information spread through the communications network, especially for doctors.

I have tried my best throughout to offer accurate and meaningful generalizations, mindful of the fact that few subjects offer so many exceptions to generalizations as drug use or the public opinion it sparked. Nearly every aspect of the subject mentioned merits further detailed study, and I have made some suggestions for further research in the bibliographical essay.

I have also respected the privacy of patients involved and cite no such names unless they appeared in public print. In noting materials from manuscript collections such as those of Harry J. Anslinger or of the Keeley Institute, I use the initials of such correspondents. The abbreviations AMA and *JAMA* stand for the American Medical Association and its journal. The spelling of certain terms, such as hashish and marihuana, vary over time, and I have usually left them in their original without using *sic*.

Terminology poses something of a problem which I hope that common sense and a desire for simplicity have solved. I have read a great deal of technical literature but do not use its language except when absolutely necessary. People still employ the word "addiction" to indicate a habit that is hard to break, though the medical and psychological meanings are more exact. I take "addiction" to involve physical and psychological dependence on a substance and the development of tolerance. A substance is addictive if its discontinuance causes a set of symptoms called "withdrawal." The term "dependence" can apply to anything that may produce habitual use, whether from conditioning or psychological need, but whose discontinuance does not cause true withdrawal symptoms. There is still considerable debate on the addictive properties of some substances, but it is clear, for instance, that opiates are addictive, while cocaine or cannabis use potentially may develop into dependence. These are twentieth century terms and ideas; prior generations used words like "habitué," and "habit-forming." The terms "abuse" or "misuse" merely indicate society's apparent disapproval of drugs taken for nonmedical or "recreational" purposes. In this sense, a substance is open to abuse if it seems harmful to society's perceived general interests or to the user, whether through affecting the body or mind.

My own interpretations are obvious, but a word of explanation about the approach and general views may be helpful. No single theory or idea fully explains why people use drugs or desire a drug experience. Such a monocausal explanation becomes so large and abstract that it eliminates the people and variables in the story. Users doubtless turn to drugs for psychological reasons, for example, but these motives are very complex. Acting out the needs involved depends on the availability of the desired drugs; the approval of peers, or the disapproval of people the user wishes to punish or defy; the desire to escape problems or relieve anxiety; the search for pleasure or for other kinds of experience beyond the daily routine, and many similar goals that often even conflict. Thus an urge that we may say is basically psychological, and that may arise in any social circumstances, may take many often puzzling or contradictory forms, depending on the environmental circumstances and conditions of the user.

Efforts to control or end the use of suspected substances show similar multiple origins. It is tempting to find only "realistic" or material motives among opponents of drug use. Thus desires to protect authority, to make people conform to certain codes of behavior, to guard social status or professional interests, or to control feared opponents become the "real" motives behind the rhetoric of efforts at control. But control movements were founded in hope as well as fear and seemed liberal and humane to their proponents. Critics opposed drug and alcohol use because they represented behavior that affected society as well as the individual, and because their continuance seemed opposed to social progress.

In my view, Americans have opposed drug use and feared drug experiences because they seemed to threaten a generally accepted set of values and aspirations that dated from the beginnings of the national experience. These involved an individualism that was responsive to larger social needs and that conformed to limits; the need for order, efficiency, and predictability that kept the entire society going; productivity that enriched the society as well as the producer; an emphasis on the observable reality of the world rather than flights of imagination; and a rational mentality and emotional stability that were the hallmarks of liberty based on conscious logic. Drug experiences and effects seemed to produce opposite results, and social disapproval was not merely repressive or irrational in its intentions. These reactions intensified after the 1870s, when the fear of enslavement to drugs entered the debate, and when the new industrial order seemed more interconnected and thus more dependent on rational behavior than ever before.

The racial imagery that was so common at peaks of concern about drug use is equally complex. Every such image represented profound conflicts and fears. The Near Easterners who figured in the early concern about cannabis use symbolized passivity and backwardness that seemed diametrically opposed to the developing American nation. Opium use appeared to be a major factor in China's apparent stagnation and inability to become modern. The black who figured in the sharp debate over cocaine represented violence and irrationality, as did the Mexican in the later debate about marihuana. And the hippie flower child, the most recent analogous stereotype, was supposedly passive, unproductive, and hostile to the basic values of thrift, productivity, rationality, and realism.

These images were powerful foci of debate, but in each case the adverse public reaction grew not only from fear of these groups or the need to control them. It also represented the desire to isolate the effects of their actions from the larger society. In this view, drugs and the drug experience were major causes of the threatening and unattractive conditions of the people involved, and drug use might cause that condition in anyone. Control, education, or prohibition were thus in order. This attitude was also clear in social disapproval of marginal groups such as bohemian intellectuals and artists, itinerant musicians, and petty criminals who seemed uninterested in accepting the society's central values. Critics saw drug use as an aspect or cause of this rejection.

The study of history can develop perspective or a sense of irony. Throughout my research I have tried to recall the implications in the observation of an anonymous morphine addict written in 1876: "This is an inquisitive, an experimenting, and a daring age, — an age that has a lively contempt for the constraints and timorous inactivity of ages past. Its quick-thinking and restless humanity are prying into everything. Opium will not pass by untampered with." This same observation is as true today as then and doubtless will merit quoting in generations to come. Every enduring social problem is rooted in some basic debate over inherited values and can neither be comprehended nor affected without an understanding of its history.

It is a pleasure to thank the many people who helped me write this book over a longer period of time than I anticipated when I started it. The staff of the National Library of Medicine is superb, and I am especially grateful for the issuance of a stack pass that allowed me to explore the medical literature in detail. In that institution's History of Medicine Division, Mrs. Dorothy Hanks, a great reference librarian, was especially helpful.

Mr. J. H. Oughton, Jr., of Dwight, Illinois, whose grandfather was a partner of Leslie E. Keeley, granted me permission to use the Keeley Collection at the Illinois State Historical Library in Springfield. He also shared some memories, and showed me around Dwight, which retains many aspects of the Keeley years.

Several friends were equally helpful. My former colleagues at the University of Texas at Austin, Clarence G. Lasby and Lewis L. Gould, both read the manuscript. I profited from their suggestions even when I did not take all of their advice. Mr. Harry Hogan of the Congressional Research Service at the Library of Congress read the manuscript in the light of his knowledge of the present-day drug problem. He was also a generous host during several of my stays in Washington. In my own department, Professors Russell D. Buhite and James L. Goldsmith were very helpful with constructive criticisms. Professor Harold M. Hyman of Rice University was a source of encouragement. Professor David Courtwright of the University of Hartford generously shared with me his great knowledge of the history of opiate addiction. Mrs. Amy Moorhead read the manuscript carefully and saved me from many stylistic lapses. As usual, my greatest thanks are due my wife Anne, who has survived the writing of yet another book.

Norman, Oklahoma   H. WAYNE MORGAN
Fall 1981

DRUGS IN AMERICA

GOD'S OWN MEDICINE

OLIVER WENDELL HOLMES was one of America's most famous nineteenth-century cultural figures. Whether as Autocrat of the Breakfast Table or genial after-dinner speaker he commanded an audience. But he was first and foremost a doctor who treated patients, wrote about medicine, and taught the next generation of Harvard MDs. He was born in 1809 and died in 1894. He lived through the twilight of colonial medicine, the age of "heroic therapy" of bleeding and purging, and the onset of dramatic discoveries in a new medicine allied with science.

In 1860 he warned colleagues against the overuse of drugs; many were irrelevant to therapy, and some were harmful to patients. He suggested in a famous sally that, with few exceptions, if "the whole materia medica, *as now used,* could be sunk to the bottom of the sea, it would be all the better for mankind—and all the worse for the fishes." Yet while attacking the vestiges of "heroic therapy," fads, and nostrums, he specifically exempted opium. It retained a majesty inherited from ancient practice and was a natural substance "which the Creator himself seems to prescribe, for we often see the scarlet poppy growing in the cornfields, as if it were foreseen that wherever there is a hunger to be fed there must also be pain to be soothed. . . . "[1] In saying this he echoed the thinking of medicine's greatest heroes and of those who dubbed opium "God's Own Medicine," even though he cautioned against its overuse.

Most opium came from Turkey or Asia but was so widely used that many writers at the turn of the nineteenth century suggested home cultivation. Some people experimented with the results on themselves and friends.[2] One Baltimore doctor suggested that it was "worth the attention of gardeners to cultivate the poppy for use as well as beauty."[3] These early growers chiefly wanted to end reliance on expensive imported opium, and to produce an American variety that was both potent and predictable in effects. By 1810 a popular dispensatory suggested that "Such is the intrinsic value of opium, and such the high price which it commands, that every method, promising to increase the quantity in the market, should be encouraged as of great importance to the community."[4]

Throughout the nineteenth century people tried poppy cultivation in many parts of the country. The southern states seemed a logical place, especially when the Civil War ended imports there. Strains of poppies grew to some extent in Virginia, Georgia, Tennessee, South Carolina, Florida, and Louisiana.[5] The dry sunny Southwest also seemed suitable, and experimenters grew them in Arizona Territory and California. The plants grew easily in California. One writer suggested in 1866 that trained monkeys or Chinese coolies could form the small labor supply needed to tend such crops there. Even if the morphine content of the resulting gum were low, the quantity would help meet the rapidly increasing demand in the United States.[6] Poppies also grew in Pennsylvania, Vermont, Massachusetts, New Hampshire, and Connecticut.[7] But the cost of producing American opium made it uncompetitive with that of Turkey and the Near East. The United States continued to import opium, which had two long-term social effects. Imports rose faster than the rate of population growth after the 1840s, and these statistics fortified the idea that opiate use was increasing rapidly. And in the long run, imports made it appear that foreigners were adversely affecting American life.

Various forms of opium became familiar as the century developed. The thick resinous variety used in smoking was not widely known in the United States until about mid-century, when it became identified first with the Chinese and then with a broader range of smokers. Gum and powdered opium were readily available but usually appeared in solutions. Mixed with alcohol and water either formed the ancient compound laudanum. The "opium eaters" of public fancy and news reports usually drank opium in this form. The drug's camphorated tincture was paregoric, a familiar weapon in the battle against dysentery and as a pacifier for infants. Opium in solution was widely used in many famous cordials, syrups and elixirs, familiar companions of the nursery or medicine chest under such titles as "Black Drop" or "Mrs. Winslow's Soothing Syrup." Opium's principal alkaloid, morphine, became available as powder, tablet, or liquid. The "morphine eater," who began to appear in the post–Civil War years, consumed the drug in tablet form. But this yielded among "morphinists" to dissolving the tablets in water or to using a prepared solution for a hypodermic injection.

Opium was familiar to both doctors and laymen. Dispensatories and home medical handbooks contained recipes for laudanum and paregoric, whose ingredients were readily available in all but the most remote places. In the 1820s, the unsuspecting bought false gum opium, like wooden nutmegs, at fairs and medicine shows.[8] Self-medication was universal, given both the lack of doctors in many sections and the public suspicion of physicians. Many home remedies contained alcohol, opium, or both; potential users at least knew that these substances had some effect in treating illnesses.

In the first decades of the nineteenth century, doctors prescribed opiates widely, often merely to help the body control symptoms that no one understood, or to ease a dying patient's last hours. Opiates were seldom prescribed as an actual cure, even in an age that did not understand the causes of most diseases. They were part of a broader therapy, used chiefly to relieve distress through sedation to help nature heal the patient if the doctor's efforts failed. In a period with few sedatives, opiates were vital to the physician. Many of opium's effects were puzzling, yet the typical doctor and patient knew enough about its actions from tradition and experience to remain positive about its use.

The maladies calling for opium ran the gamut of human experience. It was well known in controlling dysentery, since it retarded secretions in general. An Ohio doctor reported in 1852 that he had taken opium for a year to prevent contracting the widespread dysentery he treated in the district.[9] He doubtless felt unwell if he reduced or omitted the dose, which fortified a tendency to consider it a preventative.

Doctors also employed opium against the varied fevers that were so common in frontier and rural America.[10] It was recommended for inflammation and swelling.[11] Rheumatism, a constant complaint throughout the century, persistent pain resulting from pinched nerves, or "neuralgia," a catch-all category—all responded to the opiates that came so freely from the doctor's bag and apothecary's shelves.[12] In their bewilderment at certain disorders, doctors sometimes ascribed great power to opium. In 1860 one suggested that it cured pneumonia; in 1870 another recommended it to suppress urine production in diabetics.[13]

Opiates were a friend indeed in emergencies. The man run over in the street, the worker with a broken leg, the child with a cut scalp all took opium. It relieved pain and allowed the doctor control while setting bones or sewing skin. Physicians recommended opiates to relieve lockjaw, sudden spasms in childbirth, delirium tremens, persistent headache, and to relax muscles while repairing hernia.[14] By the mid-nineteenth century, opiates were gaining some use in treating mental patients. It was only a short step to using them in more subtle complaints subsumed under the rubric of nervous disorders.[15]

The early handbooks and texts were cheerful about "God's Own Medicine," while warning against overdose. "Of all the articles of the materia medica, this is, perhaps, the most extensively useful, there being scarcely one morbid affection or disordered condition of the system in which, under certain circumstances, it is not exhibited, either alone, or in combination," a writer said in 1821.[16]

This use of and faith in opiates did not imply understanding of their actions in the body. Authorities could not agree on whether opium was a stimulant or depressant, for instance. The doctor who saw an agonized patient fall asleep after a dose of opium took it to be a valuable depressant. The observer who watched an opium user in the twilight stage between sleep and wakefulness, assumed it was some kind of stimulant. The addict who prized the imaginative expansion he thought opium produced usually considered it a stimulant, however mysterious its workings.

Samuel Crumpe, an eighteenth-century English writer, concluded that opium was a stimulant which overloaded the brain as dosage increased and produced the unconsciousness that made it appear a depressant. A generation later an American writer suggested one among many interpretations, that opium increased blood circulation. It was "not improbable that it excites and subsequently disturbs the sensorial function, as a consequence of this excited arterial action," he noted in 1826.[17]

Similar uncertainties and misunderstandings surrounded the phenomena of tolerance and addiction. The need to increase dosage of opiates to obtain the same or greater effect was obvious from some symptoms of regular users. Yet the medical journals, and often the public press, reported on heavy users who attained great longevity and lived apparently normal lives. How dangerous was opium when taken regularly, even in large doses? As late as 1876 one report concerned an English sea captain who was allegedly 106 years old, and who attributed his great years and good health to the pacifying effects of opium.[18] Equally puzzling was the huge dosage that many people survived. This led one doctor to ask colleagues at a medical meeting in 1858 if they had not "somewhat overestimated the poisoning qualities of opium? If not, I would ask, what is the peculiar condition of the system, or under what circumstances, and why is it, that the system is enabled at times to withstand such monstrous quantities of opium?"[19]

How users became addicted to the drug was equally obscure yet was obvious from the symptoms of those who stopped using it. The Englishman John Jones, who wrote an early book on opium, realized that sudden deprivation made users anxious, depressed, and irritable.[20] In 1823 a medical journal warned against the problem. "Nothing makes one more miserably dependent than the use of opium, as a temporary stimulant against feelings of exhaustion attending artificial modes of life. When its excitement ceases, almost insufferable, long anxiety and irritation succeeds."[21] Yet as late as 1869 an Alabama physician reported naively that he had taken two to four grains of morphine a day for three years, chiefly to fight colds and catarrh, and clearly did not consider himself an addict.[22]

Given the differences in training among doctors, and the ignorance of the self-medicating public, these mysteries had long lives. But at the same time common sense drawn from observation sounded cautionary notes. Jones concluded that moderation was called for in using opiates, as with everything else in life. "There is nothing so good, whereof an *Intemperate Use* is not *mischievous*, God having so ordered it to deter from, and punish *Intemperance*, and the *Abuse* of his *Creatures,*" he noted. He went on to see nonmedical use as both dangerous and a moral lapse, a major idea in the later drug debate. "Therefore ill *Effects* are not always to be imputed to the *viciousness* of the things used, but frequently to the *Person* that imprudently uses them."[23]

In due course, American authorities cautioned against addiction. In 1810 a medical handbook noted: "Like spirits, tobacco, and other substances called narcotics, by frequent use the system becomes accustomed to its [opium's] stimulus, and refuses to obey without an increase of the quantity."[24] In 1822 another handbook warned against using opiates too freely with obviously nervous patients, who might overuse them.[25] These early commentators were at least aware of the general importance of psychological factors in drug use.

By the Civil War era authorities understood that dependence was somehow at work. In 1869 a medical editor told a bewildered doctor-addict trying to abandon morphine: "Rest assured on one thing—that the unpleasant sensations you experience on quitting the drug, are more owing to the loss of it than to any disease."[26] Yet clinical concepts of addiction and tolerance developed only in the 1870s and after, when opiate use began to alarm both Europeans and Americans.[27] Throughout the century authorities could not really explain how opiates worked in the body. This left open a fruitful field for speculation, invention, and error. Some users simply denied any adverse effects from opiates. Many doctors did not believe that they were addictive and overprescribed them. And a host of quacks, and even sincere "cure doctors" developed fanciful explanations of the opiates' workings to justify their theories and treatments. This confusion ultimately worked in favor of legislative control, when the public decided that all theories were suspect and that the absence of opium was the best cure for addiction.

As early as the first decades of the century, opium also began to gain adverse associations. Authorities warned against its poisonous effects, even while praising it in normal usage.[28] It became increasingly identified with unwelcome social change and human behavior, as in the case of suicide. In 1810 a medical writer warned: "It is a melancholy consideration, that the excellent, kind assuager of our bodily pains and mental distress, is frequently resorted to for the horrid purpose of self-destruction."[29] Reports that prostitutes, drunkards, and the emotionally disturbed often died from overdoses did not enhance the drug's reputation.[30] These facts reflected the human anxieties of an increasingly complex social order. But the society at large doubtless thought in smaller terms and blamed the drug. Opium was identified chiefly with healing and surcease from pain, but it always had a darker side in the public imagination.

The most curious aspect of this duality to early observers was the fascination the drug held for some users. Jones had noted early the tendency of opiates to relieve anxiety, produce psychic warmth, and create a sense of the ability to manage problems. For this reason, a Greenwich apothecary had suggested in 1763 that everyone keep silent about opium lest its appeal increase.[31] By the time Americans became conscious of an opium problem, English intellectuals like Samuel Taylor Coleridge and Thomas De Quincey had advertised the drug's psychic powers.

In the 1820s and 1830s there seemed little need to caution the public against the nonmedicinal use of opiates. This habit did not seem destined to affect America much. A reviewer of De Quincey's *Confessions of an English Opium Eater* in 1824 was confident if not smug in explaining why he bothered with the book. "We believe that very few persons, if any, in this country, abandon themselves to the use of opium as a luxury, nor does there appear to be any great danger of the introduction of this species of intemperance." He recommended the book "more as an object of taste and literary curiosity, than by way of warning persons against a pernicious practice."[32]

A decade later a major medical journal was still certain that few people used opiates to escape from anything except pain. "Of those who take opium for purposes of unnatural excitement and inebriation, we have no knowledge," the editors noted. But they indicated an already established division of approval between use for medical and nonmedical reasons. "They need less of our sympathy, and would excite us less to exertions on their behalf."[33]

The story began to change in the 1840s as opium imports rose. Doctors were using opium widely in normal practice with little thought of addiction. Patent nostrums containing opium and alcohol were increasingly popular. Perhaps there was a growing reliance on opium in areas that adopted temperance legislation.[34] At the same time missionaries and other reformers added emotional scope to the issue. They condemned as uncivilized and un-Christian American participation in the Chinese opium traffic, "this crime of freighting a poison, which leads to certain moral infatuation, degradation and death. . . . "[35] Dr. Nathan Allen of Massachusetts attacked the British during the Opium Wars for fostering China's decadence. One reviewer of Allen's book agreed that "the horrors of the opium trade beggar description, and are worse to its victims than any outward slavery."[36]

Long before drug use became a topic of national debate, an adverse image of the opium user was at hand, one that could easily transfer to users of other drugs and crystallize many social concerns. This image derived from foreign models, whether English, Chinese, or Near Eastern. It combined ill health, social irresponsibility, and personality that was degraded through enslavement. One report of an English "opium eater" in 1824 summarized many attitudes and fears. This responsible, able-bodied young man became addicted to opiates and declined into poverty, rootlessness, and imprisonment.[37] This was clearly an example Americans should note and avoid.

Fourteen years later in 1838 a major medical journal depicted the opium addict as a walking corpse, social outcast, and dead personality:

> The habitual opium-eater is instantly recognized by his appearance. A total attenuation of body, a withered, yellow countenance, a lame gait, a bending of the spine, frequently to such a degree as to assume a circular form, and glossy, deep-sunken eyes, betray him at first glance. The digestive organs are in the highest degree disturbed; the sufferer eats scarcely anything, and has hardly one evacuation in a week! his mental and bodily powers are destroyed—he is impotent. By degrees, as the habit becomes more confirmed, his strength continues decreasing, the craving for the stimulus becomes even greater, and to produce the desired effect, the dose must be constantly augmented. . . . These people seldom attain the age of forty, if they have begun to use opium at an early age. The torments of the victim of opium, when deprived of this stimulant, are as dreadful as his bliss is complete when he has taken it.[38]

This was greatly exaggerated and not the universal outcome of opiate addiction. Many addicts appeared relatively normal in their social dealings. But the public appeal of this and similar imagery over the decades to come was great and developed out of the corollary notion that opiates were enslaving. Long before the debate over drug use flared into social concern and legislation, it was clear that addiction affected the personality as well as the body. No commentators saw it as a normal or desirable condition, however much they might sympathize with an addict.

Concern about the misuse of opiates at mid-century grew out of their connection with slavery, illness, and oblivion. Yet opium retained a powerful fascination for many people. After trying to explain why it had ravaged China, Nathan Allen analyzed this attraction in prophetic words:

> There seems to be a wonderful power in the use of this drug, to attract and captivate. It holds out a temptation far more powerful than that of any other intoxicating agent. Such is the testimony of experience as well as observation in the matter. This fascination does not arise merely from that passion in human nature for excitement—that yearning after stimulus and that horror of ennui which crowd the Parisian Theater, but from having experienced or heard of that peculiar state of ecstasy which can be produced only by this drug, and which has not inappropriately in some respects, been termed the 'Chinese Heaven.'[39]

The number of users, and the likelihood of spreading use, were uncertain when he wrote in 1850. Yet addicts were hidden throughout the society. They were an irregular lot, cutting across social and occupational lines. Doctors clearly had addicted many people suffering from chronic illnesses. Still more users were "nervous," avoiding psychic pain, or seeking escape. On farmsteads and in remote villages otherwise abstemious people were addicted to medicinal opiates. There was also the occasional rebellious youth, and dissatisfied intellectual, whether at the village store or city street corner. And now and then, a traveller from an antique land told stories of wondrous substances that created dreams. In the West, the Chinese population was becoming the first group to be identified with drug use.

As the nation wrestled with slavery, transcontinental development, a growing industrial system and its attendant human problems, drug use seemed a minor question. It was still something the average American would never see or adopt. But a new society was aborning that included some groups that might find a drug experience to their liking. This new society also was emphasizing a set of standards for individual conduct that rested on sobriety, productivity, and order. It stressed the inherited ideal of individualism, but only within the confines of a system that rested on efficiency, rationality, and predictability. The concentration of people in cities, rapid communications, and the inter-locked web of production reinforced the apparent need for these per-sonal characteristics and general values and aspirations. These attitudes were as old as the nation, but the stakes were changing. The new industrial society would frown upon, ostracize, and then attempt to control deviations from this system of conduct. These values and aspira-tions might be "middle class" or "bourgeois," but they dominated all levels of American society and became something much larger than a class standard, a national consensus.

These tensions and challenges that might affect drug use were emerging by the 1850s. And the world faced changes in therapeutics that promised better health and a proliferating array of substances that might provoke social as well as medical concern.

2

THE THERAPEUTIC REVOLUTION

NATIONAL CONCERN ABOUT NON-MEDICAL DRUG USE began in the transition period between "heroic therapy" and a new age of medicine allied with experimental science. Beneath the sectarian quarrels of the homeopath, herbalist, and orthodox physician, profound changes worked to alter the thinking and practice of doctors everywhere. The country grew rapidly and unevenly, and medical practice was scarcely the same in all its sections. Yet the forces of change tended to make doctors everywhere more aware of the latest research and methods, and more willing to employ new therapeutics.

This was evident in the printed matter they read. Gone were the days when the rural physician had to rely on a wrapper of instructions around a bottle, a pamphlet from a drug house, or a handbook that might be out of date. If he wished, he could now read of new therapeutics almost as quickly as they were announced. Every major city boasted some body that issued a journal. By the 1840s, smaller cities and every region of the country produced medical journals. Newspapers and popular periodicals also reported on scientific and medical developments. A general communications network grew rapidly. The idea or method announced in a Boston or New York medical journal in November appeared in the December issue of regional publications in Chicago, Louisville, New Orleans, and San Francisco. The major reviews summarized European events, which passed through this communications network. By the post–Civil War decades medicine was subdivided enough to warrant specialized journals, including some in psychology and neurology that became important in the drug debate.

At the same time, the physician's handbooks, texts, and reference works improved. There were professional meetings almost everywhere. And while medical education lagged in many respects, it improved throughout the nineteenth century. The information and ideas at work within this system were not always correct, but the total process enhanced a general sense of intellectual and practical progress.

These abstract developments attained humanity in the physician. Each new generation of practitioners considered itself more modern and better equipped than its fathers. More and more new MDs studied abroad, first in England or Scotland until about the 1830s, then in Paris, and finally after the 1860s in Berlin or Vienna. Once in practice, the new generation of physicians slowly gained increased respect and trust, both among patients and from society at large. Medicine's bad reputation, dating from the "heroic therapy" that killed as often as it cured, lessened after mid-century. These changes in prestige also reflected advances in medical knowledge, better prevention of communicable diseases, and the growing authority of experimental science, all of which enhanced the doctor's image.

The physician remained a major figure in the social setting. Whether in rural New England or Boston, in Chicago or Peoria, hamlet or metropolis, he entered more closely into the community's life than his successors did. On the whole, he focused first on the patient, then on the disease. At the same time he gained prestige as an agent of modernization, one who knew more of the world, the body, and perhaps the personality than others did. His rising sense of self-confidence also ironically made the physician quick to use all the new discoveries, especially in the prevention of pain and production of rest. He trusted, perhaps overtrusted, the experts beyond his office who supposedly understood the complexities of new substances that in the end were liable to misuse as well as medicinal use.

The old-fashioned apothecary also changed. The drug business became the pharmaceutical profession. New journals, associations, pharmacopoeia, and educational changes there paralleled those in the physician's world. The compounds the pharmacist dispensed became more exact and predictable in actions, thanks to standardization and technological improvements in pill-making.[1] The catch-all nostrums remained on the shelf, but by the Civil War medicines were more accurately prepared than ever before. They were also easier to prescribe, dispense, and use.

The variety of those medicines increased rapidly throughout the nineteenth century. A few examples entered the public mind and symbolized the progress in chemistry. Morphine was isolated from opium in

1803 and after about the 1820s became synonymous with relief from pain. Chloroform and ether captured the public imagination after the 1840s as the first successful anesthetics in surgery. The plant products of coca and cannabis were discovered or rediscovered and refined. In the latter part of the century came a wave of new substances, often from Germany, that controlled pain or produced ease and sleep: Chloral hydrate (1869), paraldehyde (1882), sulphonal (1889), veronal (1898), and morphine's great shadow substance named heroin (1898).* So rapidly did the flood of new and often overpraised remedies come that in 1869 one journal lamented of a newly touted therapy: "We trust the method will not share the fate of nine-tenths of the new remedies and new plans, which blaze up with dazzling brightness and then vanish."[2]

The twentieth century opened the floodgates to a series of substances that altered mood and which were susceptible to nonmedicinal use. Many of the new boons to medicine, whether to relieve pain or induce sleep, seemed open to what society called abuse, or nonmedicinal use and potential dependence. Discoveries in chemistry and medicine thus had social impacts. Nor did the ironies of progress end there. For while the doctor's reputation grew steadily through his alliance with modernity and science, his actual understanding lagged well behind technological and chemical discoveries. The flood of therapeutics was far greater than anyone could master. And knowledge of the workings of these substances in the body, especially in the nervous system, remained uncertain and often erroneous.

The most magic of these substances was morphine, the major alkaloid of opium, named after Morpheus the Greek god of sleep. Its advantages over other forms of opium were numerous. In powder or tablet form it less often caused nausea, headaches, or stomach irritation than did opium in gum or solutions. More important, chemists soon prepared precise dosages, and its actions became predictable.[3] It was one of the first substances injected beneath the skin and became popular after it was packaged in bottles and then ampules for hypodermic use. By the 1860s, doctors were using it against all sorts of pain and distress, despite some warnings about addiction.[4] Morphine became and remained the doctor's constant companion because of its low cost, known action, and ease of administration. There were few regulations anywhere against its sale, and as its reputation grew countless patients purchased it and hypodermic kits for self-use.

---

*Cocaine is dealt with in the following pages for the nineteenth century; both it and heroin, which figured chiefly in the drive for regulation, are treated in Chapter 6.

Though their use did not become as widespread as morphine, chloroform and ether also went through a cycle of nonmedicinal appeal. Both substances were used as anesthetics in surgery and dentistry by the late 1840s and became fads in the next decade. The press reported that medical and dental students used them in "jags" and parties. For a time they were fashionable among young people given to hijinks, and to those in high society bent on intoxication without suffering a hangover.

Both popular and professional evaluations of chloroform remained ambivalent. It seemed to have no aftereffects and did not produce tolerance. In 1851 a doctor reported that "the intemperate use of chloroform is attended with far less danger than is the same use of alcohol or opium."[5] It was also later attractive to some people who "desired a respirable deliriant without the disreputable associations which attach themselves to the use of alcoholic drinks."[6] Toward the end of the century, chloroform still had its devotees in many hidden places. The high society matron and potential suicide, the insomniac and the bored college student alike apparently used it. As late as 1911 the *New York Times* reported on chloroform habits in the Boston area. And in 1912 a southern doctor offered several cases of its uses among young people, calling it "the devil's own embodiment."[7]

The medical profession warned constantly against the danger of death from overdose in using ether and chloroform. And outside the dentist's chair and surgeon's amphitheater, their use seemed frivolous and merely escapist. They were not addictive, but the sense of calm, ease, and freedom from anxiety they produced was attractive to many people and thus potentially habit-forming. Only the convenience of using morphine hypodermically probably kept them from becoming more popular among people inclined to employ drugs for escape or release of tensions.

The story of two other new substances, chloral hydrate and cocaine, vividly illustrated how rapidly the news travelled in the medical world, and how easy it was to overestimate new wonder drugs.

By the 1860s, an increasing number of patients crowded into doctors' offices seeking relief from insomnia and the general inability to rest. Medicine needed a safe, predictable and nonhabit-forming hypnotic to treat these disorders. In 1869 a German chemist produced chloral hydrate, which in first reports seemed a perfect solution. Once again, society's apparent needs and science had met, predisposing people to approve of a new substance.

Chloral hydrate was noted as far west as St. Louis by the end of 1869. In the spring of 1870 it was available in San Francisco. One doctor there praised it in treating delirium tremens, while another thought it was generally overrated. By November the Bay Area medical community was already suspicious. "It is wrong to claim for it a harmlessness which belongs to no active remedy yet discovered."[8] Elsewhere it seemed attractive because of its quick action in inducing sleep. It was potentially toxic but easily measured in exact doses and did not seem to cause dependence.[9]

One asylum superintendent called it "this now almost indispensable remedy in controlling the insomnia and restlessness of mania in all our insane asylums," in 1871. He even suggested a concoction: "It acts like a charm if given in half a pint of rich eggnog, at bedtime, well charged with whiskey." It seemed to be "a remedy which is now doing, in the insane hospitals of the land, more than all other remedies combined, in leading back the erratic wanderings of the insane mind to the realms of reason restored."[10]

In the years that followed, chloral hydrate developed a favorable reputation among doctors treating alcoholism, delirium tremens, and mania. One southern physician was "disposed to believe, as an internal remedy, the discovery of this drug to be the greatest boon to suffering humanity that has been discovered for the last half of a century."[11] Before long, chloral hydrate had the cachet of identification with "brain work" as well as brain disorders. "Chloral is a valuable remedy for sleeplessness in exhaustion of the brain through mental application..." one doctor noted in 1881.[12]

Opinions differed on its liability to misuse. An early analyst argued that it did not produce an imagined world of dreams and fancies like opium, or light-headed escape like chloroform. Surely no one wanted to be asleep or stupefied more than was necessary to good health. "Hence we have the full assurance that it cannot be used by the common people to abuse themselves with producing their supposed happiness."[13] Another writer in 1877 doubted that there would be any "chloral eaters."[14]

Other observers were not so sure; after all, chloral was available at the drugstore like morphine or chloroform for those inclined to use it. In 1871 a doctor feared that "with their characteristic anxiety for dosing themselves," Americans would overuse all the new remedies, especially in the absence of regulation.[15] A year later another writer saw a chloral habit developing because so many people sought rest and release from tension. "Men and women who suffer from sleeplessness habitually, are easily tempted to resort to it, and many, very many do it," he insisted. And it was no respecter of persons, an increasingly familiar pattern in drug use. "Amongst its votaries are businessmen, harassed with great anxieties, school-teachers, bookkeepers, invalid women made weaker

by family cares; in each of these instances I have seen chloral victims."
Though not in his opinion as prevalent yet as habituation to morphine or
even bromides, chloral hydrate was on its way.[16]

By the end of the 1870s, Dr. Jansen B. Mattison of Brooklyn,
emerging as a major authority on drug abuse, saw chloral's fascination
for certain kinds of people. "Chloral seems to possess a special adapta-
bility for self-taking; it has such a wonderful power in bringing sleep and
freedom from mental worry and jar, the reverse of which is so often
prominent in almost every department of active life."[17] It was thus
potentially habit-forming and escapist. Its steady use also reduced efficiency and mental power and altered the personality adversely. It also
seemed especially attractive to an important social group: middle-class
women exhausted from efforts to maintain their families' stations in life.
A rough survey in 1881, however, showed that most users were men.
And while their ages ran from 20 to 70, a majority were between 30 and
50, the prime of life.[18]

A generation after its introduction into medical use, chloral hydrate seemed a classic case of the tendency to overpraise and overuse
every new chemical discovery in modern medicine. It figured prominently in the suicide statistics and in deaths from accidental overdose.
Many people were doubtless dependent on it. And it proved the new
experts wrong. William Rosser Cobbe, a famous opium addict, noted in
his memoirs in 1895: "Physicians insisted for years that a 'habit' was
impossible for the chloral user, and there are some who still persist in the
claim that one may take the drug indefinitely without harmful results; in
the face of indisputable testimony that the country is full of chloral
habitues. There is not one town or city in the United States that is free
from slaves of the somnific, 'colorless, bitterish, caustic crystal.'"[19]

Some people became concerned precisely because chloral hydrate was attractive to important elements of the new industrial order,
the thinker, the organizer and planner, and the woman in a new social
role. The popularity of chloral hydrate was alarming in some measure
because it was liable to cause death from overdose. But it was equally
dangerous if it depressed or controlled people's minds, even while
affording some rest. If it became a habit, it then reduced the power of
their sensibilities, their reasoning, and energies, and became a matter of
social concern.

The story of coca well summarized the conflicts and ironies in the
therapeutic revolution. The coca leaf was familiar to some chemists and
travellers but was not significant in medicine at mid-century. Europeans
in the areas of South America where it grew, especially Peru, knew from
local traditions that the leaves relieved fatigue and hunger in those who

chewed them. By the late 1850s, European chemists isolated the plant's major alkaloid and christened it cocaine. There were scattered reports of its role as a mental stimulant, but coca products were not well known in America until the 1870s and 1880s.

In 1877 an article in a prestigious medical journal predicted that coca would soon attain great popularity and suggested caution in using it. Its habit-forming qualities were uncertain, but its reactions varied widely in individuals. The author warned that it affected personality and social behavior, but urged caution chiefly because the world was awash in new substances that everyone tended to overuse. "I trust that the profession will thoroughly examine into the merits and demerits of the article, and give the full negative results of their investigations," he said. "I say *negative,* for that is the evidence demanded at the present day. We are overrun with positive evidence, all virtues being ascribed to all remedies to such an extent that we become lost in seeking information. What we need to know is what medicine will *not* do."[20] The warning was timely but as was the case with other substances went unheeded. Both experts and laymen often failed to distinguish between coca and cocaine, whose effects were different. Like all alkaloids, cocaine was much more potent than its parent coca.

By the mid-1880s, cocaine appeared as another wonder drug in the growing list of new discoveries. Reports of the work of Sigmund Freud and other European experts who praised it as an anesthetic and stimulant were printed in American journals and the press as soon as received. Major drug houses offered cocaine for sale at high prices, which declined as early as the spring of 1886 when production increased to meet great demand.[21]

Various coca preparations soon went on the market as tonics and restoratives. The most famous was *Vin Mariani*, which Angelo Mariani manufactured in France for worldwide sale. In short order this and similar preparations became as popular as bottled mineral waters. Most such concoctions consisted of a good wine in which coca leaves, spices, and flavorings had soaked.

A flood of testimonials from world figures, including kings, writers, and captains of industry, preceded Mariani's salesmen to sing the praises of coca wine in alleviating depression and fatigue. As an American said of one such formula: "Indeed, this wine is beneficial in all instances in which it is desirable to increase the vital powers. Coca appears to be the one agent that can be thus employed without fear of the depression that so generally follows the use of other stimulants."[22] The various wines of coca actually contained only small amounts of the plant's active agent and were tonic in effect. They even fortified General U. S. Grant in a race against death to finish his memoirs.[23]

"Mariani Bottle" showing Shape and Label.

We are justified in saying: Never has anything been so highly recommended and every trial proves its excellence.

"Mariani Bottle" showing Outside Wrapper.

Size of Regular Bottle, half litre (about 17 ounces).

Never sold in bulk—to guard against substitution.

VIN MARIANI

Nourishes - Fortifies Refreshes

Aids Digestion - Strengthens the System.

Unequaled as a tonic-stimulant for fatigued or overworked Body and Brain.

Prevents Malaria, Influenza and Wasting Diseases.

We cannot aim to gain support for our preparation through cheapness; we give a uniform, effective and honest article, and respectfully ask personal testing of **Vin Mariani** strictly on its own merits. Thus the medical profession can judge whether **Vin Mariani** is deserving of the unequaled reputation it has earned throughout the world during more than 30 years.

Inferior, so-called Coca preparations (variable solutions of Cocaine and cheap wines), which have been proven worthless, even harmful in effect, bring into discredit and destroy confidence in a valuable drug.

We therefore particularly caution to specify always " VIN MARIANI," thus we can guarantee invariable satisfaction to physician and patient.

Advertisement for Vin Mariani, a popular wine of coca. From Angelo Mariani, *Coca and Its Therapeutic Application* (1896).

Cocaine became popular in treating another range of complaints. An 1880 article called it "a great antidote for the blues."[24] By 1885 the Parke-Davis drug company was experimenting with it in various social as well as medicinal guises. They even offered a cigar containing cocaine. "After dinner he smoked a couple of the cigars," they reported of one subject's experiences, "with the effect that the 'blues' were expelled and he felt the exhilarating effect of the drug in the same manner as after a dose of the wine."[25] The number of vague, nervous complaints increased dramatically after the Civil War, and doctors welcomed any new drug that combatted depression and anxiety without apparent side-effects.[26] Some writers also recommended it for various sexual complaints, thus beginning its long association with sexuality.[27] In short order, cocaine became the druggists' stock in trade, available to anyone who had read or heard of its virtues, to be swallowed, inhaled, or injected on demand. As with chloral hydrate, its overuse was as sudden as its notoriety.

The most dramatic suggested use for cocaine was as a specific against opiate addiction. The Parke-Davis catalog of 1885 hoped this was true. "If these claims are substantiated by more mature observation, and cocaine should prove to be, as the facts recorded would now indicate, the long sought for specific for the opium habit; the reliable antidote in poisoning by opium preparations; and the invaluable stomachic and tonic in alcoholism, it will indeed be the most important therapeutic discovery of the age, the benefit of which to humanity will be simply incalculable."[28] These early claims were false, but doctors used cocaine to relieve some withdrawal symptoms and to produce energy among addicts.[29]

There was always a shadow movement of criticism against both coca and cocaine. The sensations they caused in some minds might cause dependence, even if the substances were not truly addictive. Some critics pointed to the example of "coqueros" in Peru, users who became habituated and apparently lived only for the drug in a "blasted and desolate life...."[30] Others warned that cocaine seemed especially attractive to overworked doctors, who used it against fatigue. Cases of ruin in the medical fraternity duly entered the journals.[31]

Was cocaine habit-forming? The medical profession remained divided in a strong debate. "The habit has been formed in several instances under the direction of physicians, who, being desirous of breaking off some other habit, substituted a much worse one," a doctor held in 1886.[32] Others disagreed. In 1887 William A. Hammond, a famous nerve specialist, denied that cocaine use ended in mania or insanity. He held that "All of us feel that we have the power left us of discontinuing its use if we choose to discontinue its use. This is not the feeling of a whiskey-drinker or an opium-eater."[33] A contemporary opiate addict who also used cocaine was more accurate than the doctors, which was often true throughout the drug debate: "There is no such thing as a *true* cocaine or chloral habit; or, paradoxically as it may sound, an addiction to the use of either of these two drugs is *a matter of habit only*."[34]

Though its inflated reputation declined, cocaine remained of some use in general practice, especially as a local anesthetic. More reliable and specific substances superseded it in the new century, but it remained available in varied forms at the drugstore. It did not become a major factor in the antidrug debate until after 1900, but cocaine had a well-established image by then that was likely to result in regulation. Because cocaine excited the user, critics early linked it to irrationality and then to violence. Since it was not truly addictive, it seemed a drug of willful choice. Its use was thus a moral lapse, part of a search for escape from reality or for pure hedonism. As with chloral hydrate, though for different reasons, cocaine seemed to threaten productivity, the majority's view of normality, and predictability in persons and thus ultimately in society. It could also cause dependence in people who desired its effects. Chloral depressed, cocaine excited. In either case the result was an artificial personality that became disliked or feared because it did not seem controlled or useful.

The products of another plant, *Cannabis sativa*, which was often labelled *Cannabis indica*, caused equal interest and controversy in the medical and lay worlds. Doctors could prescribe a tincture of cannabis for oral use, and sometimes for injection. But the lay user like Fitzhugh Ludlow, the famous "hasheesh eater" of the 1860s, consumed cannabis in various forms, usually without knowing the dosage of active ingredients. The plant's resin was generally more powerful than the leaves or stems, whether eaten, smoked, or mixed with food. The psychic effects varied even more than the physiological effects of a substance whose strengths always remained uncertain. As with coca and cocaine, commentators often failed to distinguish among the plant's various products, which led to considerable confusion about their actual properties. And cannabis was available in varying strengths mixed with candy, food, and some drinks on the open market.

There was no lack of attention to cannabis, either in medical or lay circles after the 1840s. It first won American notice in reports from overseas, and doctors heard about it from respectable sources in Britain, of this emotion alone may produce greater results than any drug is capable of," one hostile doctor admitted. "Further, the intensification of this effect by bringing large numbers together with the same hope and enthusiasm is a factor that it is hardly possible to overrate."[71]

The patient who was finally cured also had a new definition of his condition. Keeley held that cure consisted of freedom from alcohol and drugs; there was no assurance of permanent abstinence. Medicine could only remove drugs and alcohol from the body and give it a chance to regenerate. Avoiding relapse into alcohol or drug use was a matter of realism, maturity, and will. As Keeley told one graduating class:

> You must remember that I cannot paralyze the arm that would deliberately raise the fatal glass to the lips. When you all go out into the new life, I will have placed you exactly where you were before taking the first drink. You will look back over the past and then contemplate the future, and you will then choose which path you will follow the balance of your days.[72]

The program at Dwight fortified whatever self-help the patient could muster, and Keeley believed chances of relapse small. The departing patient tended to be euphoric, oriented toward the future, and usually agreed. If he relapsed later, it was not the program's fault. "Yes sir, it is his own fault if he don't [stay cured], and it is not the fault of the treatment," one said. "If a man wants to behave himself, he can, and he can make a damn fool of himself if he wants to."[73]

The numbers of patients were impressive by anybody's standards. Between September 1, 1892, and September 1, 1893, some 14,991 people took the treatment, and the numbers grew with the treatment's fame and expanded facilities.[74] Keeley insisted that only 5 percent of these would relapse on an average, a figure it was impossible to check, but which was clearly too low and which applied only to alcoholics. Relapses among drug addicts were doubtless more numerous.

Keeley's chief aim was to return patients to respectability in the world. To fortify their nerve and offer fresh challenges he devised elaborate after-care programs. Patients were encouraged to take pride in their therapy and to decline alcohol or drugs with the explanation "No thank you; I've been to Dwight," a phrase that became national for a time.[75] Former patients were "graduates," each with a class that often held reunions, with distinctive paraphernalia and paper honors. Local Keeley Clubs carried on propaganda and group-help for graduates and others interested in ending an alcohol or drug problem. There were auxiliaries for wives, mothers, and children. The organization published a periodical, *The Banner of Gold,* and distributed pamphlets and leaf-lets. Keeley's own writings remained in print, and he lectured in the United States and England. There was even a "Keeley Baby," the child of an addicted mother. Both took the cure and allegedly recovered.[76] Once again, critics envied this success. "By doing this, the Keeley graduates ... have thrown around them all the moral restraints of the old-time temperance organizations that, in time past, cured as many, and perhaps more, drunkards than all the Keeley Institutes."[77]

By 1891 Keeley began to plan new facilities, and ultimately there were franchise operations in most major cities. He apparently did not supervise these himself, and with his death in 1900 the network became too much to control. Some local operations were sound, but many ran down quickly.[78] This fading reputation combined with changes in therapeutical approach and the growth of publicly funded programs to reduce the system by the time of World War I. In 1920 the U.S. govern-ment purchased the Dwight facility for a veterans hospital. It then had about 500 beds, laboratory space and equipment. Hundreds of thousands of people with all kinds of drug and alcohol problems had taken the Keeley cure at the local institutes, at Dwight, or at home over the preceding forty years.[79]

Keeley's story unfolded amid great controversy. The chief sub-ject of criticism was the Bichloride of Gold remedy. The AMA officially opposed using any compound whose contents were unknown. This was an effort to avoid identifying orthodox medicine with quackery and was also a way of controlling maverick doctors. Keeley insisted repeatedly that he would not reveal the formula because druggists, doctors, and quacks would simply reproduce it to his detriment. He shrewdly iden-tified himself with Robert Koch, whose premature announcement of tuberculin as a cure for tuberculosis had adverse effects on his reputation.[80]

He also insisted that the formula was only part of a broad treat-ment that patients at home as well as at the institute should follow. Critics charged that he touted Bichloride of Gold as a specific, like any other nostrum peddler; he insisted that it was only part of a cure pro-gram.[81] His supporters emphasized that critics did not demand the formulas of all patent medicines; their concern thus attested to the importance of Keeley's compounds.[82] Keeley also played on the public suspicion of doctors. "If I should throw open my formula to the world it would not cheapen the cure to the patient one cent," he said in 1891. "Reputable physicians would charge their regular rates, disreputable physicians would charge less in money, but by their dishonest practices would rob the poor drinking man of the thing dearest to him in this world —the chance of complete reform."[83]

"hemp, on the contrary, tends to confuse the mind, and induces a purposeless succession of ideas, which, though generally pleasing and even exciting, have no essential connection, and lead to no special result." The feeling of heightened consciousness was thus a delusion. "It does not aid the student in acquiring, nor the writer or speaker in dispensing knowledge. It is the imagination and feelings which appear to be most highly stimulated and altogether without control of reason."[51]

In 1857 a commentator gave a shrewd assessment of what society feared from drug experiences that produced uncontrolled imagination rather than controlled reason. "The most superficial observation of a case of mania, will not fail to show many and strong points of resemblance to that of a person under the influence of a powerful dose of cannabis indica," he noted. "In both there is the same excitement and abruptness of manner, the same rapidity and incoherence of thought, the same false convictions and lesions of affective faculties." He challenged the wisdom of trying to emphasize imagination at the expense of reason artificially. Such a separation of the two processes with drugs threatened the integrated personality, with obvious harm to both individual and society.[52] These ideas recurred in many forms in the long debate over drug policy to come. Once more like cocaine, cannabis seemed to have its medical uses, but none important enough to override its identification with irrationality, escapism, and mental disturbance.

As the century ended and cannabis products declined in medical use, few social commentators thought their abuse likely. But experts thought that hashish in large and steady doses led to violence or insanity. And while cannabis itself was not apparently addictive, the psychic states it produced in susceptible minds could be habit-forming.[53] A few critics warned of cannabis abuse; some intellectuals and artists, perhaps a few foreigners in the cities used it. But it did not seem a social threat. Yet like cocaine, its public image was ambiguous and easily became negative.

The greatest boon among the new therapeutic agents was not a drug but a procedure, hypodermic medication. In less than a generation the hypodermic kit took the world's medical profession by storm. In the late 1850s, few practitioners had heard of it. By the 1870s, it was a standard article in the doctor's bag. Like other products of the therapeutic revolution its sale was unrestricted. Nothing better illustrated the dangers of ignorance about body processes, or the tendency to overpraise new technology than the immense popularity of this innovation.

However dazzling to this generation, the hypodermic did not spring fullblown from the medical armory.[54] Like other discoveries it grew out of practice. In the first part of the nineteenth century, European

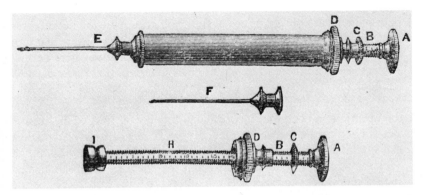

Hypodermic kit from the 1870s. From H. H. Kane, *The Hypodermic Injection of Morphia* (1880), p. 21.

doctors applied opiates and other drugs through massage, especially to inflamed joints.[55] They also dusted or dropped medicines into open wounds and sometimes used dressings treated with opiates.[56] It was easy then to make an opening in the skin with a blister, a popular procedure among the French in the 1830s.[57] The lavish use of the lancet was precedent for the next step, incising the skin and introducing medicine with a syringe. This also developed from experience with irrigating body cavities. It was difficult to gauge dosage in this procedure, which also could cause inflammation, but it had prospects of refinement. In 1849 an American army surgeon at Fort Graham, Texas, reported on injecting substances into the veins of horses without adverse effects. He saw the advantages of such a procedure if it could be perfected. It might have saved many lives in the Mexican War, when the wounded usually vomited up medicines.[58]

The final implement was as simple as most breakthroughs seem in retrospect. Its chief technical merits were the ability to deliver exact doses and to penetrate the skin easily without much pain. Its greatest therapeutic merit was the rapid relief of pain, for morphine was among the first substances used in hypodermics. Doctors in Great Britain used the procedure in the late 1840s, and a decade later several Americans had hypodermic kits. The procedure was well known in medical circles during the Civil War, when it gained some attention.[59]

In the decade after the war, the journals reported an ever-lengthening list of drugs and ailments suitable for the process.[60] Morphine injections for the pain of joint and nerve disorders became widely popular. One doctor in 1864 reported that many of his patients took poor patients at reduced prices or free.[53] This largesse did not affect his prosperity. Toward the end of his life Keeley withdrew more and more from the business and built a large home in Los Angeles where he spent winters. He died there of apparent heart failure on February 21, 1900, a millionaire.[54]

Keeley articulated a theory of addiction to explain and justify his therapeutic approach that incorporated aspects of most of the reigning ideas of his day. He focused on alcohol more than on drugs, but thought all had similar actions and effects in the body. He wrote material for opiate addicts and users of other drugs, and the therapeutic program made special allowances for them. He doubtless did not emphasize them as much as alcoholics because society was so hostile, and because their relapse rate was high.

Keeley believed that inebriety had a physiological basis. Inherited tendencies were important but not inevitable in their effects. Though his ideas changed between the 1870s and 1890s, he basically argued that alcohol and drugs were poisons that somehow altered nerve cells and other tissues, creating a self-perpetuating demand for themselves. Once these substances were removed, and the body freed of the adverse effects they caused, regeneration began. Nervous endowment and resistances varied from person to person, which explained why some users developed what the world called "habits" and others did not. "If a man who takes poison, who takes a disease, or eats opium, or drinks whiskey, cannot create in his tissue cells a variation of structure, enabling him to resist the poison," Keeley said in 1893, "then the poison will kill him, or the disease will kill him."[55] His gift for clarity in explaining the theory was appealing. "Nerve cells are very impressionable. They have the power of becoming educated," he said again in 1893. "Repeated impressions made upon them from any source will cause this training, or conduct, or mode of action, or education. When the brain cells are educated, they perform their function according to the form and type of this training. They act as they are taught to act."[56] In short, if the body could learn inebriety it could learn sobriety. This view appealed to the American ideals of education, self-help, and optimism about environmental influences while explaining addiction as basically a physiological problem that treatment could correct. At a time when no explanation of the nervous system's functioning was satisfactory or exact, Keeley's did not seem illogical.

The treatment that Keeley proposed for this disease rested first on a famous product, the Bichloride of Gold compound. He recalled his bewilderment at the excessive drinking and drug-taking among respectable people he knew and began studying the problem while a young physician. In reviewing the literature, he came upon a remark from

Paracelsus that future generations would find "Gold, the king of metals," effective against diseases rooted in heredity.[57]

He allegedly wrote some 500 doctors for their opinion of gold in therapy and began experimenting with various compounds in the late 1870s. He supposedly tried gold in pill form on an especially hardened local alcoholic. The man nearly died but stopped drinking. Keeley continued the experiments, adding and subtracting substances that were then popular in treating opiate addiction and alcoholism. He was apparently familiar with the actions of nux vomica, atropia, chloral, cannabis, coca, jamaica dogwood, bromides, and hyoscine. A former patient years later recalled helping Keeley's partner, John R. Oughton, mix a batch of the specific. He could only say for certain that well-water, willow bark, and a small amount of something in a bottle bearing a skull and crossbones went into the mixture.[58]

By the late 1870s, Keeley was ready to distribute the Bichloride of Gold remedy.[59] Aides decided upon a unique package for the product. It came in special bottles with a curved front and flat back. Two back to back made a convenient package, and Keeley sold them in pairs. The labels were ornate and impressive, and each bottle top was heavy with sealing wax. Printed instructions for using the compound also directed the recipient to break the empty bottle so that no one else could fill it with another mixture. Prices varied with the habit in question. Tobacco users paid five dollars for a pair of bottles. Neurasthenics required an eight dollar set. Alcoholics needed nine dollars worth. Opium addicts needed ten dollars worth, testifying to the difficulty of curing their habit. Keeley secured copyrights, patents, and trademarks for the bottle's shape, the label designs, and other accoutrements but never sought protection for the formula, in order to avoid stating its composition.[60] At no time did Keeley or anyone else reveal the formula, and it died with the partners.

Gold was the focus of both the popularity and the controversy that gathered around Keeley in the 1890s, but his emphasis on the metal was not intrinsically absurd or unusual. He was not the first to suggest its use against alcoholism and addiction. The heavy metals had a long history in therapeutics, though their popularity was declining, mainly because of the dangers associated with mercury. But gold was in some use for skin and venereal diseases. Some authorities recommended it for epilepsy and nervous ailments.[61] Chloride of gold increased elimination, which was important in removing toxins from the systems of addicts and alcoholics.[62]

It also seemed promising in treating addictions and alcoholism because it stimulated the brain and nervous system. An English

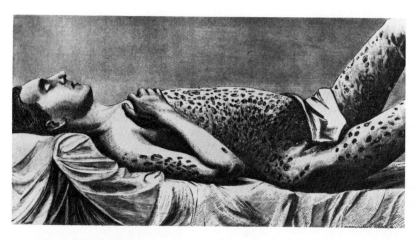

Abscesses on the body of a morphine addict. From H. H. Kane, *The Hypodermic Injection of Morphia* (1880), p. 287.

Though addiction seemed a remote threat, and in any event a puzzling phenomenon, to most users until the 1870s, other dangers were clear. Some doctors warned that hypodermic morphine after all was an opiate, liable to fatal overdose. And abscesses were an even greater danger because many physicians and laymen used unsterile needles. Still others did not even believe in the germ theory of disease. Both medical and popular literature cautioned against the dangers of skin reactions in using the hypodermic.[73] And all experts urged users to avoid hitting a vein. The result was sudden dizziness, unpleasant floating sensations, and loss of bodily control. Ironically enough, in view of the widespread use of morphine in the late nineteenth century, "mainlining," or intravenous injection, did not become popular until well into the twentieth century.[74]

Authorities also warned against allowing patients to administer to themselves, though this was hard if not impossible to prevent, given the ready availability of both drugs and hypodermics. If a patient could not get them from his doctor, he had only to send out to the nearest drugstore. One doctor told H. H. Kane in 1880 that "any of these patients having provided themselves with a syringe, take it [morphine] as regularly as the drinker does his 'nip,' and in quantities that would astound the uninitiated...."[75] Only the terminally ill should have home kits, and it was unwise even to tell a patient the dose or substance in use. "Nor can you trust the relatives or the nurses in this matter," Kane warned. "They *will* yield to the importunities of the patient."[76]

Several vague but generally held ideas kept doctors from anticipating the wave of addiction they caused with hypodermic morphine. Some experts thought that narcotics in moderation were not habit-forming and were merely dissipated in use throughout the body. Others believed that injected morphine was not addictive, though it was when taken orally. One North Carolina doctor told Kane in 1880 in perfect innocence: "On one patient I have used the hypodermic syringe between 2,500 and 3,000 times in a period of eighteen months, and so far see no signs of the opium habit."[77] He obviously arrived with his needle before the onset of withdrawal symptoms. Still others thought they might be overusing morphine, but the facts were cloudy, and its advantages outweighed the risks. There was literally little else to use. "The ability to *stop pain* in a few minutes, is a boon worth years of discussion," one physician held in 1878.[78]

As in the period before the hypodermic appeared, a concept of addiction was lacking. The early patients of the 1860s and 1870s knew that morphine relieved symptoms which they took to be some kind of illness rather than withdrawal pains. Doctors were equally puzzled. And when the idea of opiate addiction clarified in thought, they had little except more morphine to offer for the relief of this distress.

By the late 1870s, concern about both addiction and nonmedical use began to rise both in the United States and Europe. "A dangerous method of using morphine to produce pleasurable sensations is believed by physicians in this city to be a growing vice," the *New York Tribune* reported late in 1878.[79] Syringes became a fad, especially in high society, where some women reportedly wore them cleverly disguised as jewelled fobs and charms. One New York City jeweller praised his handiwork as both attractive and practical. "When in this position, it is ready for any emergency, and is not likely to be forgotten. Its moderate price should prove a recommendation."[80] Lesser mortals had only to repair to the nearest drugstore. "There are one hundred hypodermic syringes sold now for each one that found a purchaser a few years ago," a dealer in medical instruments said in 1882. "People have discovered that they are not only of great service in the alleviation of extreme pain, but that they afford a convenient sort of respectable intoxication."[81] By this he meant nonalcoholic. The hypodermic kit was preferable to the hip flask or decanter in many respectable homes. People in the countryside could easily secure a hypodermic kit, needles, morphine, and also a bottled cure for the habit by mail.[82]

Concern in the medical profession paralleled these public disclosures and debates. Reported cases of morphine habit always accompanied the flood of praise for hypodermic medication. In 1870 one doctor addiction has taught me one thing if it has done nothing else—I know that its problems will never be solved by any special remedies. I know that they will never be solved by the adoption of any routine method."[41]

The regimens that developed out of experience focused on the addict who cooperated in seeking cure. The user for pleasure, or the one who thought his case incurable was generally hopeless. The treatment programs were thus elaborate and gave the patient the sense of being at their center. Everyone involved was doing everything possible for him. More so than with purely physical ailments, the procedure was reciprocal. "No treatment requires so many *small things* to be done," a doctor from Brownwood, Texas, wrote in 1892, "with perfect submission to all the requirements on the part of the patient and special knowledge, experience and tact on the part of the physician."[42] The only suggestions lacking in these varied programs were leeching and bloodletting, and some doctors doubtless tried them without leaving a record.

Few such regimens were suitable for home use, simply because so much attention to the patient's body was necessary. All except the strongest also would return to drugs if they were available, as at home or among friends. The sympathy of loved ones was important but functioned best from a distance where it did not become pity or collusion. And leaving the familiar social or business environment was vital if the patient was to change the habits and stresses that caused or fortified the original condition. "To those who profess to think a man can stay at home, continue to attend to his business, and put a stop to the habitual use of morphine, I have only to say: If it be so easy then do it," Dr. William F. Waugh of Chicago wrote in 1895. "Go right ahead and stop; and I shall take off my hat to you, as a giant among men."[43]

Treatments usually occurred in a special facility. Comfort was all-important and restraint unpopular unless the patient was truly violent. In the first stages of withdrawal, chloral or some other hypnotic might keep him relatively comfortable while antispasmodics combatted the restlessness. Discharges from the bowels and mucous membranes emptied the body of wastes without hindrance. This necessitated frequent tepid baths, which were also soothing. After a few days, the patient might take electric shocks to relax muscles. In a few more days, he could exercise briefly and begin the arduous task of restoring normal body functions. As soon as the stomach permitted, he took nourishing foods and restoratives. Any ailment that addiction had masked received treatment. Most patients responded quickly, testifying to the human body's resilience, and gained weight, improved the muscle tone, and became more aware of the world around them.[44]

The subject then faced an indeterminate period of feeling weak and emotionally drained. The opiates were out of the system, but the memory of their action remained. Anyone who reflected solely on the past, on regrets and remorse, or the roads not taken, could relapse. The sense of care must be all-pervasive from doctors and attendants. Family and friends were welcome only to reassure the patient. Most regimens then emphasized keeping busy. Reading, gardening, doing chores, talking with other patients, group exercises, entertainments, and similar activities were all designed as small challenges the patient could fulfill. He must obtain self-respect, a sense of authority, and focus on the future. In short, he must not relapse into the situation and mental frame that sustained the addiction.[45] This psychological emphasis became dominant in the twentieth century but was always implicit in earlier therapies. Addicts clearly understood the need for affection and a kind of spiritual renaissance to develop what the world called "willpower."[46]

The next step in treatment depended on the patient's physical and emotional health, optimism and pocketbook. He could return home and hope to alter the old routines and relationships, or remain for an extended period of time at a sanitarium. By 1870 there were publicly funded asylums for inebriates in New York, Pennsylvania, and Michigan. But most such institutions were private, usually the creation of one doctor dedicated to treating alcoholics and addicts with a special approach. In the 1870s and 1880s Dr. Harry Hubbell Kane of New York City gained considerable notoriety for treating inebriates in his "home," though his reputation suffered for overenthusiasm about new and debatable therapeutics. In Brooklyn Dr. J. B. Mattison operated an important sanitarium and became a major writer on the subject of addiction and drug use. Dr. Thomas D. Crothers presided over a famous sanitarium in Hartford, and became prominent for both his theoretical and practical writings. He was also a leader of a group of physicians dedicated to refining and teaching the disease theory of inebriety, edited the *Quarterly Journal of Inebriety,* and was important in the American Association for the Cure of Inebriates.

The sanitarium movement that these and other doctors spoke for seemed a progressive innovation in both medicine and psychiatry that appealed to many kinds of reformers. Its attempt to individualize and humanize care for addicts complemented similar efforts to liberalize the treatment of insane, indigent, and impaired persons. Sanitarium treatment was also identified with the latest in technology and scientific thinking in its field. And it attempted to return the patient to "normal" society after showing him how to manage new anxieties and tensions.

to the study of inebriety used a similar figure later in the year. The numbers did not change much among knowledgeable experts into the twentieth century. Dr. Thomas D. Crothers, a well-known specialist in the treatment of drug dependence, accepted 100,000 in 1902. In the same year, a committee of pharmacists estimated that there were 200,000 addicts in the country.[2]

These figures, and the tone of reporting, changed markedly in the twentieth century, and the inflation of both peaked just after World War I. The public read more and more reports in the daily press, and in the popular weeklies and monthlies, that the number of opiate addicts was increasing rapidly. In 1909 one story held that a single sanitarium in Atlanta had treated 100,000 patients, and that other institutions had dealt with as many as 50,000. If this were true, the number of addicts, even allowing for repeaters and errors, was much larger than experts believed.[3] The alleged number of addicts and users began to grow with the demand for regulation. By 1917 one witness at a New York legislative investigation said that there were 300,000 addicts in New York City alone. A year later, another writer thought there were at least one million in New York State.[4] A special committee of investigation for the U.S. Treasury Department reported that there were one million addicts in the United States in 1918–19, concentrated chiefly in major cities.[5] The New York *Times* accepted the figure and supposed that 1.5 million was believable.[6] Stories emphasizing these large numbers flooded the news media, and many people believed that 1 to 2 percent of the population was addicted.[7]

The estimates declined in the aftermath of anxiety and hysteria surrounding the demand for regulation and as a result of some specific experiences with addicts. The relatively small number discovered among draft age men during World War I was reassuring, especially since young men were supposed to be the population element most liable to drug misuse. The equally small numbers of addicts who sought treatment at the public clinics established in most major cities during 1919–20 suggested a lower rate of addiction than the widely discussed figures indicated, if this were any kind of reliable sample. And doctors were clearly reducing the use of opiates in favor of new, less suspect pain killers. By 1924 Lawrence Kolb, of the United States Public Health Service, a close student of the drug problem, held that there were never more than 246,000 opiate addicts in the United States, plus about 18,000 cocaine habitués.[8] In retrospect it seemed clear that opiate addiction had begun to grow in the 1870s, peaked in the late 1890s, and declined thereafter.[9]

All statistics, of course, were educated estimates. Careful analyses of import figures such as Kolb's could only allow a margin of error for the opium that was smuggled to avoid tariff duties. Impressionistic evidence and police reports indicated considerable smuggling at all the major ports, and especially those on the Pacific and Gulf coasts. Kolb's figures were probably close to the mark, and there were doubtless never a million true addicts in the country. Yet as Charles E. Terry, another distinguished expert, said in 1928, "the fact that opium use in any form is regarded by the general public as alone a habit, vice, sign of weak will or dissipation undoubtedly has caused the majority of users to conceal their condition."[10] And there may well have been a million persons dependent on chloral, bromides, patent nostrums, and various new wonder drugs when the Harrison Act became law in 1914.

Throughout the long debate on national drug policy, imprecise information often shaped the views of policy-makers. The lack of precision produced anxiety, since it enhanced the idea that addiction and drug use were greater than they appeared, or at certain times such as the progressive era, were increasing and required control. The doctor who finally realized that many of his patients were opiate addicts wondered how common this was. "Allow me here to observe, the use of narcotics is indulged in by the American community to a much greater extent than is even divined by physicians themselves," one such physician wrote as early as 1860, after finding that a young male patient was addicted to large doses of morphine.[11]

The reporter who set out blithely to cover the local red-light district or tenderloin for its color or sensationalism and encountered drug use returned sobered from the experience. By 1879 the New York *Times* could editorialize: "The use of opium as a stimulant seems to be steadily growing throughout civilization, having greatly increased within a few years, even in this country, where it was almost never employed a generation ago, except as a medicine."[12]

The druggist who sold morphine to the same people year after year inevitably concluded that the habit was more widespread than the experts said.[13] The person who discovered that a relative, friend, or neighbor was addicted naturally wondered how many more people on nearby farms, or in the village, or along the city streets were in similar circumstances.

The addicts also influenced public opinion as their stories appeared in print, or perhaps from the temperance platform. Stumbling through the half-lit world of drug users, they inflated the number of their fellows, and in terms that enhanced public fears that the problem was habits, wrote in 1880.[16] By the middle of that decade a few doctors began to lecture colleagues on their moral as well as medical responsibilities toward addicts. "The person comes to us for relief *as a patient*," one wrote in 1884, "and we should treat him, socially and professionally, as a diseased person, and not as a brute or an outcast. . . . The victim needs no other judge than his own conscience, and it ill becomes us, as alleviators of pain, to add to the exquisite tortures and torments he has already experienced."[17] J. B. Mattison agreed. "In the vast majority of cases the *vice* theory of its origins is incorrect, so that, with few exceptions, the term 'opium habit' is a misnomer, implying, as it wrongly does, an opiate-using quite under individual control." A decade later he thought it clear that opiates somehow affected the nervous system and made addiction involuntary. He noted that addicted infants were born to addicted mothers; they obviously had not committed any vice.[18]

A large array of procedures to treat opiate addiction developed in the last third of the nineteenth century. By 1900 the study and treatment of addiction was a respectable, though not large, professional subdivision. But the experts and therapists in it always cautioned of the special frustrations in dealing with addicts whose illness arose from multiple and often intangible causes. Nor did they underestimate the hold that opiates had on some people. Mattison and others warned early that only comprehensive, individual programs that actually stopped opiate use, restored health, and changed the patient's environment stood any chance of success.[19]

Opiates adversely affected many body processes. They deadened appetite, slowed digestion and elimination, and suppressed secretions in general. Physical and mental reflexes, muscle tone, and attention to the environment declined under addiction. The emotional effects of opiates reinforced inattention to the body and personality, and most addicts who sought treatment were debilitated.

These general physical and emotional aspects of addiction were hard enough to treat, but specialists quickly focused on controlling the specific painful symptoms that followed witholding opiates. Most addicts abandoned self-cure when the withdrawal distress became severe. They were not likely to commit themeselves to doctors who did not understand their feelings of horror about this stage. And if they failed to get through withdrawal, the details of any subsequent regimen mattered little.

The nature of what came to be styled withdrawal was well known, if not well understood. In 1822 John Eberle, author of a popular medical guide, noted: "When the system is entirely free from the influence of the accustomed stimulant, torments of the most distressing kind are experienced."[20] A century later Edward Huntington Williams could write: "Indeed, the Inquisition missed what would certainly have been one of its choicest torture-devices by passing out of fashion before morphine came in."[21]

Addicts tried to convince the public and doctors of the terrible nature of withdrawal. Every addict-memoirist recounted experiences at cure, whether alone or with medical aid. The physical and emotional agonies were simply too much to endure. Once again, they insisted that their addiction and relapse resulted not from lack of will or the desire for normality, but because of processes beyond the control of even normal people. They along with most of the new drug experts insisted that addiction continued from the need to avoid pain rather than from any desire for pleasure.[22] The emotional dread of withdrawal reinforced the fear and expectation of misery, which naturally inhibited the will to seek cure. Charles B. Towns, who developed an elaborate cure program, summarized this view in 1916: "...the great majority of drug-users wish nothing so much as to be freed from this slavery, while at the same time they fear nothing so greatly as sudden deprivation of their drug. In the interaction of these two major impulses lies the key to the addict's psychology."[23]

The first stages of withdrawal from opiates produced symptoms that were both physically painful and emotionally exhausting. The patient experienced copious discharges from the mucous membranes, vomiting, and diarrhea. This reduced him to an infantile condition, which heightened his sense of degradation and helplessness. There was sharp pain in the muscles, often seeming to make the bones ache, spasms, and a general sense of aching throughout the body. The skin usually became hypersensitive. The prick of a needle might feel like impalement, or crucifixion, as the more florid addict-memoirists said. The craving for relief with morphine became intense. "It is generally the case, at this stage," an addict wrote in 1876, "that the opium eater would wade through blood for opium."[24]

The patient's sense of time slowed, and he was restless, semiconscious, or sleepless. The process seemed endless, which caused a general feeling of despair and misery. An addict under treatment told Fitzhugh Ludlow in 1867 that "God seems to help a man in getting out of every difficulty but opium. There you have to *claw* your way out over redhot coals on your hands and knees, and drag yourself by main strength through the burning dungeon-bars."[25]

Another genteel, well-educated patient under therapy said in 1883: "I believe hell is composed of opium eaters, and the punishment consists of withdrawing from them the drug, as that is the greatest

The growing temperance movement there supposedly fostered some of this drug use. Respectable women who would not be seen near a whiskey bottle relieved their psychic distress with laudanum or morphine.[28] And William Rosser Cobbe thought that many southern men who took the pledge against Demon Rum merely turned to the genie of opium. " ... the poor drunkards seek a substitute for the alcohol from which they have been forcibly separated, and they think they find it in the extract of the poppy."[29]

These views doubtless reflected a widespread tendency of the times to see the South as backward and southern whites as self-indulgent. But like most such generalizations there was a kernel of truth there. The region did have a larger number of genteel and medical addicts than other sections. And people in general in the South used large quantities of opiated patent medicines to combat fevers and parasitical diseases.[30]

The ethnic origins of early users were sketchy, but commentators attributed most drug use, especially of opiates, to native-born white Protestants. Some ethnic elements seemed outside the problem, perhaps for ironic reasons. "The immigrant peasantry from Ireland and Germany also seem to be, as a rule, peculiarly exempt, perhaps because whiskey in one case and beer in the other supply the means for stimulation," the New York *Times* said in 1877.[31] They also could not afford regular doctoring, with its attendant risks of addiction or dependence. Fears that drug use was undermining the so-called better elements of society developed early in the debate.

Blacks, the most prominent racial group in the country, appeared to use few drugs in the late nineteenth century.[32] This reflected their poverty and low level of medical care, and they also avoided the authorities, who reported few cases of drug use among them. Yet a few commentators adapted racial stereotypes to the role of blacks in the drug issue. In 1885 one southern doctor familiar with mental illness summarized the reigning views in analyzing a black mental patient who supposedly lost his mind through opiate use. The doctor knew of only three such cases. "We can see some reason why the colored man is not as susceptible to the habit as the white," he wrote. "He has not the same delicate nervous organization, and does not demand the form of stimulant conveyed in opium — a grosser stimulant sufficing [presumably alcohol]." He did think that the black's nervous organization became more refined and thus more susceptible to opiates as he rose on the scale of civilization. "In the large cities, especially the Northern ones, where the financial, social, and we might say, the *nervous* condition of the negro are of a higher scale, we may find the opium habit more prevalent." And, "It is a known fact that the advances made in the negro as a social being are bringing with them evils in the way of diseases incident to a higher civilization." It was also unlikely that the black became unwittingly addicted through morphine treatments for neuralgias, since "owing to his lower nervous development, [he] is not liable to diseases of this character." The subject bore watching, but the black as drug addict did not seem a threat.[33]

In an ironic way, these myths and clichés spared the black a good deal of scrutiny early in the drug debate. There were undoubtedly some black addicts, but the black was not a sinister figure in the drug issue until after 1900 when he became identified with cocaine.[34]

The Chinese were the principal racial group whose stereotype hovered over the drug question. They entered the West to work in mining and railroading, formed separate enclaves in most cities, and pursued habits and tastes brought from China. Opium smoking was among these, and by the 1870s many news reports of life in the West included accounts of opium dens. Local residents disliked the resulting bad publicity, and the desire to obliterate the dens was one public rationalization for the anti-Chinese riots that punctuated western life.[35]

By the late 1870s opium smoking was moving east and spreading to non-Chinese. Enterprising newsmen, doctors, and addicts reported dens in St. Louis, New Orleans, Chicago, Washington, and New York City. These included flophouses, "joints" for sharpers and petty criminals, and elegant turkish-style retreats that served both sexes in luxurious surroundings.[36]

Commentators were surprised at the spread of smoking, as if nothing Chinese could attract westerners. For a time, experts tried to find therapeutic reasons for smoking opium.[37] They generally agreed that it was easier to stop than was addiction to morphine.[38] But both doctors and other commentators quickly concluded that smoking was a vice, pure and simple. The user had to seek out the experience, either for sheer dissipation or to escape problems he should face. H. H. Kane thought that "opium smoking is essentially a vice, being a gross indulgence of a passion or appetite without the redeeming feature of pain to drive the victim to it. He carelessly, indolently, and voluntarily rivets upon himself shackles from which he soon finds that he is unable to free himself."[39] Many early addicts agreed. "Let there be full understanding of the matter," William Rosser Cobbe wrote, "the opium smoking habit comes of association with unholy persons and is entered into with deliberation."[40] Few smokers sought cure, which reinforced the image of wilful indulgence.[41]

Smoking, like the Chinese, was quickly identified with the underworlds of prostitution, crime, and filthiness. The den also symbolized indulgence and sensuality, and there was sexual imagery in most

5

CURES AND TREATMENTS

A SENSE OF PROGRESS animated the medical profession in the late nineteenth century. The therapeutic developments that eased pain and combatted diseases surely would produce an appropriate remedy for drug addiction. This seemed the more likely, given the apparent desire among addicts to be cured. As early as 1833 a medical journal reported that "every person of this description we have chanced to know has manifested a strong sense of the impropriety and danger of the practice, and entreated us to prescribe, if possible, some effectual remedy."[1]

Many addicts sought cure at sometime and spent lifetimes going from addiction, to temporary abstinence, to relapse. They naturally wanted to end their dependence on opiates and regain full health. But they also took repeated cure programs to demonstrate a desire for social respectability and normality. The pain and distress of withdrawal and the continued desire for opiates after treatment defeated all except a small minority. Users concluded long before doctors did that addiction to opiates was rooted in some psychological and physiological processes that willpower alone was not likely to defeat. This seemed obvious from painful experience, but it was also a way of explaining why so many people with good intentions and talent could not stop opiate use. These failures increased the addicts' sense of victimization and made their desire for sympathy more compelling. One wrote in 1876 that when the nature of addiction finally became clear to everyone, "the poor victim of its terrors will be taken by the hand and sympathized with by his fellow-man, instead of being ostracized from society, and treated with contempt and reprehension, as he now is."[2]

But a cure based on complete abstinence seemed as remote in the 1880s as in the 1930s or 1970s. As concern about addiction increased the nature of addiction still baffled doctors. Therapy for the specific symptoms during withdrawal did not stop the distress or produce any lasting cures. Willpower, persuasion, even threats seemed ineffectual. The journals were full of queries from doctors in every part of the country seeking the names of antidotes and asking advice on how to treat addicts during withdrawal.[3] In 1871 George M. Beard suggested that no subject remained so shrouded in mystery and bias. In 1895 another doctor thought that many colleagues still classed opiate addiction with the tea and coffee habits, or with excessive cigar smoking. They wondered why addicts did not simply quit.[4] At the same time, William Rosser Cobbe wrote with resignation: "The world cannot be greatly reprobated for its want of sympathy for the sufferers, since it has had no education upon the all-important subject."[5]

Doctors often shared the distaste for drug users that permeated the society. Moralism inhibited a purely clinical judgement that the addict was only a patient with a medical problem. The average practitioner was also unlikely or unable to learn much about a problem that seemed peripheral to his general practice. And physicians inevitably disliked being associated with the failure so common in treating addiction.[6]

This left a fertile field for the charlatan, and a minor industry arose to furnish nostrums and "cures" for the drug addict. The viability of this enterprise reflected many of the changes that transformed post–Civil War America. Newspapers now carried advertisements to every farm and hamlet. Low postal rates allowed many people to buy nostrums through the mails. And the plain brown wrapper that made the product anonymous hid the addict's condition from family and neighbors. Government patents and copyrights for labels, containers, and contents seemed to grant official approval, despite the complete lack of inspection or regulation of the traffic.[7]

Addicts turned to nostrum vendors out of both hope and desperation. If orthodox medicine, with all its new claims to scientific insight, had no answer, perhaps someone outside its constraints did. And the longstanding American tradition of self-doctoring combined with the normal human desire to believe in taking a chance to make these products attractive.

The quacks shared some attributes. They tended to have shadowy origins and humble beginnings. With few exceptions they were self-taught or had inferior educations and cast themselves as outsiders who established medicine feared. They often used the trappings of science and technology but also appealed to the average man's suspicion opium was threatening the next generation.[48] From the 1840s on, doctors began to connect it with ill effects of both body and mind among infants. And the threat of accidental overdose was strong with children. The unregulated patent medicine industry which used opium or morphine in many infant remedies came under increasing attack. "There is a triad of infant murderers, and their names are Godfrey's Cordial, Paregoric, and Mrs. Winslow's Soothing Syrup," a prominent doctor charged in 1882.[49]

Both mothers and physicians understood that such babies were often small, usually irritable, and in some kind of distress that opiates relieved. Once again, the lack of understanding about the addiction process caused many parents and doctors to mistake withdrawal symptoms for another illness, and to relieve them with compounds that could cause dependence. One harried mother doubtless represented many others who relied on Mrs. Winslow's Soothing Syrup to calm a child. "Why, she will get so mad if I don't give it to her, and scream and kick all morning," she said.[50] In the mid-nineties, when the fact of opiate addiction was clear, doctors were still warning against dosing children. "There is hardly a physician having experience with children who does not have to contend with ignorant mothers, stupid nurses, and careless women, who in order to get sleep at night feed their nurslings with soothing syrups, teething cordials, and other soothing liquids, not to mention the most common and also the most easily obtainable, paregoric."[51] Many addict-memoirists thought that their problem began in the childhood use of some "Nemesis of the nursery," as William Rosser Cobbe called paregoric.[52]

Similar and stronger apprehensions developed about women and drug use. This became a major topic of concern in the popular as well as medical press in the latter part of the century, attesting to changed roles and expectations of women. More women than men seemed to be drug users, and the typical addict appeared to be a respectable woman, whether in city or country, whose dependence began in prescriptions from a physician for either real or fancied ailments. Women also took a good deal of chloral hydrate and bromides as tranquilizers and for sleep. And they consumed a great deal of older compounds, such as laudanum. One druggist said in 1881 that "where twenty-five years ago he made it by the gallon, he now makes it by the barrel," and that four-fifths of his customers were women.[53] Some women reportedly used chloroform and ether, and the new chemical depressants with increasing regularity in the 1880s and 1890s. They also purchased quantities of morphine and hypodermic kits. Observers quickly assumed that they were using these drugs rather than buying them for families, or for men who were secretly addicted.

The secrecy with which women cloaked drug use added a sense of alarm to the debate because the numbers and station of those involved remained unclear. But the medical and popular journals carried many cases of women addicts. Many simply took "medicine," and told no one, not even husbands, of their need for opiates, or of their fruitless efforts to abandon them.[54] The families of some understood that they needed the medicine, without comprehending addiction. In one case of 1869, a workman accepted his wife's addiction and had spent eleven hundred hard-earned dollars on morphine, once walking twenty-four miles to obtain the needed dose.[55] Who could say how many women were involved, and with what loss to society?[56]

Doctors who over-prescribed opiates clearly caused much of this addiction among women. "We have an army of women in America dying from the opium habit—larger than our standing army," a physician said in 1894. "The profession is wholly responsible for the loose and indiscriminate use of the drug."[57] This reflected some basic facts about medical practice. Doctors saw more women than men patients. Women also reported generalized ailments, which increased the tendency to prescribe a sedative. And the profession held that women simply had more illness than men because of their reproductive tract, and because of menopause in later life. In 1879 J. B. Mattison wondered how many women were "sitting in a similar shadow" because of drugs taken to combat "female troubles."[58]

But theorists and practitioners alike saw broader social reasons behind the increased use of drugs among women. Middle-class women especially, though not exclusively, seemed increasingly liable to vague but obvious distressing nervous complaints. The categories of flighty girl, tense spinster, and nervous matron appeared more and more frequently in discussions of the problem.[59] Theorists of the nature of civilization such as George M. Beard attributed the entire generation's enhanced sense of nervousness to new pressures stemming from the modern industrial order. The impact was especially hard on women. "The general law is that the more nervous the organization, the greater the susceptibility to stimulants and narcotics," Beard wrote in 1871. "Woman is more nervous, has a finer organization than man, [and] is accordingly more susceptible to most of the stimulants."[60] As this view became more popular, some educated women at least conformed to its predictions. Nervousness proved that they were finer than men, had special natures and roles, and needed unusual care.[61]

Other causes had social roots. Whether a society matron in New York City or a rural wife in Minnesota, a woman had to conform to more conventions than did men. Pressure from peers, churches, and families

Some settle down to a certain dose and adhere to it for years; others devote their lives to the effort of absorbing all the opiate they can crowd into their systems. The life of the former runs on uneventfully. They live, perform a certain limited series of mental and physical evolutions, but their progress ceases, their career culminates. They gradually retire from the activities of the community and grow yearly more contracted in their operations and their sympathies. Ambition is dead, incentive has perished—they just live and no more. The man collects his little rents, sees to his little kitchen garden, eats a trifle, wears his old clothes and sits alone at home, reading a bit, meditating long, ruminating most of the time, producing nothing; a quiet, inoffensive, retiring hermit; of no use to himself or to anybody else, neither hated nor loved by any mortal man. Only the druggist knows the truth.[66]

No doubt many addicts went about their business with reasonable efficiency and the appearance of normality. But this image of the addict as withdrawn and passive was widespread.

Sympathy for this sense of stunted development was one point where the addict and society touched. Cure experts devised regimens that emphasized work with groups, life in natural settings, and other connections with the world to replace the addict's solitude or insulation.[67] And for all the era's vaunted emphasis on competition and freedom, it did not sanction isolation from or disregard of fellowmen. The "tendency to live apart from others, to shun companions, to avoid social engagements, and to ignore comradeship or natural affection for those entitled to it," was dangerous for both the individual and society.[68] Cure doctors often emphasized in their promotional literature the need for addicts to live among people.[69] In the end, as one commentator put it in 1918, "it is better for anyone's mental health to associate with one's fellows."[70]

Innocent people also suffered from anyone's addiction, which could not be a matter of individual freedom, since its effects were not confined to the user. The first to suffer, in this view, were family members. Addiction seemed to threaten both marriage and the family, important stabilizing institutions in a period of change. This was clear to addicts, whose writings were filled with guilt at impoverishing or disappointing loved ones. Medical and psychological experts often pointed to this social danger. "The friends and family of an opium habituate are most familiar with the degrading character of the slavery of the mind and nervous system which opium entails," a doctor wrote in 1884. "They realize how lost to the family circle as a real member of the household he or she has become, and whether it be father or mother, sister or brother, it is but natural that they should strive to reclaim that which is lost, or if not lost, at least estranged in many of those familiar mental traits with which are blended family love, esteem and reverence."[71]

The effects of the addict's rejection of "the relish for society and its enjoyments ... "[72] radiated out into the world which thus had a legitimate interest in his state. "The great trouble is that they are so oblivious to all the responsibilities of life, and so willing to become wrapped up with the exhilarating effects of this drug, avoiding all the troubles, pains, and responsibilities of life, that they cannot be brought to see that it is a duty both to themselves and to their friends to stop the habit," Dr. Charles W. Earle, a noted authority, wrote in 1886.[73] Introspection was thus not normally a social process, since it had to move beyond the personality to be truly worthwhile. "For emotion or sensation to go over into action is to follow the normal law of the mind," the educator David Starr Jordan wrote in 1900. "To cultivate sensation for sensation's sake, with no purpose beyond it, whether it be in art, music, love, or religion, is to live a sensuous life, and this is ultimately a life of weakness and decadence."[74] Pleasure and self-concern had a legitimate place only as part of a life involving friends, family and citizenship. In social terms, changing the normal personality or mind always seemed worse than affecting the body with drugs.[75]

The responses of many addicts testified ironically to the importance of these general attitudes. The literary addicts were not typical, but they had wide acquaintance with the drug world. They spoke for the aspirations and fears of those users striving to obtain or retain respectable status. While pleading for recognition of their plight, they often presented almost parallel images of the reigning critical social views of addiction and drug use. Their writings were filled with regret at unfinished projects, abandoned ideas, and with a sense of loss and failure. Few of them derived any pleasure or apparent benefit from opium, except to avoid withdrawal. Nearly all wanted to succeed in worldly terms but knew they were failures. They rebelled at their slavery as much as society feared and condemned it. "But the slave of the drug never for a moment loses the sense of his accountability or fails to measure the extent of his shortcomings," Cobbe wrote. "He is ever eager to accomplish something that will atone, in part, at least, for his many peccancies; hence, he plans and plans again; but, alas, he never executes."[76] There was also strong religious imagery, dealing with the themes of lost innocence, fall and redemption, in the confessional literature. Just as opiate addiction changed the vital personality, in this view, so it imperilled even the soul. If the alcoholic's nemesis was Demon Rum, that of the opiate addict was Mephistopheles.

dentist, or nurse to conceal use and drugs were readily available. Many also preferred them to alcohol, whose effects obviously showed, to the harm of their practice.

And the doctor's life was simply harried. Many were struggling to establish practices in areas where there was a surplus of physicians. Still others practiced in the countryside, at the mercy of inclement weather, bad roads, and great distances to travel on house calls. Time and energy vanished like water in sand for those physicians who did not have a settled practice in a major city, or who were not attached to a medical center.

As early as 1883 J. B. Mattison also thought that doctors unconsciously felt they were somehow exempt from the normal rules of addiction and habituation. There was always a fascination with drugs and procedures in the medical world, and it was easy to convince oneself that substances that relieved pain or fatigue could not really be harmful. Addiction was something that happened to other people, an attitude that ran through the lives of all drug addicts who told their stories. In the doctor's case, this feeling was also an aspect of the sense of special mission that accompanied the profession's technical progress.[71]

Many guides and handbooks warned against allowing this viewpoint, usually called a temptation, to triumph. None did so in better terms than D. W. Cathell's. "Beware of certain temptations to which the practice of medicine exposes you," he cautioned. "The irregularities, anxieties, and exhaustion; the cold, the wet, the hunger, the night work, the loss of sleep, and the hospitality of patients and other friends all unite to tempt physicians to use alcoholics, cocain, morphia, chloral, etc."[72]

Cathell warned that drug use easily ruined a practice as well as a life, and the medical literature offered some spectacular cases of physician-addicts as examples to avoid. A doctor reported in 1914 that "a physician who had taken the Keeley treatment ten times for alcoholism and four times for morphinism came to me taking whiskey, hyoscin, cocain, morphin, cannabis indica, chloral hydrate and bromide of soda."[73] And there were always the "scrip doctors" who prescribed for addicts, who became lurid examples of the need for regulation after 1900.[74]

As with women, young people, and other groups with special attributes for social progress, there were cultural explanations for addiction and abuse among doctors. They quickly took a place among the "brain workers," the sensitive and creative people who late nineteenth-century commentators thought were especially prone to drug use. As late as 1904 one doctor assumed that "Physicians, the cultured, the literary, and artistic classes yield a large percentage of cases, owing to an overendowment of nerves or because of neurotic inheritances."[75] Drug use among physicians remained a fact of life, but its decline, like its earlier rise, probably paralleled that in society after 1900.[76] But the rate of addiction doubtless was higher in the medical profession than in society at large. The medical world was a microcosm that showed how easily drugs seemed to attract people who were especially important to social progress.

Doctors were only one element of the "favored classes" who appeared liable to opiate addiction in the late nineteenth century.[77] The drug user profile changed after 1900, when the typical case was likely to be male, young, and a user by choice rather than by accident or mistake. But the opiate addict before then was middle-class, genteel in taste and demeanor, whether from the city or country, and was probably part of "the higher and more cultivated classes of the community."[78] As late as 1902 Thomas D. Crothers could say that "Morphinism is one of the most serious addictions among active brain-workers, professionals and businessmen, teachers, and persons having large cares and responsibilities."[79] And the traditional opiate addicts often held responsible positions in their communities.[80] Addicts themselves consistently agreed, to rationalize their condition, but also because of the kinds of people they encountered in the underworld. "Opium is scholarly, refined, and aristocratic in its association," William Rosser Cobbe held in his memoirs. "It has no part or lot with the ignorant and degraded. Its victims are those who build up thought, who advance material wealth, and give polish to society. Hence the destruction it works is frightful."[81]

This fear that drugs were eroding the talents of social groups especially important to progress, joined with two other points that made society increasingly concerned about drug use in the late nineteenth century. One was the fact that addiction and abuse appeared most widespread in people between the ages of twenty and fifty, the prime of productive life.[82] The other was the growing realization that opiates were in fact addictive to anybody, regardless of will. And drug experiences could be habit-forming for anyone whose psyche needed them. In short, society could not confine drugs to any marginal elements. Use cut across society, and as it seemed to become more and more widespread and often attractive to many people, society could not ignore it.

As people learned more about drug use after the 1870s and came to fear its effects on individualism, productivity, and progress, a set of attitudes developed that helped shape the long debate that ended in legal controls. Those attitudes had deep roots in social thought and expressed both powerful fears and aspirations concerning civilization and the relationships and duties of people to each other in a complex and often bewildering society.

breaking down is only one of time. Sometimes it happens very early; and then not only does an exhausted vitality require to be replenished, but the long-pent-up craving for a beauty of which business activity has said, 'It is not in me,' rises from its bonds, and, with a sad imperativeness, asks satisfaction.[49]

The idea that some drugs, especially hashish and opiates, expanded consciousness and intensified creativity became a staple in the discussion of drugs. "Again and again have I had said to me, 'I should like so to try it, to see what the visions are like,'" an anonymous addict reported.[50] This notion underlay the addict's constant refrain that opium appealed to the higher faculties, and that its users were aristocratic in taste and demeanor. Even the opium user's initial willingness to risk addiction in order to intensify experience was evidence to him of high intelligence. These same observers, and not all were actual opiate users, preferred the effects of opium to those of alcohol. Opium ennobled, alcohol degraded; the former produced serenity and creativity, the latter brutishness or violence. "A man who, sober, is a demi-god, is, when drunk, below even the beasts," Horace Day wrote in an 1868 survey of opium use. "With opium...it is the reverse..., that is, taking the mind as it is, it intensifies and exalts all its capacities of thought and susceptibilities of emotion."[51] This seemed true at least for early stages of use, though as tolerance developed the typical addict merely used opiates to avoid withdrawal pain or for rest and oblivion. Thus, to critics, bondage followed imaginative flights as a curious and ironic retribution.

An expanded sense of emotional opulence was compelling to many users, but both experts and addicts agreed that "opium will not give brains, and above all the intellectual nature of all narcotic visions, depends on the mental power, even more than on the associations, of the subject."[52] The apologetic or arrogant user assumed that intense visions or insights only registered the workings of an originally superior mind. But both the reflective addict and the careful investigator saw that opium only created in the mind new arrangements of sensations that had different relationships in the nondrug state. Drugs that produced psychic changes intensified memories and imaginative material already thought through. "Thus opium leads its new devotee along the mental paths he loves most to travel," an addict said.[53] Opium created the new out of the old, but it could not increase actual ability.

This was clear in the reported experiences, whether from De Quincey or Ludlow. These obviously reflected the subject's past reading, travel, schooling, and speculations. Among people with literary inclinations, the reveries tended to be set in exotic lands and were gorgeous and grandiose in appearance. The imagery came from gothic and romantic novels and poetry, traveller's tales, and religious symbolism. The tone was dreamy, free from anxiety, often coupled with a sense of omnipotence that the user did not feel in the work-a-day world and which was infantile in origin. But the experiences were also sometimes tinged with a sense of vague regret and disappointment, harbingers of failed ambitions rather than of fulfillment.

In most addicts these effects quickly yielded to the maintenance of a habit. Most who first praised the opium reverie ended in condemning its allurements. Nor did they think it truly creative. "Besides subduing the ordinary operations of the mind it tends to disorder," Cobbe thought, and "reason interfered with, there are ebullient, contradictory, evanescent, unreliable, and illogical thoughts, which find an expression in an irrepressible outflow of words which, perhaps, are mistaken for brilliancy because of their seeming spontaneity."[54] Later depth psychologists saw such effects as resulting from the release of repressed material in free associations that users called "imagination," as well as from actual changes of perception within the nervous system.

Some drug effects were also suspect because they released inhibitions and had strong erotic overtones. Most early commentators condemned opium smoking because of its associations with prostitution and the fear of white slavery that so fascinated and horrified the generation. They also attacked cannabis, especially hashish, which Cobbe called "that Messalina among drugs...."[55] The legend grew that some drugs that altered consciousness were also aphrodisiac, or heightened the sensuality around sexual expectation or performance.

Experts and addicts alike knew that this view was mistaken. If anything, depressants, and opiates in particular, inhibited sexual activity, at least after steady use. Yet there was a long tradition of identifying opium with sexual license because of the voluptuous feelings and imagery it supposedly produced. As so often in the drug debate, learned opinion varied. Some doctors used opium to repress what patients thought were excessive sexual drives. Others believed that opium enhanced sexual energy in releasing inhibitions. Opium varied in its effects, and in a sense the facts did not matter. The drug experience came to seem a sexual reverie, whether as an unnatural substitute for the sex act, or as an aphrodisiac. In due course, drugs also became associated with the sexual underworld of prostitution and illicit activity.[56]

Reaction to these vaunted drug experiences and effects revealed some basic social attitudes. What drug users saw as expansive and imaginative, nonusers thought was merely the inflation of an artificial personality that was divorced from reality. To critics such experiences

The idea that the increasing demands of "civilization" made people turn to stimulants, sedatives, and narcotics was equally popular. This notion derived partly from the growing debate over evolution and was part of a stage theory of cultural development. It held simply that the emotional demands of culture, or civilization as the era preferred, changed more rapidly than the individual's ability to understand or incorporate them. The temptations to increase energy, or at least the appearance of being energetic, or to find artificial rest and relaxation were thus strong.

This was all an ironic affirmation of progress. It showed how far society had come but only at great psychic cost. "We think, and we exhaust; we scheme, imagine, study, worry, and enjoy, and proportionately we waste," a popular magazine noted in 1862. "In the rude and primitive nations this holds good much less than among civilized people."[7] As another authority said bluntly in 1888: "Barbarians are not nervous."[8]

Late nineteenth-century culture thus seemed to be a major stage in man's development. This idea was a way of rationalizing the unhappy tensions that accompanied social processes whose outcome most people still thought would be beneficial. But whatever the value of progress to society in general, its effects on individuals were mixed. The era's rapid growth and changing values presented a threat as well as an opportunity, especially for ambitious, imaginative people. "A higher degree of civilization, bringing with it increased mental development among all classes, increased cares, duties and shocks," H. H. Kane wrote in 1881, "seems to have caused the habitual use of narcotics, once a comparatively rare vice among Christian nations, to have become alarmingly common."[9] There were great demands now on mental energy. Knowledge and insight were at a premium in the new scientific, technological society. "Life grows more complex with each development of science," an authority warned in 1883. "New faculties are brought into activity, new forces are called into being, and our knowledge of the relation of these to life and health is wanting. Hence inebriety, insanity, and a host of so-called new diseases, and new forms of old diseases."[10]

The processes of civilization caused nervousness, the inevitable cost of being modern and progressive. "Every advance of refinement brings conflict and conquest that are to be paid for in blood and nerve and life," a doctor warned in 1888.[11] In individual terms, the price was often insomnia and the inability to relax, major complaints in the late nineteenth century. The new therapeutics were standing invitations to avoid distress or pain that earlier generations took for granted or stoically expected from life, with the increased risk of drug addiction or habituation.[12]

There was even increasing concern about the rising consumption of tobacco, tea, and coffee, the minor deities of the household and workplace. Critics saw these as stimulants that were dangerous to an already tense and overworked people. They also feared that tea and coffee would become identified with food rather than medicine or drugs, and thus make their consumption seem normal. Government taxed alcohol and tobacco to raise revenue, but also to mark them as luxuries or their use as habits that merited disapproval.

These processes were at work in all industrializing nations but seemed especially strong in the American setting. American demands for worldly success obviously caused much strain. The increasing possibility of fulfilling dreams in the developing nation compounded the temptation of ambitious persons to over-extend their nervous resources. The imaginative, planning member of the middle class might be most prone to use a drug to relieve anxiety or promote a sense of energy. But members of every social element hoped to improve their prospects with extra mental effort and physical labor. Fitzhugh Ludlow, the "Hasheesh Eater," saw this everywhere. "The habit is gaining fearful ground among our professional men, the operatives in our mills, our weary sewing women, our fagged clerks, our disappointed wives, our former liquor-drunkards, our very daylaborers, who a generation ago took gin; all our classes, from the highest to the lowest, are yearly increasing their consumption of the drug," he wrote in 1867. "The terrible demands, especially in this country, made on modern brains by our feverish competitive life, constitute hourly temptations to some form of sweet, deadly sedative."[13]

This competitiveness radiated out from offices and mills to give the whole society a newly felt tinge of anxiety. "Anything is now dull and stupid that does not furnish excitement," a writer noted in 1879. "Nervous excitement prevails in our schools, in our homes, and in business."[14] A strong feeling of generational change flavored the discussion. Individual anxiety resulting from social changes seemed the more threatening for being sudden and unexpected. Life in general appeared to be markedly different from that of earlier generations. As an addict said by 1895, "all this is a growth so rapid, and in some respects so abnormal, that in many directions the mental strain has been too much for the physical system to bear...."[15]

Competitiveness was obviously a powerful cause of this tension, but commentators saw a larger pattern in American life. On the eve of the Civil War, a prescient doctor outlined the sources of what the next generation called neurasthenia. In his view the American's vaunted sense of individualism easily "tends to self-indulgence and excess." Freedom also caused rootlessness and the "discontented spirit" so

China remained the great emotional example of what opium allegedly did to the values necessary for modern life. She could never become great until she cast it off. It produced sloth instead of energy, drift instead of plans, dreams instead of truth. Hamilton Wright, a leader in the drive for international drug control after 1900, summarized the view in 1911: "You see, the whole world had regarded with a shudder China's flat prostration underneath the curse of the drug habit, and our shudders were, perhaps, the most vigorous of all."[24] The most progressive leaders and spokesmen of every country seeking to modernize or industrialize shared these views and opposed the use of drugs and alcohol that retarded their vision.

Closer to home, Americans began to develop critical attitudes toward drug use that involved basic values and ideals. The habits that sapped other cultures were a direct threat to the competitive work ethic. The drug user in general, and the opiate addict in particular, seemed unproductive. The reigning ideals of competition and hard work always involved the interaction of society and the individual. True individualism not only enriched the person involved. It fed the results of his energy and thought back into society to create wealth and the means for further advancement. What the individual did, therefore, directly concerned society at large. The imaginative flights that some opium users reported certainly did not seem to produce either material or intellectual benefits for society. That kind of individualism thus seemed selfish, detached from society, and passive.

Many drug users argued that they were trying to function in society's terms. Using stimulants allowed them to compete better; using depressants permitted them to control anxiety and husband energy for the world's work. Opiate addicts had worldly ambitions. In most cases they used the drug to avoid withdrawal pains and to continue functioning in their work. But the public never really accepted this idea, despite the examples of a few users who pursued successful careers. At most, both medical experts and social commentators held that they worked at reduced levels of efficiency and insight. They were not likely to originate new ideas or to pursue complex projects that required close attention to details. "Place the opium-eater in a situation where exertion is necessary, or unavoidable, and he will acquit himself with more energy and force than when in health," a medical journalist said in 1853, "but he will never seek an opportunity for distinction or effort, and never place himself in the way of labor. In a word, his will is wanting."[25] This view did not change much as the drug debate developed.

In more specific ways, the drug user wasted income as well as energy and insight, with adverse effects on family, friends, and co-workers. "The demands of the appetite are such that nearly every personal comfort is given up to satisfy and furnish the means to supply it," one observer reported of opiate addiction in 1878. "Neglect of business results, and poverty is the consequence. One correspondent who reports many opium-eaters in his vicinity says: 'I do not know a person who uses morphine (opium) whose family is not neglected and degraded thereby.'"[26] H. H. Kane agreed in his survey of opium smoking at about the same time. "Financially, the habit has but one tendency, viz., ruin, not so much from the money expended on the drug (from 50¢ to $3.00 per day) as from neglect of business and the impaired mental power brought to bear upon it for the short time that it receives any attention."[27]

This was the first generation of Americans to believe that general prosperity was attainable. The fear that drug use, and especially opiate addiction, lowered productivity or made individuals a drag on society, was important in shaping attitudes toward the problem. It seemed equally clear that innocent parties, whether in the family or community, suffered from the drug user's dependence and merited social concern and protection. The fear that drug use was spreading among the most productive elements of society increased the apprehension. And in an ironic way, its occasional appearance among the rich and frivolous merely identified it further with nonproducers.

These concerns about productivity and individualism merged with the belief that opiate use was a particularly strong form of slavery. This view reigned early in the debate. "It is not the man who eats opium, but it is opium that eats the man," Nathan Allen said in 1850, speaking of the drug's physical and psychological effects.[28] The experiences that addicts recounted with increasing frequency after the 1850s intensified this stereotype. Most held that they used opiates merely to avoid withdrawal pains, not for pleasure or escape. This viewpoint invited sympathy even while accepting the reigning social stereotype of the addict as slave. "It is not *pleasure*, then, that drives onward the confirmed opium-eater, but a *necessity* scarce less resistible than that Fate to which the pagan mythology subjected gods not less than men," an addict insisted in 1853.[29] "Men take it not for social enjoyment, but for a physical necessity," an authority held twenty years later.[30]

Addicts insisted that their efforts to be cured illustrated the desire to be free and normal members of society. Some who could not break the habit even sought freedom in death. "The awful mystery of death, which they rashly solved [in suicide], had no terrors for them equal to a life without opium, and the morning found them hanging in their cells glad to get 'anywhere, anywhere out of the world,'" an addict reported of cure failures in 1868.[31] Most simply surrendered to a life of addiction, yet they were intensely conscious of being outcasts. "But if there is ever a despairing time in life, it is when an opium eater, who has been earnest and determined in his effort to quit, sees himself forced back again into the habit, and realizes that life to him must ever be 'but a walking shadow,'" one addict said in 1876, "that he must languish out his natural existence, locked a close prisoner in the arms of a grisly demon!"[32]

A steadily increasing number of memoirs, case histories, and news stories emphasized the slavery of opiate addiction, and the only slightly lesser servitude of using some other drugs. The stories were often lurid enough but gained added force from the grandiose allusions which the educated addict loved so well. As one opium smoker told H. H. Kane in 1881: "Truly, the name 'fiend' is aptly used. It will make a villain of the best of men. There have been times when I believe that if I could not have obtained the money for opium otherwise, I would have taken the shoes from my wife's or child's feet and sold or pawned them."[33] In 1889 the New York *Times* reported the case of a bright young man who acquired the habit while working in the company business in Hong Kong. He had tried cure, only to relapse, and now required constant watching. "Would it interest you to hear the story of a man who daily suffers tortures beside which the inquisition was child's play?" he asked.[34] And the memoirs and case histories recounted many stories of the opiate addict as slave. William Rosser Cobbe heard of one man who became a medical addict after losing both legs in a railroad accident. The family cut off his supply. But he escaped, swung along the street for six blocks seeking morphine, and finally managed to take a train to get it from a friend 250 miles away.[35]

This sense of enslavement obsessed many addicts because it involved the loss of self-worth that society defined for and demanded of its normal members. "This very emasculation of the will itself, ... is in reality the most terrible characteristic of the injury wrought by these agents," Fitzhugh Ludlow wrote in 1857. "A spiritual unsexing as it is, it vitiates all relations of life which exist to its victim; by submitting to it he sows a harvest of degradation...."[36]

Even those who tried to explain or justify the moderate use of opiates to avoid withdrawal pains were sensitive about the point. "I want none of your readers to construe this article into a defense of the opium habit," a writer noted in 1878, "for I would condemn it, if for no other reason than that man should be free from all bondage, for nothing is more humiliating to a proud man than the thought that he is a *slave*."[37]

Addicts took various cures in hope of returning to the rationality, freedom, and efficiency the world defined as normal, and as especially important to the new industrial America. Many wrote memoirs to expiate guilt, or to explain their situation and their efforts to escape it. In the end, for so many, "One of the oppressive shadows of that dark night was the ever-abiding consciousness that self-mastery was utterly lost," as Cobbe said.[38] The apparent inability of addicts to end their habit, whatever its past origins or their present intentions, fortified the general view of the addict as slave. The condition became an example to avoid, and when cures and self-help failed, regulation seemed a logical answer.

Just as society had logical reasons for its apparent views of drug use, so addicts and users developed a rationale for their condition. Sometimes the imagery and explanations were parallel, if they did not touch. Many addicts accepted the reigning stereotypes about themselves. Many were not marginal members of society before, or even during, their drug use. Their constant desire to be a part of society, to have the respect of peers in the nondrug world, made them pay attention to what people apparently thought about their condition.

On both practical and theoretical levels, addicts usually understood their condition better than did most doctors. They perceived that opiates were somehow addictive long before most physicians did, if only after trying and failing to cure an obvious dependence. If willpower and the desire to quit using opiates failed, something physical was at work. Addicts also read much of the literature on inebriety. Many users who were habituated to one drug associated with users of others, and so understood several drug states. The educated and reflective addicts tried to analyze what in their lives made them start or continue drug use. They were among the first Americans to write about unconscious motivations and symbolism. This produced a sizeable body of memoirs, case histories, and press stories that revealed both the similarities and the differences of ideas in the two worlds of users and nonusers.

Addicts generally accepted the medically respectable explanations of the origins of drug use. Many began their use to control or suppress a medical problem. Yet they understood what Frederick H. Hubbard said in 1881: "Many patients feel ashamed of being addicted to the drug, and wishing to retain respect, will tell the physician of some imaginary trouble as the cause of the habit."[39] Many also began to use drugs at the hands of a careless or ignorant physician.[40] But they also would have understood the wry observation of D. W. Cathell: "The slaves of such blighting habits invariably cast the blame for their acquired passion or their withering enslavement on the physicians who first ordered the drug or stimulant for them, if they have the least ground for doing so."[41]

Many addicts of all types agreed with the hereditarian viewpoint. They saw their problem arising from "pre-natal tendencies, hereditary taints and passions. ... " that came to life under environmental stress and temptation.[42] In more subtle unconscious ways, they often blamed their addiction on parents and family upbringing. One thought that elderly parents of nervous dispositions blighted his life from infancy. Another's father died, and his mother lacked the emotional resources to rear a large family. Yet another simply recalled a strain of inebriety in the family. And an addict of the 1930s blamed his beginnings on too little discipline and poor adult role models.[43] This sort of analysis was a psychically bearable outlet for anger and resentment. But the constant effort of so many addicts to escape the blame for their drug use gained them a reputation for self-pity that was an important element in other people's dislike of them.

Many other drug users began with a different kind of fate or accident, arising from experimentation. These tended to possess in their own minds a special sensitivity, which the world in turn often viewed simply as another form of weakness or irresponsibility. The great early nineteenth-century models for this behavior were the English writers who first discussed opium, especially Thomas De Quincey and Samuel Taylor Coleridge. The careers and writings of both men offered ample warnings about the adverse effects of opium and the attitudes society was likely to take toward addiction. But the curious and confident reader often overlooked this in favor of the changed states of consciousness these authors described. In addition, they were men of talent and achievement, inevitably interesting to many young intellectuals and rebels. And the pre–Civil War generation was a time of rising interest in and production of things literary, with strong romantic images of the poet and essayist who was willing to risk much for fresh insights.

In short order, many "romantic youths have eaten the drug to be themselves the heroes of such dreams,..." as a medical writer noted in 1853.[44] Yet the glamorous drug user was not a universal image, and many people especially condemned De Quincey for leading others astray. Even those addicts who admired his *Confessions of an English Opium-Eater* (1822, rev. ed. 1856) criticized him for implying that he was cured, and for not emphasizing more strongly that opium was truly addictive. One addict's forcefulness revealed his disillusionment:

> The life of De Quincey, as gathered from his constant and unguarded, and therefore sincere, expressions of his wretched condition, which he made to others while living, shows the effects opium had upon him much more truthfully than do his writings. His extravagant eulogy of opium, and almost wildly-gay and lively manner of treating such a sardonically solemn subject as the effects of opium, though under the anomalous title, 'The Pleasures of Opium,' show the man to have been morally depraved, and utterly regardless of the influence of his writings. The result of the opium habit, first, last, and always, is to bring hopeless unhappiness.[45]

In the end, most addicts doubtless agreed with Cobbe that "these men were illustrious, not through the habit, but despite that hindrance."[46]

The American counterpart to De Quincey was Fitzhugh Ludlow (1836–70), the "Hasheesh Eater" who revealed his experiences in a book of that title in 1857. A sensitive, educated youth with literary ambitions, Ludlow summarized the public stereotype of those who deliberately experimented with drugs. Since his community and associates frowned on opium use, he turned to ether, chloroform, and finally to hashish, all readily obtainable at the local apothecary. He became famous in the literary world and the drug underground for vivid descriptions of the hallucinatory experiences that a potent form of hashish caused. Public fascination with this confessional writing helped to blight a small but interesting talent. Friends and critics remembered him as an example of the creative mind that drug use defeated, a warning against experimenting with "drugs of enchantment."[47]

Ludlow also typified the drug user who sought not to avoid pain or maintain a dosage but to enlarge his sense of life. There was a strong feeling among such users that observable reality and socially approved goals were not rewarding enough to justify life's anxieties and disappointments. There must be another realm of imagination that drugs could open. Ludlow, the writer Bayard Taylor, and anonymous reporters all emphasized the dazzling changes of actual perception they experienced after taking hashish, and in many cases opium. In broad emotional terms, "The whole East, from Greece to farthest China, lay within the compass of a township; no outlay was necessary for the journey," Ludlow said. "For the humble sum of six cents I might purchase an excursion ticket over all the earth; ships and dromedaries, tents and hospices were all contained in a Box of Tilden's extract." In personal perceptual terms, "the hasheesh-eater knows what it is to be burned by *salt* fire, to *smell* colors, to *see* sounds, and, much more frequently, to *see* feelings."[48]

Ludlow thought this urge to experiment was especially strong in the sensitive, educated people he saw drawn into the sharp competition for worldly success. "An intensive devotion to worldly business in our representative man often coexists with a stifled craving for something higher," he wrote as the new industrial society took form:

Beginning, for the sake of advancement, at an age when [people in?] other nations are still in the playground or the schoolroom, he continues rising early and lying down late in the pursuit of his ambition, to a period when they have retired to the ease of travel or a villa. Yet from the very fact that his fathers have done this before him, he inherits a constitution least of all fitted to bearing these drafts upon it. The question of his breaking down is only one of time. Sometimes it happens very early; and then not only does an exhausted vitality require to be replenished, but the long-pent-up craving for a beauty of which business activity has said, 'It is not in me,' rises from its bonds, and, with a sad imperativeness, asks satisfaction.[49]

The idea that some drugs, especially hashish and opiates, expanded consciousness and intensified creativity became a staple in the discussion of drugs. "Again and again have I had said to me, 'I should like so to try it, to see what the visions are like,'" an anonymous addict reported.[50] This notion underlay the addict's constant refrain that opium appealed to the higher faculties, and that its users were aristocratic in taste and demeanor. Even the opium user's initial willingness to risk addiction in order to intensify experience was evidence to him of high intelligence. These same observers, and not all were actual opiate users, preferred the effects of opium to those of alcohol. Opium ennobled, alcohol degraded; the former produced serenity and creativity, the latter brutishness or violence. "A man who, sober, is a demi-god, is, when drunk, below even the beasts," Horace Day wrote in an 1868 survey of opium use. "With opium...it is the reverse..., that is, taking the mind as it is, it intensifies and exalts all its capacities of thought and susceptibilities of emotion."[51] This seemed true at least for early stages of use, though as tolerance developed the typical addict merely used opiates to avoid withdrawal pain or for rest and oblivion. Thus, to critics, bondage followed imaginative flights as a curious and ironic retribution.

An expanded sense of emotional opulence was compelling to many users, but both experts and addicts agreed that "opium will not give brains, and above all the intellectual nature of all narcotic visions, depends on the mental power, even more than on the associations, of the subject."[52] The apologetic or arrogant user assumed that intense visions or insights only registered the workings of an originally superior mind. But both the reflective addict and the careful investigator saw that opium only created in the mind new arrangements of sensations that had different relationships in the nondrug state. Drugs that produced psychic changes intensified memories and imaginative material already thought through. "Thus opium leads its new devotee along the mental paths he loves most to travel," an addict said.[53] Opium created the new out of the old, but it could not increase actual ability.

This was clear in the reported experiences, whether from De Quincey or Ludlow. These obviously reflected the subject's past reading, travel, schooling, and speculations. Among people with literary inclinations, the reveries tended to be set in exotic lands and were gorgeous and grandiose in appearance. The imagery came from gothic and romantic novels and poetry, traveller's tales, and religious symbolism. The tone was dreamy, free from anxiety, often coupled with a sense of omnipotence that the user did not feel in the work-a-day world and which was infantile in origin. But the experiences were also sometimes tinged with a sense of vague regret and disappointment, harbingers of failed ambitions rather than of fulfillment.

In most addicts these effects quickly yielded to the maintenance of a habit. Most who first praised the opium reverie ended in condemning its allurements. Nor did they think it truly creative. "Besides subduing the ordinary operations of the mind it tends to disorder," Cobbe thought, and "reason interfered with, there are ebullient, contradictory, evanescent, unreliable, and illogical thoughts, which find an expression in an irrepressible outflow of words which, perhaps, are mistaken for brilliancy because of their seeming spontaneity."[54] Later depth psychologists saw such effects as resulting from the release of repressed material in free associations that users called "imagination," as well as from actual changes of perception within the nervous system.

Some drug effects were also suspect because they released inhibitions and had strong erotic overtones. Most early commentators condemned opium smoking because of its associations with prostitution and the fear of white slavery that so fascinated and horrified the generation. They also attacked cannabis, especially hashish, which Cobbe called "that Messalina among drugs...."[55] The legend grew that some drugs that altered consciousness were also aphrodisiac, or heightened the sensuality around sexual expectation or performance.

Experts and addicts alike knew that this view was mistaken. If anything, depressants, and opiates in particular, inhibited sexual activity, at least after steady use. Yet there was a long tradition of identifying opium with sexual license because of the voluptuous feelings and imagery it supposedly produced. As so often in the drug debate, learned opinion varied. Some doctors used opium to repress what patients thought were excessive sexual drives. Others believed that opium enhanced sexual energy in releasing inhibitions. Opium varied in its effects, and in a sense the facts did not matter. The drug experience came to seem a sexual reverie, whether as an unnatural substitute for the sex act, or as an aphrodisiac. In due course, drugs also became associated with the sexual underworld of prostitution and illicit activity.[56]

Reaction to these vaunted drug experiences and effects revealed some basic social attitudes. What drug users saw as expansive and imaginative, nonusers thought was merely the inflation of an artificial personality that was divorced from reality. To critics such experiences were escape from responsibilities and often seemed a kind of madness. Much of the addict-memoir literature revealed that drugs, especially opiates, allowed users to work out repressed fantasies centering on power, punishment, and other antisocial drives. In many ways, addicts controlled these impulses with opiates, but observers usually thought that drugs threatened to release them.

Most of all, imagination was intangible and thus suspect to a generation and a people that prized the concrete over the abstract. Reality was better than unreality, fact superior to fancy. Knowledge and insight won through working in the world and with other people were more important to both the individual and society than that supposedly raised up genielike without effort. In the end, people could agree with the anonymous addict who came to prize what the world called normal: "When a man is once a confirmed opium eater, all the pleasure he can derive from opium would not equal the enjoyment a well man receives from the animal spirits alone; and all the intellectual force obtainable from stimulation can never approach that which would have been his own freely in a natural condition."[57]

The opium experience thus seemed to alter the personality fundamentally. It became internal rather than external in orientation, focused more on the self than on friends, family, or society. The concern that addicts were not productive involved more than a fear that they were a drag on others. True social and mental health arose from relationships with other people and the world. Production or accomplishment thus represented emotional as well as material success, a real individualism derived from testing and expanding the abilities.

Many addicts struggled to achieve some great success that the world would acknowledge, both to prove their own worth and to conform to worldly standards. The literature of addiction was filled with stories of users who were going to write great books, discover great inventions, and make major breakthroughs in their business or profession. In the end, the dream usually sufficed for the reality. Society's stereotype about the addict and work seemed too often correct. "The evil lay in the utter inability to pursue extended and connected labor," William Rosser Cobbe said from the personal experience of one who longed for fame as a writer.[58]

The slavery image was strong among both addicts and laymen, and emerged early in the discussion. "There is but one all-absorbing want, one engrossing desire, his whole being has but one tongue—that tongue but one word—morphine," a popular magazine reported in 1868. "Place before him all that ever dazzled the sons of Adam since the fall, lay sceptres at his feet and all the prizes of vaulting ambition ever sighed and bled for, unfold the treasures of the earth and call them his: wearily he will turn aside and barter them all for a little white powder."[59] If anything, this stereotype grew stronger in the twentieth century when the addiction process clarified in medical thought and after most cure regimens had failed.

This dependence on a drug supply caused the addict to develop other qualities that people disliked and feared. He became deceitful, whether to hide his condition, or obtain drugs. "No sooner did opium *enter in* than conscientiousness *walked out*," Alonzo Calkins said in 1871.[60] A newspaper report agreed. "Like other secret vices the use of morphine gains a stronger hold over the will because of the deceit which it engenders," the New York *Tribune* reported in 1878. "A victim of the morphia crave [*sic*] might be trusted in everything else, but he will descend to the lowest deceit to obtain and use his favorite drug."[61]

The average doctor knew many people with imaginary ailments that required narcotics. And the addict who was always looking for something else, who bought a dozen items to conceal the desire for only one, who filched drugs from the shelves was familiar to pharmacists everywhere.[62] A medical journal warned in 1884: "Persons addicted to the use of opiates usually seem kind, well-disposed, meek and benevolent. At the same time they are perfectly unreliable in all their dealings; are untruthful and dishonest; neither their word nor their oath should be taken as true."[63] Here was a circular problem so common to the drug question: society disapproved of the addict, who pretended to be something else, only to win further disapproval for dishonesty. This all made the addict seem untrustworthy, whether as producer, citizen, or community member. And the society at large needed and prized a reliability he did not have.

Knowledge of the public's dislike, as well as the physiological actions of opiates, further turned the addict inward. This reinforced the world's tendency to see his state as passive, self-absorbed, and indifferent to the needs of others. Alonzo Calkins commented in 1871 on the typical addict's "amiable self-complacency ... ," and "self-satisfied disposition. ... "[64] The addict Henry Cole noted the tendency to withdrawal and solitude. "Opium, like liquor, gives an abandonment to the soul that makes it indifferent as to coming events," he wrote in 1895. "It lives in the present. It knows no tomorrow."[65]

This inwardness took intelligence and energy from society. But it seemed distasteful chiefly because it was negative and artificial, and involved brooding rather than thinking, somnolence instead of reflection. One doctor caught this viewpoint in a striking passage in 1908, perhaps drawn from the experience of someone he knew:

Some settle down to a certain dose and adhere to it for years; others devote their lives to the effort of absorbing all the opiate they can crowd into their systems. The life of the former runs on uneventfully. They live, perform a certain limited series of mental and physical evolutions, but their progress ceases, their career culminates. They gradually retire from the activities of the community and grow yearly more contracted in their operations and their sympathies. Ambition is dead, incentive has perished—they just live and no more. The man collects his little rents, sees to his little kitchen garden, eats a trifle, wears his old clothes and sits alone at home, reading a bit, meditating long, ruminating most of the time, producing nothing; a quiet, inoffensive, retiring hermit; of no use to himself or to anybody else, neither hated nor loved by any mortal man. Only the druggist knows the truth.[66]

No doubt many addicts went about their business with reasonable efficiency and the appearance of normality. But this image of the addict as withdrawn and passive was widespread.

Sympathy for this sense of stunted development was one point where the addict and society touched. Cure experts devised regimens that emphasized work with groups, life in natural settings, and other connections with the world to replace the addict's solitude or insulation.[67] And for all the era's vaunted emphasis on competition and freedom, it did not sanction isolation from or disregard of fellowmen. The "tendency to live apart from others, to shun companions, to avoid social engagements, and to ignore comradeship or natural affection for those entitled to it," was dangerous for both the individual and society.[68] Cure doctors often emphasized in their promotional literature the need for addicts to live among people.[69] In the end, as one commentator put it in 1918, "it is better for anyone's mental health to associate with one's fellows."[70]

Innocent people also suffered from anyone's addiction, which could not be a matter of individual freedom, since its effects were not confined to the user. The first to suffer, in this view, were family members. Addiction seemed to threaten both marriage and the family, important stabilizing institutions in a period of change. This was clear to addicts, whose writings were filled with guilt at impoverishing or disappointing loved ones. Medical and psychological experts often pointed to this social danger. "The friends and family of an opium habituate are most familiar with the degrading character of the slavery of the mind and nervous system which opium entails," a doctor wrote in 1884. "They realize how lost to the family circle as a real member of the household he or she has become, and whether it be father or mother, sister or brother, it is but natural that they should strive to reclaim that which is lost, or if not lost, at least estranged in many of those familiar mental traits with which are blended family love, esteem and reverence."[71]

The effects of the addict's rejection of "the relish for society and its enjoyments ... "[72] radiated out into the world which thus had a legitimate interest in his state. "The great trouble is that they are so oblivious to all the responsibilities of life, and so willing to become wrapped up with the exhilarating effects of this drug, avoiding all the troubles, pains, and responsibilities of life, that they cannot be brought to see that it is a duty both to themselves and to their friends to stop the habit," Dr. Charles W. Earle, a noted authority, wrote in 1886.[73] Introspection was thus not normally a social process, since it had to move beyond the personality to be truly worthwhile. "For emotion or sensation to go over into action is to follow the normal law of the mind," the educator David Starr Jordan wrote in 1900. "To cultivate sensation for sensation's sake, with no purpose beyond it, whether it be in art, music, love, or religion, is to live a sensuous life, and this is ultimately a life of weakness and decadence."[74] Pleasure and self-concern had a legitimate place only as part of a life involving friends, family and citizenship. In social terms, changing the normal personality or mind always seemed worse than affecting the body with drugs.[75]

The responses of many addicts testified ironically to the importance of these general attitudes. The literary addicts were not typical, but they had wide acquaintance with the drug world. They spoke for the aspirations and fears of those users striving to obtain or retain respectable status. While pleading for recognition of their plight, they often presented almost parallel images of the reigning critical social views of addiction and drug use. Their writings were filled with regret at unfinished projects, abandoned ideas, and with a sense of loss and failure. Few of them derived any pleasure or apparent benefit from opium, except to avoid withdrawal. Nearly all wanted to succeed in worldly terms but knew they were failures. They rebelled at their slavery as much as society feared and condemned it. "But the slave of the drug never for a moment loses the sense of his accountability or fails to measure the extent of his shortcomings," Cobbe wrote. "He is ever eager to accomplish something that will atone, in part, at least, for his many peccancies; hence, he plans and plans again; but, alas, he never executes."[76] There was also strong religious imagery, dealing with the themes of lost innocence, fall and redemption, in the confessional literature. Just as opiate addiction changed the vital personality, in this view, so it imperilled even the soul. If the alcoholic's nemesis was Demon Rum, that of the opiate addict was Mephistopheles.

Since the world's approval as well as a sense of personal worth determined anyone's feelings of success, addicts keenly resented their separation from society. Like so many other aspects of the drug situation, this reinforced the external actions that society found alarming or distasteful. Unsure of what the world really thought of them, they boasted, lied, and dissimulated. They misread social signals, creating grievances from mere accidents or unintended slights. In their fear of being discovered, many avoided society or turned to each other, which fortified the sense of isolation. Like society at large they despised their servitude. But if they sought cure and failed, the sense of bondage increased. If people expressed sympathy, they felt unworthy or did not believe the sentiment.[77] Few ever abandoned what Cobbe called "the never-lost desire to be continued in the self-respect of their neighbors."[78] In the end, as a group, they developed an almost unique sense of isolation and of general hopelessness about changing their condition.[79]

In the decades after 1900 there were many shifts of emphasis and concern in the discussion of drug use. The user population changed, which caused fresh social anxieties. The substances involved varied, as did their perceived effects and social importance. But a body of ideas and attitudes developed in the late nineteenth century that remained fairly constant and had a long life. Stereotypes to which the public responded were set, and policy-makers in medicine, law, or politics found it increasingly difficult to make qualitative judgements about the varied kinds of drug users. The drug experience, whether from opiates, cannabis, chloral, or other substances that changed the users' functioning seemed suspect or dangerous.

The antidrug consensus rested on attitudes that involved basic social aspirations, values, and fears. The opiate addict and some other drug users seemed enslaved, unproductive, or at least inefficient, escapist, and self-centered. Western man was always suspicious of introspection and generally preferred to subdue or control the world rather than to analyze or intuit its hidden meanings. These emphases on action, rationality, and predictability were always strong in American life. But they were unusually potent in the complex, interdependent industrial order of the late nineteenth century. The heart of the antidrug consensus was the fear of an alternate personality and way of life that threatened these generally held social views, and which might retard accepted ideas of progress and civilization. It also seemed that many people were liable to become dependent on opiates, or seek the effects of other drug experiences, to the detriment of society.

This body of ideas had not developed into a prohibitory mentality by the end of the nineteenth century. Few people desired to persecute or outlaw the addict or drug user. But any efforts at regulation would have to call upon this broad concern for support. Because they involved public fears and hopes, these and similar ideas would rise into life in the heat of debate about drug use after 1900.

5

CURES AND TREATMENTS

A SENSE OF PROGRESS animated the medical profession in the late nineteenth century. The therapeutic developments that eased pain and combatted diseases surely would produce an appropriate remedy for drug addiction. This seemed the more likely, given the apparent desire among addicts to be cured. As early as 1833 a medical journal reported that "every person of this description we have chanced to know has manifested a strong sense of the impropriety and danger of the practice, and entreated us to prescribe, if possible, some effectual remedy."[1]

Many addicts sought cure at sometime and spent lifetimes going from addiction, to temporary abstinence, to relapse. They naturally wanted to end their dependence on opiates and regain full health. But they also took repeated cure programs to demonstrate a desire for social respectability and normality. The pain and distress of withdrawal and the continued desire for opiates after treatment defeated all except a small minority. Users concluded long before doctors did that addiction to opiates was rooted in some psychological and physiological processes that willpower alone was not likely to defeat. This seemed obvious from painful experience, but it was also a way of explaining why so many people with good intentions and talent could not stop opiate use. These failures increased the addicts' sense of victimization and made their desire for sympathy more compelling. One wrote in 1876 that when the nature of addiction finally became clear to everyone, "the poor victim of its terrors will be taken by the hand and sympathized with by his fellow-man, instead of being ostracized from society, and treated with contempt and reprehension, as he now is."[2]

But a cure based on complete abstinence seemed as remote in the 1880s as in the 1930s or 1970s. As concern about addiction increased the nature of addiction still baffled doctors. Therapy for the specific symptoms during withdrawal did not stop the distress or produce any lasting cures. Willpower, persuasion, even threats seemed ineffectual. The journals were full of queries from doctors in every part of the country seeking the names of antidotes and asking advice on how to treat addicts during withdrawal.[3] In 1871 George M. Beard suggested that no subject remained so shrouded in mystery and bias. In 1895 another doctor thought that many colleagues still classed opiate addiction with the tea and coffee habits, or with excessive cigar smoking. They wondered why addicts did not simply quit.[4] At the same time, William Rosser Cobbe wrote with resignation: "The world cannot be greatly reprobated for its want of sympathy for the sufferers, since it has had no education upon the all-important subject."[5]

Doctors often shared the distaste for drug users that permeated the society. Moralism inhibited a purely clinical judgement that the addict was only a patient with a medical problem. The average practitioner was also unlikely or unable to learn much about a problem that seemed peripheral to his general practice. And physicians inevitably disliked being associated with the failure so common in treating addiction.[6]

This left a fertile field for the charlatan, and a minor industry arose to furnish nostrums and "cures" for the drug addict. The viability of this enterprise reflected many of the changes that transformed post–Civil War America. Newspapers now carried advertisements to every farm and hamlet. Low postal rates allowed many people to buy nostrums through the mails. And the plain brown wrapper that made the product anonymous hid the addict's condition from family and neighbors. Government patents and copyrights for labels, containers, and contents seemed to grant official approval, despite the complete lack of inspection or regulation of the traffic.[7]

Addicts turned to nostrum vendors out of both hope and desperation. If orthodox medicine, with all its new claims to scientific insight, had no answer, perhaps someone outside its constraints did. And the longstanding American tradition of self-doctoring combined with the normal human desire to believe in taking a chance to make these products attractive.

The quacks shared some attributes. They tended to have shadowy origins and humble beginnings. With few exceptions they were self-taught or had inferior educations and cast themselves as outsiders who established medicine feared. They often used the trappings of science and technology but also appealed to the average man's suspicion of experts, portraying their discoveries as the fruits of pragmatic work with a broad spectrum of people. They were especially active in the Midwest and South, and played on resentment of the East, which was the center of establishment medicine, as it was of finance and culture.[8]

Samuel Collins of La Porte, Indiana, was among the best known of this breed. A bricklayer turned medico, he developed a thriving business selling a bottled cure nostrum via the mails. As his success grew, Collins built impressive looking offices, a fancy home, and a sanitarium for resident patients. He also published a magazine called *Theriaki*, replete with addict confessions, articles on the drug question, and testimonials for his medicine. Basil M. Woolley of Atlanta operated in much the same way, as did countless other such "doctors" across the country.[9]

Most of the mail-order doctors followed procedures that allayed the patient's skepticism, fed his hopes, and made him seem important and unique. Each buyer filled out a personal history, with attention to how long he or she had taken the particular drug, in what dosage, and with what effects. The vendor then appeared to tailor the compound for them. He encouraged the user to report on progress, and if "cured," to endorse the product. Many such testimonials were false, but most doubtless were genuine, written in the euphoria when the patient thought himself cured. Relapses were not recorded; nor were the users who became addicted to the nostrum.

The simple fact, of course, was that no antidote or cure for opiate addiction existed. Each product contained drugs that allayed withdrawal distress, usually bromides, alcohol, perhaps cocaine, or a hypnotic and morphine. The patient might reduce a large opiate habit with decreasing doses. He could report progress, and if a novice, was sure that he was on the road to recovery. In the end, the typical purchaser reached a maintenance dosage below which he experienced withdrawal pains and either stayed at that level or relapsed to his prior usage.[10]

The widespread sale of these compounds illustrated the extent of addiction and the effort of many people to seek anonymous cure. Countless addicts spent their incomes on such products.[11] No chemical assay was as attractive to them as the label on the bottle they so eagerly unwrapped in the privacy of home. And doctors and health reformers inveighed in vain against these peddlers. In 1885 Albert B. Prescott, professor of chemistry at the University of Michigan, gave an opinion in language more colorful than scientific: "And for this nostrum vendor, certainly, the symbol of the spider and the fly would be too tame a trademark, and his own service with chain and ball not too severe a retribution."[12] The cure compounds came under regulation with national pure food and drug regulation after 1906, when their sales declined.

In an ironic way, these vendors were part of the first stage of an emerging specialty devoted to drug dependence and addiction. They at least defined the nature of a health problem that orthodox medicine could not solve and was avoiding. Even as the nostrums went out across the country, a number of physicians demanded closer investigation of addiction and more sympathy for the addict who sought medical help. Some argued simply that doctors had a special responsibility, since they made so many addicts.[13] By the Progressive era, some medical commentators held that the very fact of failure should be a challenge, and physicians ought to stop avoiding or repelling addicts seeking help for what seemed to be a disease.[14]

The search for the causes of addiction, whether rooted in heredity, personality, or environment, inevitably created a body of thought oriented toward seeing drug use and addiction as a disease. By 1877 the New York *Times* reflected some medical opinion in holding that "It is not a vice which afflicts them [addicts], but a disease, which presents as marked and as specific a symptomatology as do many of the better known diseases, and requiring, as they do, proper medical aid and systematic treatment to effect a cure.... "[15]

Spokesmen of the disease theory developed a variety of explanations for addiction that tried to free the user from self-deprecation and to soften social criticism. Specialists oriented toward physiology proposed that opiates, and alcohol, somehow altered nervous tissue in the brain and spinal cord to create what appeared to be a compulsion to use certain substances whose effects counteracted these changes and seemed to the user to restore normality and a sense of well being. Other thinkers refined hereditarian ideas and saw addiction as rooted in poor physical endowment or in inherited tendencies. Still others held that even if drug use began accidentally from experimentation it became a compulsion grounded in psychological and physiological change. It was thus a disease rather than a mere vice, open to treatment and cure through changing the patient's physical and emotional habits and outlook. This general body of thought and practice created a respectable speciality, a network of sanitaria whose practices usually reflected the ideas of a dominant personality, and a body of writing in books and journals that tried to inform the profession at large about the problem of addiction and dependence.

The idea that addiction was a disease gained ground slowly but steadily. "The habitual use of opium is a disease, and a formidable one ...," Frederick H. Hubbard, author of studies on the drug and alcohol habits, wrote in 1880.[16] By the middle of that decade a few doctors began to lecture colleagues on their moral as well as medical responsibilities toward addicts. "The person comes to us for relief *as a patient,*" one wrote in 1884, "and we should treat him, socially and professionally, as a diseased person, and not as a brute or an outcast.... The victim needs no other judge than his own conscience, and it ill becomes us, as alleviators of pain, to add to the exquisite tortures and torments he has already experienced."[17] J. B. Mattison agreed. "In the vast majority of cases the *vice* theory of its origins is incorrect, so that, with few exceptions, the term 'opium habit' is a misnomer, implying, as it wrongly does, an opiate-using quite under individual control." A decade later he thought it clear that opiates somehow affected the nervous system and made addiction involuntary. He noted that addicted infants were born to addicted mothers; they obviously had not committed any vice.[18]

A large array of procedures to treat opiate addiction developed in the last third of the nineteenth century. By 1900 the study and treatment of addiction was a respectable, though not large, professional subdivision. But the experts and therapists in it always cautioned of the special frustrations in dealing with addicts whose illness arose from multiple and often intangible causes. Nor did they underestimate the hold that opiates had on some people. Mattison and others warned early that only comprehensive, individual programs that actually stopped opiate use, restored health, and changed the patient's environment stood any chance of success.[19]

Opiates adversely affected many body processes. They deadened appetite, slowed digestion and elimination, and suppressed secretions in general. Physical and mental reflexes, muscle tone, and attention to the environment declined under addiction. The emotional effects of opiates reinforced inattention to the body and personality, and most addicts who sought treatment were debilitated.

These general physical and emotional aspects of addiction were hard enough to treat, but specialists quickly focused on controlling the specific painful symptoms that followed witholding opiates. Most addicts abandoned self-cure when the withdrawal distress became severe. They were not likely to commit themselves to doctors who did not understand their feelings of horror about this stage. And if they failed to get through withdrawal, the details of any subsequent regimen mattered little.

The nature of what came to be styled withdrawal was well known, if not well understood. In 1822 John Eberle, author of a popular medical guide, noted: "When the system is entirely free from the influence of the accustomed stimulant, torments of the most distressing kind are experienced."[20] A century later Edward Huntington Williams could write: "Indeed, the Inquisition missed what would certainly have been one of its choicest torture-devices by passing out of fashion before morphine came in."[21]

Addicts tried to convince the public and doctors of the terrible nature of withdrawal. Every addict-memoirist recounted experiences at cure, whether alone or with medical aid. The physical and emotional agonies were simply too much to endure. Once again, they insisted that their addiction and relapse resulted not from lack of will or the desire for normality, but because of processes beyond the control of even normal people. They along with most of the new drug experts insisted that addiction continued from the need to avoid pain rather than from any desire for pleasure.[22] The emotional dread of withdrawal reinforced the fear and expectation of misery, which naturally inhibited the will to seek cure. Charles B. Towns, who developed an elaborate cure program, summarized this view in 1916: "...the great majority of drug-users wish nothing so much as to be freed from this slavery, while at the same time they fear nothing so greatly as sudden deprivation of their drug. In the interaction of these two major impulses lies the key to the addict's psychology."[23]

The first stages of withdrawal from opiates produced symptoms that were both physically painful and emotionally exhausting. The patient experienced copious discharges from the mucous membranes, vomiting, and diarrhea. This reduced him to an infantile condition, which heightened his sense of degradation and helplessness. There was sharp pain in the muscles, often seeming to make the bones ache, spasms, and a general sense of aching throughout the body. The skin usually became hypersensitive. The prick of a needle might feel like impalement, or crucifixion, as the more florid addict-memoirists said. The craving for relief with morphine became intense. "It is generally the case, at this stage," an addict wrote in 1876, "that the opium eater would wade through blood for opium."[24]

The patient's sense of time slowed, and he was restless, semiconscious, or sleepless. The process seemed endless, which caused a general feeling of despair and misery. An addict under treatment told Fitzhugh Ludlow in 1867 that "God seems to help a man in getting out of every difficulty but opium. There you have to *claw* your way out over redhot coals on your hands and knees, and drag yourself by main strength through the burning dungeon-bars."[25]

Another genteel, well-educated patient under therapy said in 1883: "I believe hell is composed of opium eaters, and the punishment consists of withdrawing from them the drug, as that is the greatest torture I can imagine."[26] Some observers believed that addicts shammed or greatly exaggerated these effects to get sympathy and explain subsequent relapse. Psychology played a part, and reactions varied in individuals. But most addicts before 1914 employed morphine in pure states and developed high tolerances that intensified the withdrawal process.

Three approaches to getting through this crucial first phase of treatment developed in the late nineteenth century.[27] All authorities agreed that none was pain free. Doctors who promised painless cures were thus probably giving patients opiates, and patients who claimed to have no distress were secretly using them.[28]

The first method came from Germany, especially from Dr. Edouard Levinstein, who argued that addiction to opiates was physiological, with anyone liable. The point was to rid the system of them and begin the process of rebuilding immediately. He recommended abrupt cessation, what later generations called "cold turkey," with physical restraint if necessary and some control of symptoms with other drugs. The suffering might be intense, but it was emotionally better than prolonging the ordeal.[29]

This idea was popular briefly during the late 1870s and early 1880s but yielded under the pressures of reality. J. B. Mattison thought it invited failure. "This course, if it be appreciated by the patient, will be very apt to give rise to a spirit of insubordination quite fatal to the success of the movement, standing, as it inevitably would, in the way of keeping up the courage and co-operation to the desired degree."[30] Addicts and their sympathizers agreed. As James Coulter Layard wrote the New York *Times* in 1878: "If you were on the top of a six-storey building, Mr. Editor, and wishing to come down to the street, would you jump out of the window, at the imminent risk of breaking your limbs, or maybe your neck, or would you come down by the stairs, step by step."[31] This approach usually only made the physician a villain to the addict, someone to avoid in the future.[32] Such therapy also smacked of moralistic punishment, aimed at establishing a memory that would prevent relapse but which instead more likely kept the addict from trying treatment again.[33]

A second approach rested on withdrawal of opiates in a week or so, while using drugs to alleviate distress. This gained approval, and blended into the third general method, a "humane" program that relied on gradual withdrawal, with supportive drugs and emotional therapies. This was expensive and ran the risk of never quite ending, but when done firmly, the patient supposedly cooperated while the body began to recover smoothly.[34]

These systems shared many procedures. The treatment of drug addiction quickly became eclectic because of the varying reactions in individuals, the state of knowledge, and the roles of the many doctors involved. And the parallel search went on for a specific remedy, or "magic bullet," that somehow would kill addiction. Even if such a substance was not a substitute for opiates, it might at least alleviate major symptoms and be usable in the average doctor's office rather than in a sanitarium or hospital.

The plant kingdom seemed to offer some hope. The enthusiasm for coca was widespread in the early 1880s. "Coca is to be used as a *substitute* for the opium," one writer held in 1880. "It is therefore to be taken as freely as the cravings of the system for opium may demand.... The 'break off' is to be made at once and for all, and coca is the staff upon which the sufferer is to throw his whole weight."[35] For a time, drug houses could not produce enough coca extract to meet the demand such announcements generated. Many practitioners failed to note that most authors saw coca, and then cocaine, not as antidotes or substitutes for opiates, but as aids to getting through withdrawal. Coca and cocaine failed to fulfill these expectations and also became a source of dependence for some patients.

Cannabis went through a similar cycle of appeal and favor. It gained some importance as a tranquilizer and was more useful in treating chloral or bromide habits than opiate addiction.[36] Among the more surprising plant specifics was one derived from common oats, *Avena sativa*. Packaged in a suitable compound, this allegedly cured some opiate addicts. But J. B. Mattison demolished the product's credentials, and in the end, in an all too familiar cycle, it became part of a quack nostrum for the opium habit that contained morphine, "Scotch Oats Essence."[37] Some more exotic plants seemed attractive. In 1898 Dr. W. W. Winthrop of Fort Worth, Texas, suggested that the Florida plant called "husa," or *Viola sagittata,* the spear-eared violet, was "an infallible cure for the opium habit." It produced a mild euphoric effect, and several of his acquaintances claimed that it cured their opiate addiction.[38]

The search for a nonaddictive narcotic also began. Codeine, then heroin, gained a good deal of attention until familiarity demonstrated that they too caused addiction.[39] Some experts used hypnotism, a popular procedure for alleviating the psychic tension that supposedly underlay addiction.[40] By the beginning of the new century, addicts and experts alike had experimented with almost everything that conceivably could affect the withdrawal process. There was no magic bullet. As Ernest S. Bishop said in 1915: "My work and experience with narcotic drug addiction has taught me one thing if it has done nothing else—I know that its problems will never be solved by any special remedies. I know that they will never be solved by the adoption of any routine method."[41]

The regimens that developed out of experience focused on the addict who cooperated in seeking cure. The user for pleasure, or the one who thought his case incurable was generally hopeless. The treatment programs were thus elaborate and gave the patient the sense of being at their center. Everyone involved was doing everything possible for him. More so than with purely physical ailments, the procedure was reciprocal. "No treatment requires so many *small things* to be done," a doctor from Brownwood, Texas, wrote in 1892, "with perfect submission to all the requirements on the part of the patient and special knowledge, experience and tact on the part of the physician."[42] The only suggestions lacking in these varied programs were leeching and bloodletting, and some doctors doubtless tried them without leaving a record.

Few such regimens were suitable for home use, simply because so much attention to the patient's body was necessary. All except the strongest also would return to drugs if they were available, as at home or among friends. The sympathy of loved ones was important but functioned best from a distance where it did not become pity or collusion. And leaving the familiar social or business environment was vital if the patient was to change the habits and stresses that caused or fortified the original condition. "To those who profess to think a man can stay at home, continue to attend to his business, and put a stop to the habitual use of morphine, I have only to say: If it be so easy then do it," Dr. William F. Waugh of Chicago wrote in 1895. "Go right ahead and stop; and I shall take off my hat to you, as a giant among men."[43]

Treatments usually occurred in a special facility. Comfort was all-important and restraint unpopular unless the patient was truly violent. In the first stages of withdrawal, chloral or some other hypnotic might keep him relatively comfortable while antispasmodics combatted the restlessness. Discharges from the bowels and mucous membranes emptied the body of wastes without hindrance. This necessitated frequent tepid baths, which were also soothing. After a few days, the patient might take electric shocks to relax muscles. In a few more days, he could exercise briefly and begin the arduous task of restoring normal body functions. As soon as the stomach permitted, he took nourishing foods and restoratives. Any ailment that addiction had masked received treatment. Most patients responded quickly, testifying to the human body's resilience, and gained weight, improved the muscle tone, and became more aware of the world around them.[44]

The subject then faced an indeterminate period of feeling weak and emotionally drained. The opiates were out of the system, but the memory of their action remained. Anyone who reflected solely on the past, on regrets and remorse, or the roads not taken, could relapse. The sense of care must be all-pervasive from doctors and attendants. Family and friends were welcome only to reassure the patient. Most regimens then emphasized keeping busy. Reading, gardening, doing chores, talking with other patients, group exercises, entertainments, and similar activities were all designed as small challenges the patient could fulfill. He must obtain self-respect, a sense of authority, and focus on the future. In short, he must not relapse into the situation and mental frame that sustained the addiction.[45] This psychological emphasis became dominant in the twentieth century but was always implicit in earlier therapies. Addicts clearly understood the need for affection and a kind of spiritual renaissance to develop what the world called "willpower."[46]

The next step in treatment depended on the patient's physical and emotional health, optimism and pocketbook. He could return home and hope to alter the old routines and relationships, or remain for an extended period of time at a sanitarium. By 1870 there were publicly funded asylums for inebriates in New York, Pennsylvania, and Michigan. But most such institutions were private, usually the creation of one doctor dedicated to treating alcoholics and addicts with a special approach. In the 1870s and 1880s Dr. Harry Hubbell Kane of New York City gained considerable notoriety for treating inebriates in his "home," though his reputation suffered for overenthusiasm about new and debatable therapeutics. In Brooklyn Dr. J. B. Mattison operated an important sanitarium and became a major writer on the subject of addiction and drug use. Dr. Thomas D. Crothers presided over a famous sanitarium in Hartford, and became prominent for both his theoretical and practical writings. He was also a leader of a group of physicians dedicated to refining and teaching the disease theory of inebriety, edited the *Quarterly Journal of Inebriety,* and was important in the American Association for the Cure of Inebriates.

The sanitarium movement that these and other doctors spoke for seemed a progressive innovation in both medicine and psychiatry that appealed to many kinds of reformers. Its attempt to individualize and humanize care for addicts complemented similar efforts to liberalize the treatment of insane, indigent, and impaired persons. Sanitarium treatment was also identified with the latest in technology and scientific thinking in its field. And it attempted to return the patient to "normal" society after showing him how to manage new anxieties and tensions.

There were probably a hundred such sanitaria in the country in 1910.[47] Even those in urban areas emphasized the need for fresh air, pastoral settings, calm, and physical labor, testifying to the belief that urban-industrial tensions caused addiction and drug use. There were occasional fund drives in cities like New York to raise money to send addicts to rural retreats away from the temptations and pressures of urban life.[48] The health reformers who ran the Battle Creek Sanitarium in Michigan even used organic foods, exercise, and natural remedies in treating addiction.[49]

By the turn of the century the sanitarium business was important. It was well organized, in the hands of acknowledged experts, and had many standardized procedures that allowed for individual variations. In some towns the sanitarium tower rivalled the railroad station as a sign of progress. The movement testified to the organizational changes that had transformed the nation's medicine as well as its economy.

Many of these therapeutic and organizational methods met in Leslie E. Keeley, the late nineteenth-century's most controversial cure doctor. Mystery shrouded his origins, and even as a figure of national importance in the 1890s, he seldom spoke about his background, focusing instead on the specific remedy and general treatment he developed

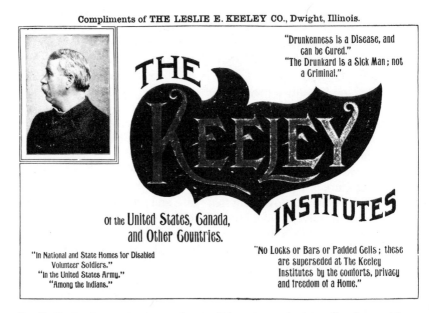

Compliments of **THE LESLIE E. KEELEY CO.**, Dwight, Illinois.

THE

KEELEY

INSTITUTES

Of the United States, Canada, and Other Countries.

"Drunkenness is a Disease, and can be Cured."
"The Drunkard is a Sick Man; not a Criminal."

"In National and State Homes for Disabled Volunteer Soldiers."
"In the United States Army."
"Among the Indians."

"No Locks or Bars or Padded Cells; these are superseded at The Keeley Institutes by the comforts, privacy and freedom of a Home."

Leslie E. Keeley on the cover of one of his company's promotional pamphlets. Courtesy National Library of Medicine.

for alcoholics and drug addicts. He led people to believe that he was born in St. Lawrence County, in upstate New York, probably in Potsdam, in 1832. As a young man he apparently moved west to Beardstown, Illinois, and began studying medicine with a local doctor. He took an M.D. at Rush Medical College in Chicago. During the Civil War he was a post surgeon at Jefferson Barracks, St. Louis, and then settled in Dwight, Illinois. He was division surgeon for the Chicago and Alton Railroad and gained local fame for organizing a relief expedition after a particularly terrible railroad accident.

Drinking among the soldiers he dealt with during the war apparently made Keeley wonder about the causes of inebriety. The youthful practitioner supposedly experimented with various compounds and substances, including gold, and announced in 1879: "Drunkenness is a disease and I can cure it."[50] Keeley then began distributing a specific, the Bichloride of Gold remedy, and established a sanitarium at Dwight. In 1891 the famous and influential publisher of the Chicago *Tribune*, Joseph Medill, anonymously sent Keeley a random sample of derelicts and other confirmed alcoholics. They apparently stopped drinking after the treatment, and Medill became a formidable supporter of Keeley and his methods.

The complex at Dwight prospered thereafter, and Keeley's name became almost a household word after his corporation granted franchises for similar operations in many cities. The billboards and wall-sized signs proclaiming the presence of a Keeley Institute were almost obligatory for a city to be up-to-date from the 1890s to the first World War.

Keeley began his experiments with a few friends and ultimately had two partners, but his organization and therapeutic system were extensions of a strong personality. He insisted that his name appear prominently on the operation's advertising, literature, and products. Frederick Hargreaves, an early helper who became a hostile critic, agreed that "he was a man of strong personality. He dominated everybody, or ruled everybody, and made them do as he wanted to do, and if they would not do it, he would make them do it, or have nothing to do with them at all. That was Keeley's character."[51] Keeley cultivated an attitude of remoteness and mystery. This doubtless reflected experience with alcoholics and addicts who needed firm authority but was basically a reflection of his personality. "Dr. Keeley was a born autocrat," Nate Reed, another associate, recalled. "He brooked no interference. Had he gone upon the stage he would have had few if any superiors."[52]

For all his formidable demeanor, Keeley could be generous and sympathetic. He spent large sums on charity cases and treated many poor patients at reduced prices or free.[53] This largesse did not affect his prosperity. Toward the end of his life Keeley withdrew more and more from the business and built a large home in Los Angeles where he spent winters. He died there of apparent heart failure on February 21, 1900, a millionaire.[54]

Keeley articulated a theory of addiction to explain and justify his therapeutic approach that incorporated aspects of most of the reigning ideas of his day. He focused on alcohol more than on drugs, but thought all had similar actions and effects in the body. He wrote material for opiate addicts and users of other drugs, and the therapeutic program made special allowances for them. He doubtless did not emphasize them as much as alcoholics because society was so hostile, and because their relapse rate was high.

Keeley believed that inebriety had a physiological basis. Inherited tendencies were important but not inevitable in their effects. Though his ideas changed between the 1870s and 1890s, he basically argued that alcohol and drugs were poisons that somehow altered nerve cells and other tissues, creating a self-perpetuating demand for themselves. Once these substances were removed, and the body freed of the adverse effects they caused, regeneration began. Nervous endowment and resistances varied from person to person, which explained why some users developed what the world called "habits" and others did not. "If a man who takes poison, who takes a disease, or eats opium, or drinks whiskey, cannot create in his tissue cells a variation of structure, enabling him to resist the poison," Keeley said in 1893, "then the poison will kill him, or the disease will kill him."[55] His gift for clarity in explaining the theory was appealing. "Nerve cells are very impressionable. They have the power of becoming educated," he said again in 1893. "Repeated impressions made upon them from any source will cause this training, or conduct, or mode of action, or education. When the brain cells are educated, they perform their function according to the form and type of this training. They act as they are taught to act."[56] In short, if the body could learn inebriety it could learn sobriety. This view appealed to the American ideals of education, self-help, and optimism about environmental influences while explaining addiction as basically a physiological problem that treatment could correct. At a time when no explanation of the nervous system's functioning was satisfactory or exact, Keeley's did not seem illogical.

The treatment that Keeley proposed for this disease rested first on a famous product, the Bichloride of Gold compound. He recalled his bewilderment at the excessive drinking and drug-taking among respectable people he knew and began studying the problem while a young physician. In reviewing the literature, he came upon a remark from

Paracelsus that future generations would find "Gold, the king of metals," effective against diseases rooted in heredity.[57]

He allegedly wrote some 500 doctors for their opinion of gold in therapy and began experimenting with various compounds in the late 1870s. He supposedly tried gold in pill form on an especially hardened local alcoholic. The man nearly died but stopped drinking. Keeley continued the experiments, adding and subtracting substances that were then popular in treating opiate addiction and alcoholism. He was apparently familiar with the actions of nux vomica, atropia, chloral, cannabis, coca, jamaica dogwood, bromides, and hyoscine. A former patient years later recalled helping Keeley's partner, John R. Oughton, mix a batch of the specific. He could only say for certain that well-water, willow bark, and a small amount of something in a bottle bearing a skull and crossbones went into the mixture.[58]

By the late 1870s, Keeley was ready to distribute the Bichloride of Gold remedy.[59] Aides decided upon a unique package for the product. It came in special bottles with a curved front and flat back. Two back to back made a convenient package, and Keeley sold them in pairs. The labels were ornate and impressive, and each bottle top was heavy with sealing wax. Printed instructions for using the compound also directed the recipient to break the empty bottle so that no one else could fill it with another mixture. Prices varied with the habit in question. Tobacco users paid five dollars for a pair of bottles. Neurasthenics required an eight dollar set. Alcoholics needed nine dollars worth. Opium addicts needed ten dollars worth, testifying to the difficulty of curing their habit. Keeley secured copyrights, patents, and trademarks for the bottle's shape, the label designs, and other accoutrements but never sought protection for the formula, in order to avoid stating its composition.[60] At no time did Keeley or anyone else reveal the formula, and it died with the partners.

Gold was the focus of both the popularity and the controversy that gathered around Keeley in the 1890s, but his emphasis on the metal was not intrinsically absurd or unusual. He was not the first to suggest its use against alcoholism and addiction. The heavy metals had a long history in therapeutics, though their popularity was declining, mainly because of the dangers associated with mercury. But gold was in some use for skin and venereal diseases. Some authorities recommended it for epilepsy and nervous ailments.[61] Chloride of gold increased elimination, which was important in removing toxins from the systems of addicts and alcoholics.[62]

It also seemed promising in treating addictions and alcoholism because it stimulated the brain and nervous system. An English homeopath noted in 1879 that it caused a sense of well-being and energy in the aged and infirm and even aroused sexual functions.[63] An American authority reported in 1893 that a careful mixture containing gold and arsenic was a good tonic. "It stimulates the brain, incites a flow of spirits, gives sleep to the sleepless, courage to the despondent, and intensifies sexual desire and power," he said in recommending it for "those in middle life and in old age."[64] Another wonder drug seemed available, but experts cautioned that gold preparations were difficult to regulate and uncertain in action. Too much of the metal or its salts caused kidney damage, and its actual workings remained unknown.

Keeley soon developed an elaborate regimen for patients who stayed at the institute in Dwight, but continued to sell the home cure via the mails. Like other cure doctors, he tried to tailor this to individual needs and followed up on progress. He cautioned home users to rest, exercise, and develop new interests while taking the compound. Those with low level dependencies thus might benefit from self-dosage; others had to come to Dwight. Keeley also left the strong impression that the home cure was a way of helping poor people, and of reaching those who would not visit a sanitarium for fear of exposure. Just when the organization stopped selling the home remedy was unclear, but probably about the time of Keeley's death in 1900. By then there were enough franchise institutes to handle the volume of applicants, and new ideas of treatment emphasized custodial care.[65]

The facilities at Dwight gained a reputation for being modern, efficient, and humane. There was no restraint of patients unless they requested it. They could have alcohol or drugs on request; the treatment would simply stop their cravings. They were free to walk around town, visit each other, or drive in the countryside. There was some dormitory space and a fairly large hotel, and many patients rented rooms from local residents. There were special facilities for women who desired privacy. The treatment might last from four to six weeks, and in 1914 it cost $100 for four weeks plus about $20 for board.[66] This was not excessive in comparison to other programs, or to such care from a private physician.

The regimen aimed at developing a sense of responsibility and heightened self-esteem among recovering patients and rested on the psychic reassurance of a basic routine. At stated hours during the day, patients lined up for "malted milk," and "lemonade" compounds, and after the mid-1880s, a "barber pole" hypodermic shot that was red, white, and blue in color.[67] Keeley understood the importance of gesture and symbolism. He also retained absolute authority. A wealthy patient once objected to waiting in line and offered him a thousand dollars for private treatment. The Doctor did not hesitate: "My friend, I cannot do

Patients awaiting hypodermic injections at the Keeley Institute, Dwight, Illinois. From Leslie E. Keeley Co., *The Keeley Institutes of the United States, Canada and Other Countries* (1895), p. 33, courtesy of National Library of Medicine.

what you ask; but never mind; get into the 'line,' and if you behave yourself for a couple of weeks you will be just as good as any of them."[68]

This attitude pointed to other qualities of the program that many patients remembered all their lives, whatever the controversies around Bichloride of Gold. The person arriving at the train station in fair weather or foul usually saw a group bidding goodbye to an apparently cured patient, exhorting him or her to keep the newly found faith. Once in the clinic the newcomer ceased to be defensive or ashamed. On all hands, he encountered alcoholics or addicts eager to discuss their lives and help each other. Here was a cross section of humanity, volunteering for a cure program, each member reinforcing his reviving strength of body and mind through contact with others.[69] The orientation was toward the future and a new beginning in life. As a former patient said: "The whole atmosphere of the place was that of a camp meeting or a revival."[70] Even critics recognized the therapeutic value of this redemptive psychology. "An enthusiastic hope is engendered and the operation of this emotion alone may produce greater results than any drug is capable of," one hostile doctor admitted. "Further, the intensification of this effect by bringing large numbers together with the same hope and enthusiasm is a factor that it is hardly possible to overrate."[71]

The patient who was finally cured also had a new definition of his condition. Keeley held that cure consisted of freedom from alcohol and drugs; there was no assurance of permanent abstinence. Medicine could only remove drugs and alcohol from the body and give it a chance to regenerate. Avoiding relapse into alcohol or drug use was a matter of realism, maturity, and will. As Keeley told one graduating class:

> You must remember that I cannot paralyze the arm that would deliber-
> ately raise the fatal glass to the lips. When you all go out into the new life,
> I will have placed you exactly where you were before taking the first
> drink. You will look back over the past and then contemplate the future,
> and you will then choose which path you will follow the balance of your
> days.[72]

The program at Dwight fortified whatever self-help the patient could muster, and Keeley believed chances of relapse small. The departing patient tended to be euphoric, oriented toward the future, and usually agreed. If he relapsed later, it was not the program's fault. "Yes sir, it is his own fault if he don't [stay cured], and it is not the fault of the treatment," one said. "If a man wants to behave himself, he can, and he can make a damn fool of himself if he wants to."[73]

The numbers of patients were impressive by anybody's standards. Between September 1, 1892, and September 1, 1893, some 14,991 people took the treatment, and the numbers grew with the treatment's fame and expanded facilities.[74] Keeley insisted that only 5 percent of these would relapse on an average, a figure it was impossible to check, but which was clearly too low and which applied only to alcoholics. Relapses among drug addicts were doubtless more numerous.

Keeley's chief aim was to return patients to respectability in the world. To fortify their nerve and offer fresh challenges he devised elaborate after-care programs. Patients were encouraged to take pride in their therapy and to decline alcohol or drugs with the explanation "No thank you; I've been to Dwight," a phrase that became national for a time.[75] Former patients were "graduates," each with a class that often held reunions, with distinctive paraphernalia and paper honors. Local Keeley Clubs carried on propaganda and group-help for graduates and others interested in ending an alcohol or drug problem. There were auxiliaries for wives, mothers, and children. The organization published

a periodical, *The Banner of Gold,* and distributed pamphlets and leaf-
lets. Keeley's own writings remained in print, and he lectured in the
United States and England. There was even a "Keeley Baby," the child
of an addicted mother. Both took the cure and allegedly recovered.[76]
Once again, critics envied this success. "By doing this, the Keeley
graduates ... have thrown around them all the moral restraints of the
old-time temperance organizations that, in time past, cured as many, and
perhaps more, drunkards than all the Keeley Institutes."[77]

By 1891 Keeley began to plan new facilities, and ultimately there
were franchise operations in most major cities. He apparently did not
supervise these himself, and with his death in 1900 the network became
too much to control. Some local operations were sound, but many ran
down quickly.[78] This fading reputation combined with changes in
therapeutical approach and the growth of publicly funded programs to
reduce the system by the time of World War I. In 1920 the U.S. government purchased the Dwight facility for a veterans hospital. It then had
about 500 beds, laboratory space and equipment. Hundreds of
thousands of people with all kinds of drug and alcohol problems had
taken the Keeley cure at the local institutes, at Dwight, or at home over
the preceding forty years.[79]

Keeley's story unfolded amid great controversy. The chief subject of criticism was the Bichloride of Gold remedy. The AMA officially
opposed using any compound whose contents were unknown. This was
an effort to avoid identifying orthodox medicine with quackery and was
also a way of controlling maverick doctors. Keeley insisted repeatedly
that he would not reveal the formula because druggists, doctors, and
quacks would simply reproduce it to his detriment. He shrewdly identified himself with Robert Koch, whose premature announcement
of tuberculin as a cure for tuberculosis had adverse effects on his
reputation.[80]

He also insisted that the formula was only part of a broad treatment that patients at home as well as at the institute should follow.
Critics charged that he touted Bichloride of Gold as a specific, like any
other nostrum peddler; he insisted that it was only part of a cure program.[81] His supporters emphasized that critics did not demand the
formulas of all patent medicines; their concern thus attested to the
importance of Keeley's compounds.[82] Keeley also played on the public
suspicion of doctors. "If I should throw open my formula to the world it
would not cheapen the cure to the patient one cent," he said in 1891.
"Reputable physicians would charge their regular rates, disreputable
physicians would charge less in money, but by their dishonest practices
would rob the poor drinking man of the thing dearest to him in this world
—the chance of complete reform."[83]

Throughout the 1890s the medical journals and the popular press ran various chemical analyses of Bichloride of Gold. Most revealed simple ingredients such as water, alcohol, glycerine, willow bark, ginger, ammonia, and hops. Some assays also turned up traces of coca, aloes, atropine, pilocarpine, apomorphine, and strychnine. Some showed traces of gold salts, others did not. Most critics thought gold useless anyway but saw its promotional value "as a concession to prevailing materialism ... ," something "'solid' and of the *earth,* [that] can be grasped and appreciated."[84]

In 1893 one Chauncey Chapman worked undercover in a Keeley Institute then wrote a lengthy article for a Chicago medical journal charging that Bichloride of Gold and other Keeley compounds contained no gold. They were composed instead of drugs that merely sedated patients during withdrawal and created a temporary aversion to alcohol and drugs through producing nausea. The entire Keeley "cure" was a fraud.[85]

Keeley responded with bluntness and vigor. The gold cure was "the medical child in the manger," and these "pretended formulae" were false. "The remedy I use is a secret. It has never been analyzed; it never will be," he insisted. "The formula has never been published or printed. In my opinion, it never will be." He could hardly have been firmer. "I use no strychnia, aloes, atropia, muriate of ammonia, barber pole, bichloride of gold, tonic, dope or apomorphine, or the other drugs mentioned." He admitted that the term "bichloride of gold" was a technical misnomer. He preferred "double chloride of gold and sodium," but a patient "wanted a convenient title for his club. He called it 'bichloride' because he found difficulty in naming the organization the 'Double Chloride of Gold Club,' or the 'Chloride of Gold and Sodium Club.'" In the end he flung down a simple challenge: the issue was results, not formula contents. If he cured no one, he was a fraud; if he did cure people, the profession owed him recognition. He believed he had cured thousands if not millions of people.[86]

Chapman's reply further clouded the issue, as was so common in the debate about Keeley. He insisted that Keeley could not have devised a formula beyond chemical analysis. But he admitted that "I do not claim to give Keeley's exact formulae, but I do claim to give formulae which are identical therapeutically with his; I claim that Keeley does use strychnia, he does use atropia, he does use apomorphine, or principles identical with these in therapeutic effect."[87] The debate continued to no one's satisfaction but did not slow Keeley's progress. He won the endorsement of churches, temperance groups, and even the U.S. Army, which used the treatment for alcoholic soldiers. Ironically enough, many doctors who did not believe in "Keeleyism" sent hopeless patients to Dwight, just in case the program worked.

What did Bichloride of Gold and the other compounds contain? It seemed certain that the critics were right — Keeley could not have a formula that no chemist could analyze. Much of the debate concerned terminology. What critics called "poisons" or "narcotics" Keeley could style something else. Every pharmaceutical had numerous variations, with different names, and Keeley doubtless denied using certain specific substances or names to evade critics. Whatever the precise nature of the compounds, they clearly relied on tranquilization and antagonism for effect. Some relaxed and stupefied the patient while others created a temporary distaste for alcohol or drugs.[88] As for gold, its presence was always hard to detect, yet traces of it were in almost everything. It had no therapeutic value in the minute doses the Bichloride of Gold compound apparently contained but had strong symbolic appeal.

At some point in the 1890s when he was successful and a national figure, Keeley may have rued his original reliance on a nostrum. Without it, his necessary defense of it, and the confusion surrounding its composition, he would have seemed a prophet ahead of his time. His real contribution lay in the routine at Dwight. It integrated medicine, self-help, and group therapy, which in various guises were all the wave of the future in drug treatment. His career also showed the importance of having a strong personality at the center of such a program and organization.

Keeley died in 1900 just as a new sense of optimism entered the debate over addiction treatment. Medicine was more than ever identified with experimental science, especially body chemistry. Discoveries in bacteriology and immunology seemed now to offer new explanations of the body processes that were relevant to addiction.[89] The reformist spirit of the progressive era also fortified the belief that a solution based on empirical evidence was near, especially in the hands of a new generation of experts oriented toward a humane and rational treatment program for addicts.

The idea that opiates somehow poisoned cells and thus produced the symptoms associated with addiction became dominant in various forms. Belief in toxemias was always included in the eclectic explanations of addiction. Even in 1833 Dr. C. L. Seeger of Northampton, Massachusetts, thought that such a process was at work. His answer was to eliminate the waste matter with purgatives and emetics and restore the patient's normality with good food, rest, and fresh air.[90] Variations of this idea underlay the later sanitarian treatments and the disease theory of addiction.

Refinements of this view gained ground in the 1890s, including the idea that the body produced antitoxins to cope with the poisons that wastes and drugs caused. Dr. William F. Waugh of Chicago argued in 1895 that withdrawal pains resulted from toxic substances the blood absorbed from the intestinal canal. "The reason men who are addicted to a drug can take enormous doses of it is that in the body there is developed an antidote to that drug—just as the laborer's hands develop callosities," he suggested. "When the drug is discontinued, the production of the antidote continues, and the withdrawal symptoms are due to poisoning by this antidotal toxine."[91] The goal of the first treatment programs was chiefly to remove opiates from the system to allow for regeneration. This now seemed insufficient. The drugs somehow caused additional poisoning that required further treatment, a view that seemed logical given the new work in bacteriology and immunology.

Variations of this kind of explanation gained fresh appeal as the new century developed. Dr. George E. Pettey became a strong spokesman for the idea of toxemia, the basis of a regimen he used at his Memphis clinic. The positivistic neurologists who found no organic lesions that explained addiction concluded that it was psychological, the result of some nervous or mental imbalance. Pettey disagreed and adopted a materialism somewhat more subtle than the endless search for lesions that so fascinated the preceding generation. He insisted in 1913 that "the condition is not in any true sense a neurosis; *but it is purely and solely a toxemia, and as such belongs to the field of internal medicine and not to neurology.*" He went further, believing that "if a drug patient could be made *cell clean*; that is if every cell and structure of the body

Advertisement for Dr. George E. Pettey's sanitarium. From *Medical World* 30 (December 1912): xxii.

could be entirely freed from toxic matter, there would be no nervous manifestations or suffering incident to or following the withdrawal of the opiate."[92] As for the addict's compulsion, which society so strongly disliked: "The 'habit' of using drugs is only a symptom, just as the habit of coughing is the symptom of some chronic ailments. The use of the drug produced the disease; the disease produced the habit."[93]

Dr. Ernest S. Bishop of New York, a leader in the movement to regulate drugs while treating addicts as medical patients, developed a similar approach. He saw addiction as:

> A definite physical disease condition, presenting constant and definite disease symptoms and signs, progressing through clean cut clinical stages of development, explainable by a mechanism of body protection against the action of narcotic toxins, accompanied by inhibition of function and autotoxemia, often displaying deterioration and psychoses which are not intrinsic to the disease, but the result of toxemia, malnutrition, anxiety, fear and suffering.[94]

Bishop relied on purgation, and especially on opening the bile ducts and mucous membranes, to detoxify the cells. Charles B. Towns, a layman who became a major spokesman for drug regulation, joined with Dr. Alexander Lambert of Cornell University to establish a famous treatment that relied on purging the body of wastes and toxins.

The general idea that addiction involved poisons, or antibodies, or antitoxins had a powerful clinical aura and was identified with science. It suggested a practical cure that satisfied a public opinion now moving toward drug regulation, yet concerned with what to do about addicts. It also relieved the addict of responsibility for his condition and promised him a new life as a normal member of society.

But the toxemia theory was more the result of intuition and analogy than actual experimentation. Dr. Christian Laase of New York inadvertently revealed the conflicting ambivalences and certitudes in this theory in 1919 as it passed from the scene:

> Substances floating in the blood—antidotal substances, antitoxins, antibodies—call them what you will—protect the organism against the toxic action of the drug itself and enable the body to tolerate enormous quantities of the drug; and yet when the drug is withdrawn, leaving these antidotal substances free and uncombined, the latter are themselves poisonous to the body and produce the abject sufferings of the addict when deprived of his drug. The addict takes the drug to neutralize these antidotal substances—but he doesn't know it—all he knows is that the

drug will keep away those pains that we now know are caused by
antidotal substances. And he doesn't take the drug for the pleasure of it
or the satisfaction of it; but because on account of these antidotal
substances there is a real body need for it.[95]

This general theory was as erroneous and the treatments it created were
as fruitless in results as their many predecessors. By the time of World
War I there was yet another dispensation on the cause and management
of drug addiction and abuse.

Fifty years of elaborate treatments based on cleansing the body of
wastes and drugs and trying to restore it to normality had clearly failed.
Theorists and practitioners now increasingly relied on psychology to
explain why so many people were unable to attain permanent abstinence
once their bodies were drug-free. It now seemed that some intangible,
psychological factors were at work.[96]

The newly fashionable psychological explanations did not come
unannounced. In a very real sense there were no new ideas, only
periodic new emphases in the theories of cause and treatment of addiction. Even the narrowest medical experimenter understood that psychology played a role in the patient's behavior. The early hereditarian
theories involved psychology in explaining why some personalities fal-
tered under environmental pressures and others did not. The authorities
agreed that only patients who truthfully wanted to be cured had any
chance for success. The addict who candidly used drugs for pleasure or
escape was always beyond the medical and social pale.[97] The emphasis
on postwithdrawal care, institutionalization, and changes of environment in most regimens indicated that some psyches could not stand
external environmental or internal emotional pressures.[98] Even during
the optimistic progressive era when cure seemed attainable, an authority
warned: "One great fallacy, particularly in morphine addiction, is the
belief that the individual is well as soon as the drug is discontinued."[99]

Psychological explanations became fashionable in part because
approaches based on physiology had clearly failed. Society also began to
accept them for more and more human behavior. And like earlier ideas in
medicine and science, they seemed sophisticated and modern. But both
addicts and specialists had always understood that drugs appealed to
some people as a way of seeming normal in both physical and emotional
terms. In 1833 a report held that most users took opiates "to strengthen
and balance the nervous system and enable them to attend to business,
and to appear like other people."[100] An addict-memoirist of 1876 understood this in a deeper psychological sense: "I craved something eter-
nally which seemed absolutely necessary to make up the proper con-

stitution of my stomach: —and of my happiness, also, I should add, for this is the whole truth."[101]

This need to seem normal represented a desire to correct a sense of personal inadequacy and to control the anxieties it produced. But it was one more evidence of the addict's goal of integration into the world. As Dr. Curran Pope mused in 1904: "It has often seemed to me that it is the desire to imitate the feeling of health and strength, the well-being and happiness of perfect functioning, the bodily strength and mental activity, that compels many to continue to use, and finally abuse, stimulant drinks and narcotic drugs."[102]

If this were so, the ideal of total abstinence as cure lay beyond the reach of many if not most addicts. Medicine as such could not redress psychological defects. Cleansing the body of opiates only at best restored its original emotionally unsound condition. "Everything points to a diseased mental state beyond the power of any drug to reach it as an antidote," a doctor had warned even in 1896.[103]

By the 1920s, drug treatment had moved through all the phases that marked both medical and social change. The first experts thought and hoped that narcotics caused a specific ailment they could cure. The idea that addiction was a more general disease then produced therapies aimed at removing drugs from the body, while allaying the addict's fear of pain, and changing his environment. But the disease concept now widened to include the mind as well as body. Treatment must draw on ideas from psychology and psychiatry, sociology, public health, as well as medicine and pharmacology. "Cure" for the drug addict would become as endless as living itself.

6

REGULATION

S THE NEW CENTURY DAWNED reformers set out to curb the power of business to affect individual lives and the larger society. They were equally determined to make politics more responsive to the popular will. And while they were as individualistic as their fathers or grandfathers, their definition of freedom changed along with the complex, interdependent society that competition ironically had produced. Personal actions that seemed to affect social institutions or stability faced the test of popular opinion. What people did as individuals now affected others in ways undreamed of only a generation before. A powerful urge to "purify" American life thus accompanied reforms in business and politics. This involved struggles against prostitution, alcohol, and drugs as much as it did efforts to improve the lot of women, children, and the poor.

The temperance movement began in pre–Civil War America as part of a concern in the western world about alcohol's adverse effects on individuals and society. It provoked great tension among ethnic, religious, and economic interests and had many motives and aims. On a purely human level, it represented simple disgust at the consumption of spirits among Americans. It also involved confrontations among religious groups with differing interpretations of Christian conduct and responsibilities. It was an effort to make established middle-class sobriety the general standard of conduct at a time when America's disparate population seemed dangerously fragmented, at least to people who judged personal conduct by its effects on social order. Temperance and then prohibition appeared necessary to curb the adverse effects of alcohol on the individual personality, the family, and future generations. Liquor also seemed to threaten rationality, production, and efficiency, all of which also figured in the adverse image of drug use.

Despite the tensions and struggles involved, an antiliquor consensus was appearing by the beginning of the new century. Efforts to regulate the drug traffic and drug use paralleled the drive for temperance and then prohibition but had different qualities. Society always retained some ambivalence in its views of the effects of both alcohol and opiate use. As long as these were purely private matters, it tended to inaction, however disagreeable or unattractive they were. But when they seemed to affect society at large, regulation or prohibition became popular.

There were frequent comparisons of alcohol and opiates during the nineteenth century. Until the nature of addiction became clear, they were often in favor of opium. If alcohol had some sanctions drawn from history and realism about man's use of relaxants, opium was identified with relief from pain. Late nineteenth-century experts generally doubted that opium damaged the body as much as alcohol did. Nor did it seem to cause organic changes that might be passed on to offspring.[1]

Opium seemed more respectable than alcohol in its observable effects on individuals. A medical journal noted in 1832 that a doctor might not realize that a patient used opium, since unlike alcohol, it did not produce violent outward signs.[2] Walter Colton, who reported on opium use in the Near East in the 1830s, recommended it over alcohol precisely because it seemed genteel in effects. It "never makes a man foolish, it never casts a man into a ditch, or under a table, it never deprives him of his wits or his legs," he wrote. "It allows a man to be a gentleman; it makes him visionary, but his visions create no noise, no riots; they deal no blows, blacken no one's eye, and frighten no one's peace. It is the most quiet and unoffending relief to which the desponding and distressed, who have no higher resources, can appeal."[3] The notion that opiates attracted the sensitive and intelligent, "that class who look with horror upon the dram shop or fashionable saloon," paralleled the fear that they were threatening that very class, whose talents were so needed for further progress.[4]

Opium also appeared less destructive than alcohol in social terms. The latter often caused violence and disorder that represented a prior stage of development in both the individual and society. "Liquor generally arouses the animal, the brutal part of man's nature," the New York *Times* held in 1878, "but opium subdues this completely, and in its place awakens the diviner part and brings into full activity all the nobler emotions of the human heart."[5] This rather romantic view changed as knowledge and fear of addiction increased, and no one really recommended opiates any more than alcohol to the normal person. But as late as 1893 the New York *Tribune* editorialized about one kind of opium use: "The long and short of it is that while it is impossible to recommend or defend the practice of opium-smoking, yet it is not worse than the alcoholic habit. Both are vices, but of the two, the opium eater is a much less dangerous and offensive member of society than the one who is a victim of the curse of drink."[6]

Occasionally, some of the early doctors who studied opium use even suggested substituting it for alcohol in hopeless cases. It was cheaper, its effects easier to conceal, and created the appearance of respectability while controlling "baser passions." Opiates even reduced the sex drive so that the worst offenders would not transmit their affliction to posterity.[7]

But the stream of comparison and comment turned against opiates because they seemed more enslaving, and their effects more debilitating and passive than alcohol. Addict confessions, debate within the medical profession, and press reports fortified this view.[8] And the alcohol user simply seemed more normal than the opiate addict because he was historically more familiar. Alcohol appeared to exaggerate rather than replace the user's normal personality. And the drinker could be cheerful, amusing, and apparently intelligent if he did not lapse into violence. Opinion of the opiate addict was different, as William Rosser Cobbe knew: "The drunkard displays pleasurable emotions at times; his neighbors find excuse for him in his good fellowship; but the opium 'fiend' is silent, gloomy, repressive."[9]

In the largest sense, whatever the controversy over its excessive use, alcohol appeared more suited than opiates to the American experience. Alcohol represented external action, competition, manliness, and strength. Opiates appeared defeatist, introspective, unnatural.[10] There were always spokesmen to oppose prohibition, if not to praise alcohol. But opiates had no such constituency except among addicts and some doctors. By the time prohibition became a national issue, drug use and addiction seemed as dangerous to society as alcohol. To reformers they were all counterproductive, enervating, and irrational. The drive to prohibit alcohol did not cause the movement against drugs, but it helped make it seem logical and necessary.

The effort to regulate drugs in the progressive era had special aspects, whatever its relationship to the broader drive to purify American life and morality. Two substances, cocaine and heroin, focused new attention on the question of the social effects of drug use in general. The imagery that developed in the debate over them helped to increase popular support for regulation.

Both coca and cocaine had declined in use after the first flush of enthusiasm following their discovery in the 1880s. Other drugs seemed safer and more predictable than cocaine, though it was a useful local anesthetic. Coca was still included in some tonics and nostrums, but it never developed a strong separate identity apart from cocaine and lost in appeal to newer drugs.

Cocaine also had gained an adverse reputation outside of limited medical uses. It became identified with unpredictable and often bizarre behavior. The cocainist who felt endowed with superhuman strength or intellect might casually offer to jump over a building or solve an impossible problem. He could as easily feel persecuted or the center of a universal plot, and strong changes of mood characterized steady or heavy users. Physical symptoms following overuse were often equally unsettling, as the user thought that insects were crawling beneath his skin, or had hallucinations. To the critic, cocaine seemed to produce a kind of temporary insanity that threatened both the individual psyche and social relationships.[11]

Cocaine was not addictive but gained a reputation for causing dependence. From the first, it was loosely identified with the drug world in general, so that superficially it sometimes seemed part of a true addiction cycle.[12] The new disease concept of addiction also made cocaine use appear a mere dissipation. It was a voluntary act or habit that the user could stop without withdrawal; society thus need not sympathize with him, as it often could with the opiate addict. The cocainist also won a reputation for lying, evasiveness, and boasting that even surpassed that of the opiate addict.[13]

Of even greater importance, cocaine's constituency changed during the progressive period, with profound effects on public opinion. Coca and cocaine originally seemed attractive to sensitive and intelligent people seeking to maintain energy in order to work harder at socially acceptable tasks.[14] Early users warned of its attractions to people seeking escape, but by and large saw it as a restorative.

But after about 1900 a new generation of users discovered cocaine. It soon became identified with criminal elements and with denizens of the tenderloin districts of large cities. The image of the young tough who wasted the day in a billiard parlor and stole at night to buy cocaine gave an added dimension to the older stereotypes of the antisocial threats in drug use. Police spokesmen now came to the fore for the first time in the drug debate to link cocaine with crime against both persons and property. This naturally enhanced general fears of drug use and helped to blur distinctions about the impact on society at large of different kinds of drug users.[15]

Cocaine also seemed unusually attractive to young people, always a critical constituency in determining attitudes toward drugs. And lack of regulation combined with ease of preparation to make it available nearly everywhere. The sober citizen might never encounter opiates except briefly as medicine. But now he could hear about cocaine use from the daily papers, weekly and monthly magazines, government reports, and a host of other sources. He might discover that it was readily available in mixed drinks at bars, or even at soda fountains in some parts of his city or town. Pure food and drug reformers sought to remove it from soft drinks that were popular with children.[16] Cocaine thus vividly summarized the growing public tendency to think that drug use was suddenly increasing, emerging into the light, ceasing to be something that society could merely disapprove of or isolate.

Identification of cocaine with blacks intensified this adverse imagery. After the turn of the century, increasing reports of cocaine use among blacks aroused all the lurid stereotypes and fears in American racism. There was a modest scare about cocaine use during the Spanish-American War. Innocent soldiers supposedly acquired the vice from visiting red-light districts in southern ports, which were often identified with the black population. In 1898 a New Orleans doctor warned that cocaine sniffing was on the rise among blacks there.[17] In short order, the stereotyped external effects of cocaine use began to match hidden fears about black behavior. A 1903 report on drug use for the American Pharmaceutical Association said: "The negroes, the lower and immoral classes, are naturally most readily influenced, and therefore among them we have the greater number [of users], for they give little thought to the seriousness of the habit forming."[18]

The South inevitably received the most attention in the discussion of cocaine use among blacks. It was apparently a familiar item among work gangs in the fields, on railroads, or at port facilities throughout the region. "In the South the use of cocaine among the lower order of working negroes is quite common," the New York *Times* reported in 1911. "Inquiries have shown that contractors of labor in the South, under the impression that cocaine stimulates the negro laborers to a greater output of work, wink at the distribution of the drug to them."[19] In the shanty towns cocaine peddlers allegedly went from door to door, or sold "heaven dust" along with other merchandise.[20]

This traffic was difficult if not impossible either to verify or control. Many blacks supposedly used cocaine because local authorities monitored liquor consumption among them so closely. The Gulf Coast and South Atlantic ports were sieves through which drugs passed unhindered. And the black population seemingly developed an effective distribution system of railway personnel, shoeshine boys, porters, bellhops, and similar service people.[21]

White fears about the consequences of cocaine use among blacks inevitably focused on murder and sex. The myth that the drug increased the physical powers of criminals became national currency. Some police departments insisted that ordinary police revolvers lacked the power to kill cocaine-crazed blacks, and increased the caliber of their weapons. In one typical report in 1907 from Augusta, Arkansas, a black using cocaine allegedly shot seven whites before a posse managed to kill him.[22] A writer for *Everybody's Magazine* noted in 1914 that "the cocaine which throws the victim into a frenzy increases the vitality to such an extent that 'ordinary shootin' don't kill him,' as the officers say. And this observation is confirmed by clinical observation and laboratory experiment."[23] The scientific details of the story went unproved.

The fear that cocaine might lessen the black's inhibitions and increase his sexual impulses also ran through the discussion.[24] And a member of the Philadelphia pharmaceutical board managed to include nearly every white stereotype of blacks in testimony to a committee of the national House of Representatives in 1910:

> The colored people seem to have a weakness for it [cocaine]. It is a very seductive drug, and it produces extreme exhilaration. Persons under the influence of it believe they are millionaires. They have an exaggerated ego. They imagine they can lift this building, if they want to, or can do anything they want to. They have no regard for right or wrong. It produces a kind of temporary insanity. They would just as leave rape a woman as anything else and a great many of the southern rape cases have been traced to cocaine.[25]

Concern crossed the Mason Dixon Line. By the mid-1910s there was considerable comment on cocaine use in the black populations of northern cities.

The black thus became another potent racial image in the drug debate. He was not the first or the last. The Near Easterner had symbolized apprehensions about the adverse personal and social effects of cannabis use. Stereotypes of the Chinese had summarized fears about the social dangers of opium smoking. In decades to come the Mexican and marihuana, and the black or Puerto Rican and heroin would figure in the debate. This imagery revealed apprehensions about these ethnic groups and a desire to control their behavior or isolate them. But in more subtle ways the racial imagery coincided with deeper social and psychological fears. It became part of the larger idea that drug use was backward, premodern, unproductive, as these ethnic groups appeared to be to most Americans. Race as such merely added an edge of specific fear and immediacy to the general stereotype of the effects some drugs had on users. And nonusers in the "normal" society feared that anyone risked becoming like the black, Mexican, oriental, or Near Easterner if he permitted drug use to detach him from majoritarian values.

Heroin aroused anxieties and reactions similar to those around cocaine, and the two substances had a synergistic effect on public opinion. The London chemist C. R. Alder Wright developed a "tetracetylmorphina" in 1874, but it did not become well known until after 1898 when the famous chemist H. Dreser and the Bayer Company in Germany christened a similar compound "Heroin." The very name seemed to guarantee this opiate a bright future, for this substance allegedly had heroic properties in therapy.[26]

As so often in the past, word of this discovery flashed through the medical and pharmaceutical worlds. Within a year heroin figured in reports in the professional journals, then became an ingredient in some over-the-counter medicines and in some regular practice.[27] It seemed especially useful against coughs and congestion, asthma, bronchitis, and catarrhs. Early reports insisted that it was not addictive. Pharmaceutical houses sent out thousands of free sample tablets, and lay people used it in self-medication.[28]

Heroin seemed to answer many problems for both doctors and patients. "Probably no remedy ever was heralded so enthusiastically as was heroin," Charles Terry and Mildred Pellens noted a generation later. "It was apparently the ideal preparation, — potent analgesic and sedative, — at the same time possessing other qualities highly desirable in certain ailments, above all freedom from the dreaded so-called 'habit-forming' qualities of the parent drug."[29]

In 1906 the AMA's Council on Pharmacy and Chemistry endorsed the use of heroin in small amounts but cautioned that it was addictive in large or prolonged doses. Dr. George Pettey was among the first to insist that it was addictive. Heroin had advantages over morphine, " but the same precautions should be exercised in its use as in the use of other opium preparations. Be not deceived, it is an opiate," he warned fellow practitioners in 1903.[30] Other doctors suggested using simple common sense. "It has been urged as a substitute for morphine in the treatment of morphine habit," one wrote in 1905, "but to me this suggestion seems fallacious, as heroin is itself an opium derivative, viz., the diacetyl of morphine, and the habit it may itself induce is really an opium habit."[31] Further experiments on animals and the accumulating statistics of its effects on humans made it clear by about 1910 that heroin was yet another wonder drug gone wrong.[32]

The medical profession did not use heroin as widely as it once had used morphine and did not in fact cause a fresh wave of medical addiction. But as with most drugs in the past that produced psychic effects, heroin quickly moved beyond the medical community's purview in any event. Potential users discovered its ability to produce euphoria and pleasure. It was popular among New York City users by the early 1910s and attracted the attention of police, social workers, and hospital doctors who treated overdose and addiction cases.[33] The pattern was similar in other large cities. By 1913 the New York *Times* reported that heroin was "sold so openly in one district of Boston that the vicinity of the drugstore which markets it has become known as 'heroin square.' The victims, who have increased by the hundreds within the last few months, hold regularly what are known as 'sniffing parties' when the drug is passed around occasionally as the chief means of entertainment."[34] A year later the famous pure food and drug reformer Dr. Harvey W. Wiley reported that one Philadelphia druggist bought heroin tablets in lots of 25,000.[35] Many urban druggists noted the growing use of heroin as a snuff, even though it seemed clear to everyone now that it was addictive.[36] This nonmedical use indicated both how easy it was to secure and employ heroin, and the appeal of any new fashionable substance in the drug world. And many users in states that regulated other drugs turned to heroin.[37]

The characteristics of heroin's users were as significant as its addictive properties in shaping negative public opinion. Most were young, white males, whose future social roles and general productivity heroin seemed especially to threaten. They lived in large cities, which aroused the old suspicions of urban life. They also tended to be unemployed or underemployed, and apparently stole or robbed to finance their drug use.[38] The durable identification of heroin use with crime against property and robbery against persons formed and hardened.

Equally important to public opinion, these users seemed more interested in developing a defined subculture, what the newspapers called "gangs," than in conforming to broader social rules and expectations.[39] The understandable desire of some young people to be special thus developed into rejection of society. Critics thought this merely narrowed the drug user's knowledge of the world and stunted his life. It also supposedly fortified the tendency to use more drugs, and to recruit others, whether to allay guilt or provide companionship, in a widening stain that ultimately would affect society at large. "Heroin addiction is spread almost altogether by infection," an authority warned in a familiar image in 1915.[40] And criticism or concern did not seem to affect this new kind of user. As a New York doctor noted by 1918, "publicity has thrown an appealing glamor of romance about the addict."[41] This seemed to link

heroin use to unsettling generational changes of attitude about individualism and social responsibilities.

Sarah Graham-Mulhall of New York, a leader in the drive for
regulation, later summarized both the perceived facts and the social
fears involved in heroin use. Heroin was easy to obtain, potent and
addictive and "a certain amount of freemasonry and cooperation ... "
developed among users. They created a social life centered on pool
halls, skating rinks, alleys, and other places that reinforced the out-
sider's image of degraded and dangerous activity. The heroinists were
passive and threatened to become a drag on society. "Once the habit is
established, interest is lost in work," she noted. "The addicts become
late and irregular in their hours of work and finally they throw up their
positions. Many are good workmen, but they only work long enough to
procure money with which to buy the drug."[42]

Heroin use thus intensified the older image of the addict as
self-centered, enslaved, and antisocial. But unlike the earlier
nineteenth-century opiate addicts, heroinists appeared sinister for
choosing the drug and for displaying little desire to function in the
mainstream of society. As with cocaine, heroin use seemed a mere
dissipation, identified with wayward youth, irresponsibility, and crime.
As Dr. Alexander Lambert wrote in the 1920s after the first heroin scare
had passed and left its enduring imagery:

> Heroin addiction is a public menace, as it increases the rebellious at-
> titude of antisocial youth, and obliterates all controlling influences of the
> herd instinct. Heroin, under these circumstances, is naturally the drug of
> choice of the criminal class. It gives them the desired inflation of person-
> ality, the reckless daring, the indifference to crime, and the lack of all
> remorse, no matter what crime is committed. Its good effects can be
> obtained by other salts of opium, its evil effects are its own, not shared by
> the other opiates.[43]

Another anonymous doctor summarized the extreme view that differ-
entiated older addicts from heroinists: "The morphinist has guts, while
the heroinist has only bowels."[44]

The debate over cocaine and heroin intensified the sense that the
kind as well as number of drug users had changed. The older stereotype
of the middle-class addict, or even occasional user, trying to seem
"normal" yielded to the new image of the user who defied social conventions and threatened progress and stability. Throughout the progressive
years, the fear that drug use was spreading also gave the debate a new

sense of urgency. Commentators increasingly relied on metaphors drawn from bacteriology and public health. A New York judge recalled that in the years before 1914 there seemed to be "a large number of addicts in the underworld, and this large number seemed to have come almost as an epidemic would."[45] The fear grew that drug use was a plague, a communicable disease for which there was no treatment except prevention. The growing sense that it was a national problem coincided with other forces that pointed toward regulation. The movement to control or outlaw undesirable behavior gained added force for being international. The traffic in drugs, alcohol, slaves, and women became targets of attack from nations and spokesmen that saw them as relics of a preindustrial and barbarous past. Whatever their variations, such activities were all forms of bondage that inhibited individual and national growth. In this liberal view, liberty, affluence and progress were possible if societies disavowed these older habits and activities. Powerful religious spokesmen in most western countries decried drug use in the Orient for its adverse effects on individualism and productivity as well as for its threats to religion.

In larger terms, the United States sought recognition as a major power because of goodness as well as greatness. It wanted to be set apart from older nations in order to gain future influence among emerging peoples. Its spokesmen in and out of government naturally assumed this would follow from emphasizing personal liberty, representative government, and economic development. These all now required regulating dangerous or unsettling personal activity in the name of the common good. In slaying the dragon of opium, the United States would help make its preachments and performance in the world arena match.

The drug problem seemed especially significant among the oriental peoples the United States hoped to affect both practically and morally. To the Reverend Charles H. Brent, first Episcopal bishop of the Philippines, this ambition clearly set the nation apart from the older imperial powers. Brent became a leader in the international movement against opium and thought that ending the drug traffic could not rest with European countries. The French did not care about opium use in their colonies and often even used it themselves. Opposition within Britain to the oriental opium traffic dated from the early nineteenth century. But British colonial officials often took the stoical view, when not actually profiting from opium, that these old habits could not be rooted out. Other colonial powers were indifferent or frankly welcomed drug use among potentially dangerous elements of the populations they controlled. Such fatalistic or opportunistic views would not do for the Americans, who were devoted to the future instead of the past.[46]

The first focus was on the Philippines, which had a longstanding opium problem that missionaries, reformers, and officials immediately equated with the islands' poverty and lassitude. Opium also seemed to threaten the American servicemen stationed there and elsewhere in the east. The Americans tackled the problem as part of a general effort to make the islands more orderly, productive, and enlightened according to their standards. They also wanted to make them an example of the progressive values the United States thought it represented. They identified opium with crime and waste and saw it as an obstacle to productivity as well as enlightenment. After considering many ideas, Congress finally adopted a kind of national reduction cure that curtailed opium use in the islands in stages, with prohibition after 1908.[47]

China posed a more complex problem. Increased trade there caused stirrings of an anti-Americanism that resembled an all too familiar anti-imperialism. Diplomats and businessmen wanted to prosper but to differentiate American ambitions from those of the Europeans. Missionaries and other reformers hoped to foster a liberalism in China that accorded with Christian values and American ideals. These multiple ambitions met in the westerner's horror of opium. Hamilton Wright, prominent spokesman for international control who worked with both the State Department and private groups, emphasized the point. "Our move to help China in her opium reform gave us more prestige in China than any of our recent friendly acts toward her," he told Secretary of State Philander C. Knox in 1909. "If we continue and press steadily for the Conference, China will recognize that we are sincere in her behalf, and the whole business may be used as oil to smooth the troubled waters of our aggressive commercial policy there." The secretary simply said: "Go ahead."[48]

Wright was a major human catalyst in the drive for both domestic drug control and American participation in the international anti-opium movement. He was born in Cleveland, Ohio, in 1867 into a family of British and Canadian antecedents. He studied medicine in Canada, Europe, and the United States, and at the beginning of the century did research on beri-beri in the Straits Settlements. He concluded erroneously as it later turned out, that the disease was infectious, which did not harm his reputation at the time. He was also an able organizer, ambitious for fame and a career in diplomacy or other government service, and had well-connected friends. He was a major force behind the drive for domestic legislation that resulted in the Harrison Act of 1914 but died young in 1917 before the period of enforcement began.[49]

Dr. Hamilton Wright, leader in the international war against opium. From *American Review of Reviews* 51 (May 1915): 518.

In 1908 President Theodore Roosevelt appointed him, Bishop Brent, and Charles C. Tenney, a former China missionary and then secretary of the legation in Peking, as American members of the International Opium Commission. The energetic Wright immediately set about investigating drug use in the United States, prior to the antiopium conference scheduled to meet in Shanghai in January 1909. He wrote hundreds of letters to doctors, druggists, drug dealers and importers, and law enforcement personnel to discover how much opiates and cocaine were flowing into nonmedical usage. Wright was already convinced that the country had a major drug problem, and that Americans could not lead the international crusade without regulatory legislation. Perhaps unconsciously, perhaps not, he phrased his inquiries to produce answers that matched his views. Did medical practice, he asked, really need the current level of opiate imports for legitimate purposes? Was it true that criminals in big cities, prostitutes, and other socially suspect groups used opiates and cocaine? To what extent was the "better class" addicted to opiates, and with what apparent social results?

The respondents to this survey offered varied opinions. Few thought that a large percentage of the "better elements" of society were in fact addicted to opiates, but their numbers were considerable, and the social impact of their condition important. The country did seem to import more opiates and cocaine than medical practice warranted. Law enforcement agents strongly believed that petty criminals, prostitutes, and tenderloin dwellers used opiates and cocaine. So did numerous druggists and other observers, who also held that cocaine use was increasing among blacks. Most who answered Wright's queries agreed that it was simply impossible to produce exact statistics about either actual drug consumption or the number and nature of opiate and cocaine users.

The dominant impression in the survey replies was one of genuine ignorance about what happened to these drugs outside of medical practice. There was also a general sense that control was in order, and that drugs were undermining basic values in reinforcing the activities of threatening elements in society. The response from the Merck Drug Company summarized a good deal of this feeling. "While there are no tangible figures on which to base an opinion, there certainly must be a foundation of fact underlying the widespread conviction that Morphinomania is on the increase," they wrote. "We share this belief, not on analysis of any available data, but on general principles." Much of this apparent increased drug use seemed to reflect social change. "The very conditions of progress, with its refinements in all directions, may readily induce, and no doubt are responsible in part for such practices as ether smelling, cocaine sniffing, morphinomania," they held. "Medical men agree that all forms of these deplorable practices are widespread. Education and sale-restriction for all narcotics are the remedies."[50]

Wright and other drug reformers used this and similar information to create public and congressional support for control. The United States needed domestic regulatory laws in order to conform to any agreements it signed resulting from the international antiopium meetings it supported between 1911 and 1914.

The public the reformers spoke to was prepared to accept national antidrug laws for reasons other than implementing international control. Demands for action against opiates and other drugs had paralleled increased consumption. If nothing else, many such substances were poisons, and the community should regulate their sale.[51] This seemed logical enough, and most states and localities in the latter part of the nineteenth century had required the purchaser of many drugs to sign a poison register. Even this minimal rule was generally a dead letter, and prevented few addicts from buying drugs.[52] Enforcement was nil, and the typical police force had other things to do than check druggists' sales records.

Going beyond this seemed difficult in a period of strong individualism and strict construction of governmental police powers. The Constitution reserved such powers to the states, and special interest groups easily defeated most control efforts. It was one thing to secure passage of an act outlawing opium smoking or dens. It was quite another to secure one that required someone other than the police, such as the druggist or doctor, to monitor the drug traffic. Advertisements for opium-laden nostrums filled the newspapers, magazines, and mails, and druggists sold the pure drugs without compunction.[53] One said in 1877 of his opium sales: "If it were not for this stuff and my soda-water I might as well shut up shop."[54]

Anyone was free to buy in practice. "At present it would not be difficult for a lunatic or a child to obtain at the drugstore all the opium he called for, provided he told a plausible story and had the money to pay for it," O. Marshall said after his survey of opium use in Michigan in 1878.[55] The situation was not much different in most places a generation later. "Often and even, a child of less than ten years of age, steps into a drugstore with a fifty-cent piece and a small scrap of paper, inscribed with one word, 'morphine,'" a Tennessee doctor noted in 1895. "No name is signed. No questions are asked. The bottle of morphine is wrapped up and passed to the child over the counter."[56] This lack of regulation in the name of individualism and profit increasingly seemed grotesque as well as dangerous.

The progressive years brought demands for local regulation of drugs, especially in states like New York that had large user populations. Measures aimed at indiscriminate sales, unlimited prescription refills, and the purchase of paraphernalia such as hypodermic kits and smoking layouts ran the gauntlet of opposition from private interests.[57] Even if states and localities passed laws, their jurisdiction was not adequate. Nor could they affect sales to persons crossing state lines, or those using the mails or parcel post. The federal Pure Food and Drug Act of 1906 regulated proprietary medicines but did not eliminate opiates entirely from them. By 1912 the distinguished U.S. Public Health Service officer

Martin I. Wilbert could say truthfully that "There are few if any subjects regarding which legislation is in a more chaotic condition than the laws designed to minimize the drug-habit evil."[58]

The welter of easily evaded local and state laws combined with the frustrations of enforcement to make national legislation seem logical as well as necessary by 1914. "There are fewer safeguards around morphine than there are around beer," Charles B. Towns reminded the New York *Times* in 1913. "Its production is unhindered and conducted without supervision; its manufacturer does not even pay a license fee to city, state or nation. He is as free to make his poison as a hatter is to make his hats. The contents of the workman's pipe are guarded by far more effective legislation than the contents of the 'dope fiend's' hypodermic."[59]

These concerns and demands for regulation naturally affected the interests of druggists and doctors, whose professions were changing. Both were expanding and attracting varied kinds of practitioners. The role of the pharmaceutical industry was especially complex. Wholesalers had different interests from retailers. The retail druggist's concerns did not match those of his fellows who were increasingly interested in the scientific aspects of pharmacy. New pharmacists were more attuned to social changes and more keen to modernize their profession and its views than were older practitioners.

But nearly all druggists and pharmacists were aware of the adverse public image that indiscriminate sales of habit-forming drugs gave them. At some point this might negatively affect their economic interests more than regulation would. Their spokesmen insisted, like doctors, that only a minority of their number served illicit needs. But as the controversy over drug use and regulation rose after 1900, many people in the pharmaceutical enterprise feared identification with drug users. The American Pharmaceutical Association formed a Committee on the Acquirement of the Drug Habit in 1901. Its reports and recommendations, along with other information emanating from the pharmacy world, opposed nonmedical drug use and perhaps unwittingly helped in the drive for regulation.[60]

Between 1908 and 1914 the pharmaceutical organizations carefully watched the progress of proposed legislation. They were chiefly concerned about new taxation, record keeping, and the fear that any law might permit prosecution for sales made in good faith, no matter how carefully it was drawn. They were also adamant that regulation apply to doctors who dispensed their own drugs, and that the medical profession not evade similar controls.[61]

Collier's
THE NATIONAL WEEKLY

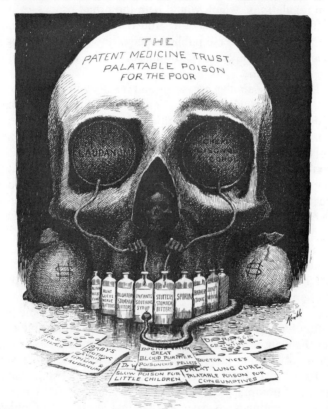

DEATH'S LABORATORY

Patent medicines are poisoning people throughout America to-day. Babies who cry are fed laudanum under the name of syrup. Women are led to injure themselves for life by reading in the papers about the meaning of backache. Young men and boys are robbed and contaminated by vicious criminals who lure them to their dens through seductive advertisement

DRAWN BY E. W. KEMBLE

Cover of *Collier's,* June 3, 1905, part of the war against drugs and poisons.

In the end the reformers trying to regulate drug use had the advantage. Like counterparts in the wars against trusts, they shone as champions of the public welfare against vested interests. Victories for pure food and drugs in 1906 also helped make wider drug regulation seem logical and the necessary next step by 1914. Like so many other interests that faced regulation in the progressive years, the pharmacy profession opted to help shape the inevitable. There was much to be said for uniform regulations, which would help the broad processes of professionalization and modernization. And the business clearly could not afford the growing adverse public image of the individual druggist, the pharmaceutical manufacturer, or salesman who profited from selling cocaine or morphine.

There were similar pressures and results within the medical profession. As a practical matter physicians did not object to reducing the role of opiates in therapy. A generation of warnings had finally made the point that they were addictive, and that doctors were responsible for much of the country's addiction problem. Improved education and accurate textbooks reinforced the fact. The oldtime handbook that genially recommended morphine for insomnia, or to calm a hysterical housewife, yielded to more cautious advice. And yet another cycle of medical research had produced safer hypnotics and pain relievers. There was even some irony in this sense of progress. One doctor noted in 1902 that "the present generation has been so thoroughly warned, both by teaching at college and by observation, that now they are in many instances so very afraid to give it [morphine], even for the worst pain, that the patient suffers agonies worse than hell for want of one-eighth grain of morphine."[62] Hamilton Wright thought that while doctors of the preceding generation had unwittingly created most of the respectable opiate addicts in the drug problem, they were now more cautious. "There is a consensus of opinion from all medical men that the profession, as a whole, have prescribed much less morphine in the last ten years than in any ten years before," he wrote Bishop Brent in 1908.[63] This doubtless fortified his tendency to assume that increased use of opiates was nonmedicinal.

The same was generally true of cocaine, which had faded from medical practice except as a local anesthetic, and in dentistry and veterinary medicine. Few respectable doctors were likely to prescribe it as a tonic or stimulant, given its widespread reputation for causing dangerous or irrational behavior. Like other Americans, they saw its nonmedicinal use as dissipation.

But other aspects of dispensing drugs increasingly seemed to warrant control. It was still easy to buy addictive drugs, even in wholesale lots, since few if any state laws required records of transactions. Anyone could print a pad of false prescription blanks and go into business for himself or others. This was common in large cities where druggists would not likely know doctors outside their neighborhoods, and among those people who ordered drugs from other states. But the most notorious offenses involved the "scrip doctor" who simply wrote narcotic prescriptions for a fee, or who maintained a clientele of addicts. He might have an office in a bad part of town, or in a big city tenderloin, but often drew patients from a wide area.[64]

Like druggists, physicians resented being identified with drug use and addiction. They also dreaded the record keeping, paperwork, and taxation that would follow regulation. But it might be worth it to drive out the scrip doctors and to remove even the hint of trafficking in drugs. "For the sins of these few the many conscientious physicians must suffer the inconvenience of keeping records of their dealings in these drugs," the *New York Medical Journal* admitted reluctantly in 1913, as that state began to regulate cocaine and other drugs.[65]

The demand for national antidrug legislation also coincided with the high point of optimism about the treatment and cure of addiction. Many doctors who wanted drugs regulated felt responsible for addicts. Countless physicians kept at least one respectable member of the community on a maintenance dose of opiates. Absolute prohibition, with no regard for the addict as patient seemed cruel and unnecessary, if a law's main intent was to affect criminals, profiteers or wilful addicts.

More and more experts like George Pettey, Charles B. Towns, and Alexander Lambert insisted that cure was now possible. If this were true, the profession could treat the addicts that regulation left behind. If control worked, there would be no new ones except for incorrigibles, liable to prosecution and incarceration, and the long-standing drug problem would disappear gradually and in humane terms. Of course, it was also possible to argue the opposite. If cure was in fact impossible, regulation seemed the only way to prevent new cases of addiction.[66]

The AMA favored controlling habit-forming drugs and narcotics for both moral and practical reasons. Its most prominent spokesmen prior to the World War accepted the broad goals of the purity movement, especially those related to public health. Like most Americans, doctors linked drug addiction and abuse with unhappiness, inefficiency, and now crime. Medical spokesmen, like counterparts in pharmacy, saw the advantages to professionalization of being linked with progressive reforms. And they wished to eliminate the marginal doctors who gave the profession a bad name.

The legislative antecedents of federal regulation developed within this larger context. Congressional action against opium use in the Philippines beginning in 1905 indicated some sentiment for control that might ultimately affect the domestic scene. In 1906 Congress enacted the District of Columbia Pharmacy Act, which regulated the nonmedical use of opiates, cocaine, and chloral in that federal jurisdiction. The act required a doctor's written order to renew narcotics prescriptions. And it established the principle that doctors could prescribe for addicts "in good faith" only as part of an effort to cure, and not merely to maintain a drug dependency. At about the same time, the national Pure Food and Drug Law went into effect.

These developments were part of a movement toward some kind of national legislation and reflected the concern of reformers on both the domestic and international scenes. Wright drafted model legislation in 1909, which he circulated among friends and potential supporters, and he gradually came to accept the facts of political life. Congress, especially the Senate, was unlikely to pass a simple prohibition measure or one that greatly extended the federal police power. A revenue measure thus seemed the safest approach, with primary enforcement devolving on local and state authorities. Wright also hoped that any law would produce statistics and other information that would help an aroused public opinion press local agencies for strict enforcement. He wanted a firm federal presence in managing the problem. But "it would be a too ardent extension of the federal police powers if the Bureau of Internal Revenue was charged with guarding, prescribing and dispensing," he wrote a friend in 1909.[67]

On April 30, 1910, Representative David Foster of Vermont, chairman of the Committee on Foreign Affairs, introduced a comprehensive measure designed to eliminate the nonmedical use of opiates, cocaine, chloral, and cannabis. The bill required careful record keeping, bonding, and reporting from those dealing in these drugs, and prescribed harsh penalties for violators. It did not exempt over-the-counter compounds containing small amounts of these substances and inevitably faced opposition from wholesale and retail drug interests.

This effort also occasioned a debate about drug use in the United States and the merits of regulation, complete with congressional hearings and press reporting. Wright strongly supported the Foster bill in testimony before the House Ways and Means Committee. He drew on the information about drug use he had gathered earlier. He wanted to eliminate the nonmedical use of the stated drugs and believed that drug use was widespread in the United States. He also linked some drugs to crime, and emphasized the alleged use of cocaine among southern blacks, doubtless in order to win support from that section's congressmen. In addition, he suggested that women and children were special objects of concern. And, as always, he emphasized the need for the United States to take the lead against the international traffic with a comprehensive law regulating nonmedical drug use at home.[68] For all the expressed concern, however, Wright and like-minded reformers lost to the interests that opposed the record keeping, taxation, and potential loss of business involved. The Foster measure died in the lame duck session that followed the congressional elections of November 1910.

In the next two years drug reformers worked to reconcile their interests with those of the professions involved. The new Wilson administration favored regulation and on June 10, 1913, Representative Francis B. Harrison of New York introduced the measure that finally bore his name in law. For all the efforts involved in securing such legislation, the debates on the Harrison bill were somewhat anticlimactic. There was the usual display of the power of special interests, which modified the measure. But most of the discussion focused on it as related to treaty obligations, foreign policy goals, and the general desire to regulate dangerous drugs. Congress did not debate addiction and did not perceive the Harrison bill as a prohibition measure or as the foundation of any apparatus of federal law enforcement.

The Harrison Anti-Narcotic Act passed Congress on December 14, 1914. President Woodrow Wilson signed it on December 17, and it took effect on March 1, 1915. It was a revenue measure, and everyone dealing in the specified drugs had to register and buy tax stamps. The drug trades won their battle against total regulation, and over-the-counter preparations containing minimal amounts of opiates remained unaffected. Chloral hydrate and cannabis were not included. Federal authorities retained records of transactions in the regulated drugs. If the law withstood the test of constitutionality, it laid the groundwork for an expandable system of federal control of drug use and users, especially through bureaucratic enforcement regulations from the Treasury Department.

In the narrowest sense, the government adopted the Harrison Act as part of its support for international opium control. But the law represented a popular consensus against drug addiction and the drug experience that had been building since the 1870s. It was the result of incremental growth in regulation, from local ordinances to a national law. By 1914 it seemed logical, the customary cap on a pyramid of legislation that had strong public support. Like so many similar progressive laws, it represented general public fear of disorder and inefficiency, and the belief that society could purify individual conduct in the name of a common good.

The struggle over national alcohol prohibition continued after 1914, but the Harrison Act occasioned little public comment, so strong was the antidrug consensus. Early enforcement problems chiefly concerned bureaucrats, addicts, and those doctors who doubted that legislation would solve the drug problem. The country as a whole continued an agenda of domestic reform and then faced the problems arising from the European war. The conflict and its aftermath produced some new public reactions against drug use and the process of shifting drug policy almost totally to regulation began.

Public concern about drug use among the young men who entered the armed forces after 1917 was strong. Authorities warned that they were in the most susceptible age group and expected a high rate of addiction and use among them. This was not a new attitude. Addicted Civil War veterans were a major object of concern in the late nineteenth century. Morphine addiction then even earned the name "army disease." Their numbers were exaggerated, but many men were addicted from using morphine for the pain of wounds and from the opium compounds that controlled fever and dysentery.[69] These military addicts gained some public sympathy because their condition resulted from ignorance or the need to alleviate pain rather than any search for pleasure or escapism.

There was also concern during and after the Spanish-American War. Public health officers and military spokesmen reported that some soldiers experimented with cocaine and other drugs as they waited in Gulf ports to be shipped to Cuba. In the Philippine campaign many soldiers and sailors regularly took "C and O," camphor and opium, to combat dysentery. And there was always the lure of the opium dens in the darker parts of Manila. Some men on the China station, in the units that policed the Caribbean nations, and in the Mexican expeditionary force of 1916 allegedly used opium, cocaine, and marihuana. As the United States became a world power, contact with foreigners, especially the "backward" peoples already associated with decadence and drug use, seemed to threaten the highly visible group called servicemen.[70]

By 1914 some commentators noted that soldiers and sailors were experimenting with cocaine and heroin like their counterparts in civilian life. This supposedly resulted from association with bad company, boredom, and resentment at controls. This all seemed a logical manifestation of their youth. But because they were concentrated in forts and camps, or around naval facilities, servicemen seemed easy targets for the peddlers the public thought so instrumental in spreading drug use.

The dire predictions about a high rate of drug use among servicemen after 1917 turned out to be false. Only about 6 percent of the men examined as of May 1, 1919, were addicts or alcoholics. These generally did conform to the new image of the drug user, young, white males, usually undereducated, chiefly from urban areas, who allegedly acquired their habits through bad associations. There was a final spasm of public concern about drug problems among the veterans returning from Europe. But despite a few lurid confessions their number was small.[71]

These actual low figures became common knowledge only later and there was a widely held idea that drug use increased between 1914 and 1919 despite the Harrison Act and new state statutes. The concern about servicemen enhanced the images of the pusher and of the relation of drugs to crime and vice. This scare also coincided with wartime intolerance of anyone and anything that seemed to weaken the country's unity and war effort. For the first, though not the last time, drug use appeared un-American and unpatriotic.

The direction of drug control and the relationship of medicine to law enforcement underwent tests throughout the war years and after. As state and local enforcement measures, along with the Harrison Act, began to take effect after the spring of 1915, everyone involved in the drug question faced the growing problem of what to do with addicts cut off from their supplies. What fate awaited them if doctors would not treat them as patients and they could not legally buy drugs under the new laws?

The medical profession was divided. Some doctors simply favored law enforcement and enforced abstinence. Others wanted special public health facilities to treat addicts. Spokesmen for the old "humane" approach favored simply allowing physicians to maintain addicts as patients to avoid driving them to illicit sources or ruining their lives.

By April 1915, this was a real problem. In New York City, confusion about the impact of the new Harrison Act and the refusal of doctors to treat addicts drove the street price of opiates sky high. Addicts crowded into police stations, hospital emergency wards, and other public facilities seeking help. Even the police were sympathetic. One Lieutenant Scherb, head of the city's "dope squad," reported panic among the addicts. "Many of them are doubled up in pain at this very minute and others are running to the police and hospitals to get relief," he said. "Those who have been getting their drugs from dope-doctors and fake-cure places are not so hard hit, because these traffickers have not been touched by the laws, but the poorer people, the men and women we call the 'bums,' who have always bought from street peddlers, are really up against it. The suffering among them is terrible."[72] The New York *Times* editorialized that the best policy was sympathy and treatment for the deserving addicts and harsh penalties to prevent new addiction. The authorities permitted maintenance, a pattern followed elsewhere simply because there was no other recourse.[73]

From the first, the Treasury Department held in regulations and through its agents that the law did not permit maintenance of addicts. Doctors thus could prescribe for them only as part of a cure. This viewpoint doubtless reflected the department's traditional approach to problems. Accustomed to dealing with smugglers, tax evaders, moonshiners, and similar lawbreakers, Treasury personnel could not see addicts as medical patients or drug use as a health problem. The department's close working relationship with law enforcers in other federal agencies and on the state level doubtless fortifed this viewpoint, which became stronger with the need to enforce alcohol prohibition after 1920.

In the first months of enforcement, the lower courts tended to view the Harrison Act chiefly as a revenue measure, and denied the government the power to forbid possession of the regulated drugs. The final determination of the law's scope rested with the United States Supreme Court, which laid down its first interpretation in June 1916, in the case of *U.S.* v. *Jin Fuey Moy.* Dr. Jin Fuey Moy of Pittsburgh had prescribed small amounts of morphine for an addict. The government held that the doctor had not acted in good faith or for professional reasons to help him seek a cure but merely to maintain his dependence. The addict was not registered to deal in narcotics, and the government further held that his possession of morphine was illegal.

In a seven-to-two decision, the court denied the government broad powers in a strict interpretation of what it took to be a revenue measure. Congress surely had not intended, in its view, to make mere possession of a small amount of a regulated substance a crime. And it found such terms as "good faith" and "professional practice" overly vague.

This development made the antimaintenance policy impossible to enforce. The Treasury Department could only urge Congress to restrict dealing in regulated drugs to legitimate persons and to make possession of them without a tax stamp illegal. This would at least make it easier to prosecute dealers in illicit drugs.

But events worked to the government's favor in the period immediately following the Jin Fuey Moy case. Wartime concern about any lawbreaking or deviant behavior further strengthened the adverse image of addicts. The obvious coming of alcohol prohibition also made the maintenance of drug addicts appear anomalous. And the war years and immediate postwar period saw a sharp increase in public concern about allegedly spreading drug use.

The government persisted and made the most of this climate of opinion in presenting two crucial cases to the Supreme Court. The court seemed to respond, though by five-to-four votes, in judgements delivered on March 3, 1919. *U.S.* v. *Doremus,* concerned a San Antonio doctor who had prescribed large amounts of opiates to addicts. The court held the Harrison Act constitutional, which validated the government's power to regulate this aspect of medical practice. Physicians thus could prescribe narcotics only in the course of recognized medical practice. In *Webb et al.* v. *U.S.*, the court ruled against prescribing solely for maintenance.

These judgements caused doctors to refuse to prescribe for addicts, creating panic among them. In view of the inflated estimates of the number of addicts in the country, and especially in large cities, authorities feared an outbreak of violence and impossible burdens on public health facilities. They cooperated in establishing municipal clinics to treat addicts, and between 1919 and 1921 there were an estimated forty-four such facilities in the nation's cities.[74]

The New York City clinic inevitably became the major example of this effort, for better and worse. Authorities insisted that such a

Exterior of New Orleans drug clinic, 1920. From M. W. Swords, "A Resume of Facts and Deductions Obtained by the Operation of a Narcotic Dispensary," *American Medicine* 26 (January 1920).

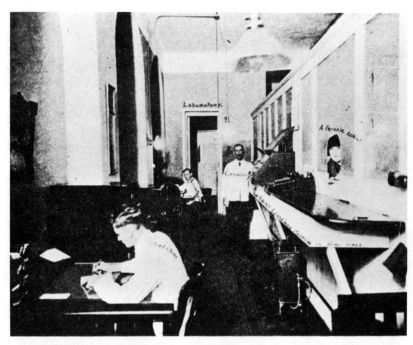

Reception area of the New Orleans drug clinic, 1920. Note the "female addict" at right. From M. W. Swords, "A Resume of Facts and Deductions Obtained by the Operation of a Narcotic Dispensary," *American Medicine* 26 (January 1920).

program was necessary because hospitals were full and other facilities lacking. They proposed to send addicts to special treatment centers as they became available. The goal was cure in some kind of custodial situation, and temporary ambulatory treatment would prevent suffering and the growth of an illicit market. Between April 1919 and March 1920, the clinic on Worth Street registered about 7,700 addicts. The first were young, white males, but the median age rose as these users who were uninterested in cure turned to illicit supplies. The addicts' occupations cut across the spectrum, and there were more men than women. The most reassuring result of the clinic experience was the failure of predicted hordes of addicts to appear. The high estimates of their number were obviously wide of the mark.[75]

Though most of the clinics were well run under medical supervision, they were never popular with the public. And the medical and public health professions were always sharply divided about this approach. The facility in New York City seemed to symbolize all the

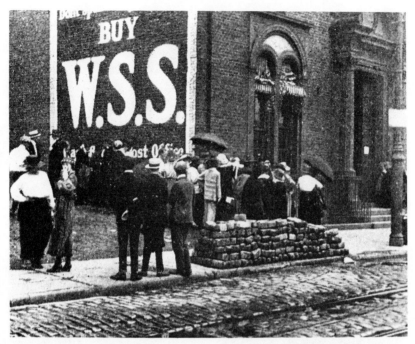

Outside the New York City drug clinic, 1920. From Alexander Lambert, "Underlying Causes of the Narcotic Habit," *Modern Medicine* 2 (January 1920).

problems inherent in stereotyped drug use. Peddlers roamed the adjacent streets despite the police. Most addicts seemed interested in cheap supplies rather than any long-term cure. Some used drugs in nearby parks, even in the presence of school children. Tawdriness reached some kind of apogee as sightseers took bus tours to see the "great and only dope line" of addicts waiting to receive medication on Worth Street. Enterprising reporters filled the newspapers and magazines with accounts of the clinic's operation, pictures of addicts with suitable human interest stories, and the comments of a cross section of humanity. The dominant tone was not one of dispassionate medical care.[76]

By the spring of 1921 the experiment was generally over, a failure in almost everyone's terms. Those doctors interested in a humane approach could not honestly say that the clinics were a doorway to cure for many addicts. Most of those who went through the prescribed hospital treatment were back on the streets in no time. A black market was ready at hand. The police saw ambulatory treatment as a simple evasion of the law, since it did not produce permanent cures. This was especially true

Addicts outside the New York City drug clinic, 1920. From Alexander Lambert, "Underlying Causes of the Narcotic Habit," *Modern Medicine* 2 (January 1920).

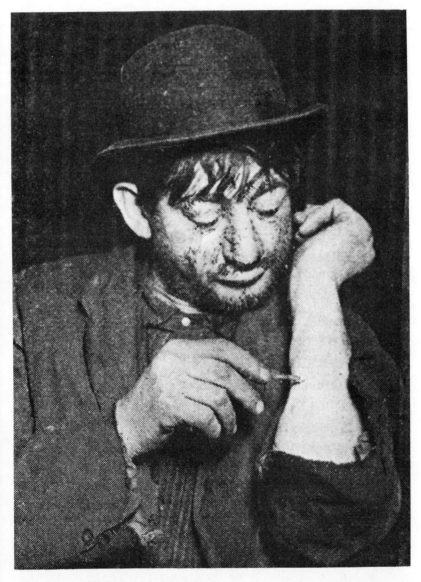

This photograph, probably posed, shows one of the popular stereotypes of the drug addict in the 1920s. From *Literary Digest* 90 (August 28, 1926): 25.

of federal agents, who looked upon local police as soft and who led determined efforts to close the clinics and to discredit the clinic idea. The AMA and important medical spokesmen soon opposed further experiments in ambulatory treatment, especially if they involved self-medication. "So long as addicts can obtain cheap supplies of drugs without personal risk, very few will apply for hospital curative treatment," Dr. S. Dana Hubbard, who worked with the New York City clinic insisted.[77] Few experts any longer believed that enforced abstinence would kill addicts, and prohibition looked like a necessary policy to end the drug problem. "If the addicts cannot obtain a supply of their drug, they will reform, and not a fatality will be recorded," Hubbard insisted in the *JAMA* in May 1920.[78]

The postwar period marked the end of an era in thinking about drug policy. The progressive optimism that underlay both efforts to find a cure and to begin regulation was gone. The first efforts at regulation at both state and federal levels offered mixed results. The critics of control who saw drug addiction as a medical problem had predicted that law would fail. In 1915 the *New York Medical Journal* had lamented the first panic among addicts when the Harrison Act went into effect but saw much worse results coming than a temporary rise in the crime rate or the number of hospital admissions. "The really serious results of this legislation, however, will only appear gradually and will not always be recognized as such," it warned. "These will be the failures of promising careers, the disrupting of happy families, the commission of crimes which will never be traced to their real cause, and the influx into hospitals for the mentally disordered of many who otherwise would live socially competent lives."[79] Control would make all addicts criminals in the world's eyes, with adverse results for respectable "honest addicts."[80]

Perhaps most important of all, as early critics of the Harrison Act insisted, legal regulation would separate doctors from the addiction problem. Their fear of prosecution and social disapproval would justify avoiding this professional responsibility. "Honest medical men have found such handicaps and dangers to themselves and their reputations in these laws ... that they have simply decided to have as little to do as possible with drug addicts or their needs," *American Medicine* editorialized in 1915, a foretaste of things to come.[81]

This attitude steadily hardened, and even doctors sympathetic to addicts accepted the changed viewpoint. "The addict is seldom benefited and the physician becomes the depository for censure, criticism and failures to cure through the law's unintelligence," Dr. J. C. Densten of Scranton noted.[82] By the beginning of the 1920s this gulf between addicts and the medical community was unbridgeable. Dr. Oscar Dowling, head of the Louisiana State Board of Health that operated the New Orleans clinic, summarized the facts. "Already many physicians have written the State Board of appeals to be relieved of the writing of prescriptions for incurable addicts," he said in 1919. "Any physician is more than willing to write a prescription, if need be, every other day for patients with incurable diseases, but he does not want on his mind or in his visiting clientele the average users. The druggist, likewise, does not want the burden of constant watchfulness as to prescriptions and amounts, with the clerical work and responsibility entailed."[83]

A sense of bewilderment returned to the discussion of drug policy. Even by 1916 there was an illicit market in most cities; stronger enforcement only raised its prices.[84] Cure seemed impossible, actual prohibition unlikely. Perhaps the only approach was to combine everything: institutional care for the willing addict, ostracism for the wilful; destruction of the sources of supply; propaganda and education to prevent future addiction; and the hope of an as yet undiscovered panacea through research.[85]

7

SOCIETY WITHDRAWS
The 1920s to the 1950s

AS THE NATION MOVED INTO THE 1920s, new concerns replaced the purity crusading and reformist drives of the preceding generation. Disillusionment with both progressivism and the war, along with growing economic affluence, fostered a tendency to focus on personal concerns. Alcohol prohibition obviously would have mixed results as the ideas that supported it faded, but the consensus against opiate and cocaine use remained intact. This fortified the tendency to turn away from belief in a final cure, or the merits of prolonged treatment, to a reliance on law enforcement to control drug use. The dominance of this attitude was clear in the aftermath of the postwar drug scare and the clinic experiment. The popular *Outlook* magazine was only one of many voices that supported a new approach. "There would seem to be no question that national and state investigation and legislation, and the more rigid enforcement of existing laws, are seriously needed," it intoned in 1919.[1]

The Treasury Department was responsible for enforcing the Harrison Act and organized a Narcotic Division of the Prohibition Unit in 1920. Regulation proceeded from this base until national narcotic control gained separate status in 1930 in a new Federal Bureau of Narcotics. Congress amended the Harrison Act in 1919 to forbid possession of regulated drugs without a tax stamp. The Narcotic Drugs Import and Export Act of 1922 permitted the federal government to monitor the movements of legitimate narcotics and to check on the illicit traffic. In 1924 Congress forbade the importation of opium for the manufacture of heroin. But the government expanded its war against drugs more through Treasury Department regulations than new laws. These had the force of law unless Congress or the courts dictated otherwise. They were a powerful weapon in attacking both the drug traffic and drug use, since few of the interested parties cared to face a court test of the department's interpretations.[2]

Narcotic control was always a cooperative enterprise within the federal government, involving people in the Customs Service, Border Patrol, Coast Guard, and Justice Department, as well as the special agents. And most actual regulation occurred on the state and local levels, though the federal agencies usually won the limelight. The number of federal agents was never large. There were about 175 in 1920, and an average of 270 in the field in any year during the 1930s.[3] But they developed a strong cohesion and sense of purpose. In a period of narrow interpretation of individual civil rights and legal procedures, they also had latitude in fighting the drug traffic.

This set of attitudes and approach characterized their long-time chief, Harry J. Anslinger. Born in 1892 in Altoona, Pennsylvania, Anslinger worked briefly for the local railroad police as a young man but came to narcotics control by chance. He was with the Ordnance Division of the War Department in 1917, then went to the Netherlands for the State Department. After the war he was in the consular service there and in Hamburg, Germany. He moved on to similar duties in Venezuela and in the Bahamas, where he secured the cooperation of local authorities against some aspects of the illegal liquor traffic with the United States. He then joined the foreign control division of the Prohibition Unit and became Commissioner of Narcotics in 1930, a post he held until 1962.[4]

Anslinger was a figure of both national homage and controversy during his long tenure as federal narcotics czar. Supporters saw him as a stalwart opponent of the insidious drug traffic that threatened the nation's vitality. His belief in strong law enforcement won their approval, as did his opposition to what they saw as soft-minded theorists and humanitarians. Critics saw Anslinger as a persecutor of hapless addicts, foe of enlightened medical and psychological reforms, and builder of a tyrannical bureaucratic empire.

The commissioner's effectiveness and longevity in office stemmed from considerable shrewdness and energy. He developed a professional force committed to his ideals of enforcement. He understood that nothing fails like failure in police work and never sought more duties than the bureau could perform well. Tireless attention to detail allowed him to quash many critics with a flood of bureau-inspired information. He cultivated the media and effectively used citizen groups that opposed narcotics. He maintained strong ties with Congress, the

U.S. Commissioner of Narcotics Harry J. Anslinger. Courtesy Pennsylvania Historical Collections, Pennsylvania State University Library.

federal bureaucracy, and local law enforcement officials. And he was the acknowledged national spokesman at the endless gatherings dedicated to suppressing the international drug traffic. For thirty years very little happened in the world of drugs that Anslinger did not know about. He helped shape the nation's attitudes against drug use and in favor of law enforcement, but he only employed and developed the broad national consensus against drugs.

The federal war against drugs had many fronts. One natural focus was smuggling, and narcotic agents gained public notoriety for helping to interdict supplies. Newspapers and magazines carried a steady stream of stories about the techniques that smugglers used and how the agents foiled them. Paraffin soaked in heroin, raisins steeped in morphine, frozen sheep carcasses laden with packages of opiates were only three of the smugglers' efforts that agents stopped.[5]

The war against smuggling was part of a broad drive for international control. The federal narcotics establishment believed that drying up supplies would force both sellers and users into the light, where law enforcement would send them to jail or hospitals as the cases warranted. Only this would stop the creation of new addicts and users. "When narcotics become scarcer, when their use is restricted as far as possible to legitimate needs, we shall find a decrease in the number of new addicts," a popular magazine reported in 1931, in a variant of the official line.[6] Field agents took heart from occasional successes, as in 1931, in closing off imports and causing panics in the addict communities of major cities.[7]

Narcotics authorities also had an elaborate network of stool pigeons and spies. They were not above using entrapment and legal harassment, or threatening to file indictments, or offering to drop shaky charges in order to keep suspected doctors and users in line. The arrest statistics seemed to prove the effectiveness if not the gentility of these

Federal narcotics officers and a haul of confiscated opiates in the 1920s. From *Literary Digest* 76 (February 24, 1923): 34.

methods. Federal narcotic convictions averaged about 5,000 a year from 1923 to 1930, then about 2,500 a year in the 1930s, with a low of 1,120 in 1945.[8] The law enforcers naturally used such figures to demonstrate their success in halting the drug traffic. But declining arrest rates in the 1930s reflected in part budget cuts of personnel in both federal and state enforcement agencies and did not necessarily reveal a true lessening of drug use or of the number of addicts. The wartime curtailment of shipping had more to do with interruptions of the illicit traffic than did enforcement.

Federal agencies cooperated with state authorities in tightening the controls against drugs. By 1931 the possession of opiates was illegal in thirty-five states, of cocaine in thirty-six, and of hypodermic paraphernalia in eight.[9] Anslinger also kept watch on domestic suppliers of narcotics and other drugs. Pharmaceutical houses complied with the law and supported the commissioner's broader efforts. "The manufacturers have recognized that they have a public trust in the manufacture and possession of these drugs," one pharmaceutical executive wrote a bureau office in 1933, "and I have supported all legislation and enforcement of legislation to restrict these drugs to legitimate medicinal and scientific needs."[10]

Federal narcotics control also benefited from the propaganda efforts of citizens groups, service clubs, and religious bodies. The most famous of these educational efforts against drug use developed in the mid-1920s, and involved Richmond P. Hobson, a hero of the war with Spain and a progressive-era congressman from Alabama. Though his information and statistics were often imperfect, the courtly Hobson was a potent force in the campaign against drugs, whether speaking from a temperance platform or on the radio. He helped organize the International Narcotic Education Association in 1923, and the World Narcotic Defense Association in 1927. These and similar organizations provided speakers and printed matter for schools, service clubs, and churches across the country. They staged Narcotic Education Weeks for school children and lobbied for federal funds for a nationwide campaign against drugs. Such groups focused on prevention through law enforcement and education. They cared little for sophisticated theories about the causes and treatments of addiction. "We shall need to preach the gospel of narcotic abstinence from the pulpit, to flash it on the screen, to proclaim it from the platform, to depict it in the press and above all, to teach it in the public schools," an agency of the Women's Christian Temperance Union proclaimed in 1923.[11]

These antinarcotic crusaders had their critics, who attacked their statements about the effects of opiates and cocaine, and their estimates

Richmond P. Hobson, popular crusader against drug use in the 1920s, and his family. From *Literary Digest* 81 (May 24, 1924): 32.

of the number of users. The focus on the alleged dangers to children seemed especially thoughtless to some critics. Carleton Simon of the New York City Police Department's narcotics squad objected to identifying children with drug use. And any dramatic educational campaign against drug use ran the risk of making it attractive to impressionable youngsters. Within the U.S. Public Health Service, Dr. Lawrence Kolb waged a considerable battle to blunt Hobson's impact on government agencies. And the well-known Dr. Alexander Lambert assured a correspondent that these organizations had dramatically overstated their cases. He thought their information on drug effects often incorrect and misleading. And in his view, the number of addicts was clearly declining. "There are less addicts than there were," he insisted gently. "There are more being jacked up and coming to the surface. They seem to be more."[12] These experts helped deny Hobson federal funding and support but could not reach any large popular audience.

These antinarcotic efforts in the mid-1920s coincided with another drive for international control, and fresh concern that the United States was once again the target of foreign drug devils. "The United States is assailed by opium from Asia as a base, by cocaine with South America as a base, and by heroin and synthetic drugs with Europe as a base," the New York *Times* proclaimed in 1924.[13] At the same time, these propagandists argued anew that "No state is exempt; there is no small town or big city in which this danger is not found."[14] The activities of citizen groups became less hysterical after the 1920s, but remained important in sustaining the antidrug consensus.

By the time Anslinger headed the federal antinarcotic effort in 1930, the patterns of law enforcement were well set. He merely made them more efficient. They seemed a little more successful each year in curtailing drug use, or at least in driving it out of sight. But the heavy-handed emphasis on law enforcement had pernicious long-term effects. It made everyone involved in the drug question hesitate to innovate or take responsibility for any new public departures. Practicing physicians avoided addicts or the study of drug use. Federal researchers on the subject feared moving beyond the controls of their bureaucracies. The criminal justice system developed a powerful intolerance for the drug user as well as the drug supplier. And the addict who once might have won some understanding if not approval for his condition was now merely a criminal.[15]

The general public doubtless approved of strong law enforcement without much thought. But as in the past, drug use was not likely to affect the typical citizen's life. This was not the case with the medical profession, whose members now became subject to routine police observation. The Supreme Court's early interpretations of the law seemed to disfavor maintenance. But in the case of *Linder* v. *U.S.* (1925), it opened the door to treating some addicts as patients, provided the doctor acted in good faith and was obviously not merely selling narcotics.

This general viewpoint became the overt basis of federal law enforcement relating to doctors. Anslinger spelled it out carefully. "If a physician in good faith, and in the course of his professional practice, prescribes, administers, or dispenses narcotic drugs to a patient under his care, he should have no fear of prosecution under the Harrison Narcotic Law," he told an inquirer in 1936, "and no administrative ruling could have any valid effect in imposing a penalty upon a practitioner thus acting in good faith in the course of his professional practice." This included maintenance for "aged and infirm persons who being already addicted to the habit, would collapse from infirmity if the drug were withdrawn." But such treatment or maintenance could not include the ordinary drug addict, "merely to keep him comfortable by maintaining his customary use." The policy remained twofold, to compel the addict to seek cure and to stop the supply of drugs. "It is reasonable, because the ordinary addict, with proper treatment, may be reclaimed as a useful member of society and may, in the opinion of this Bureau, remain cured if sources of supply are so regulated as to make it difficult or even impossible for the addict to relapse into the habit."[16]

The Bureau of Narcotics thus quietly sanctioned maintenance for numerous cases, chiefly respectable members of society whose addiction dated from before 1914, and publicly focused on the wilful or criminal user. But this policy was not designed to bring the medical profession back into the drug controversy, nor did it. The crucial and dangerous test for the doctor in dispensing narcotics was still the interpretation of such words as "good faith," "professional practices," and "proper treatment." Any contest in the courts of public opinion over such words meant ruin for the physician's practice and life.

The bureau also kept close watch on the flow of legal as well as illegal drug supplies. Any doctor who purchased or dispensed an unusual amount of narcotics was suspect.[17] Agents also knew most of the poorer or criminal addicts and often used them to entrap suspected doctors. Such practices declined after the first dramatic bursts of police enthusiasm or harassment in the mid-1920s, but never disappeared and left an indelible memory among physicians. To critics of law enforcement the whole process seemed sleazy and somehow un-American. "When American physicians advocated laws regulating narcotics, they had in mind the kind of laws in force in most western European countries," Lawrence Kolb recalled. "What our physicians did not foresee was that they would be bound by police interpretations of the regulations; and that doctors who did not accept police views might be tricked into giving an opiate to an informer, who pretended to need it for pain or disease."[18]

These specific rules and the general atmosphere of distrust and suspicion steadily combined to prevent most doctors from dealing with addicts. Before regulation, a physician gave an addicted patient the necessary drug to relieve distress, or simply to be rid of him. He might believe that he was helping a diseased patient, the equal of one suffering from tuberculosis or an accident with a handsaw. Or he might be simply indifferent yet convinced that the pain was a legitimate medical concern. Now he had to assess such cases carefully. The patient in distress could be a decoy. Even worse, he might be the advance agent of an army of addicts seeking a new source of supply, whose mere presence would bring the narcotics squad. The law and its possible interpretations or the appearance of the case to the community rather than medicine dominated the situation. Few doctors would risk much for an addict, however real his distress, unless he was clearly certifiable. The addict thus turned to the illicit market, the narcotic agent to his statistics, and the doctor to his normal rounds.

The apparent decline in the number of addicts seemed to justify strict law enforcement. In 1924 Lawrence Kolb predicted that the combination of police action and declining use of narcotics in general medical practice ultimately would solve the country's addiction problem. "From the trend which narcotic addiction in this country has taken in recent years as a result of the attention given the problem by the medical profession and law enforcement officers," he wrote in a Public Health Service report with A. G. DuMez, "it is believed that we may confidently look forward to the time, not many years distant, when the few remaining addicts will be persons taking opium because of an incurable disease and addicts of the psychopathic delinquent type, who spend a good deal of their lives in prison."[19] A rise in the median age of known addicts, which the Bureau of Narcotics doubtless overemphasized, seemed to fortify this ironic optimism about ending the problem.[20] Until the mid-1930s, few authorities believed that young people would become new addicts in significant numbers.[21] In the end, the inherited addict population would simply die off, leaving a small number of criminal and deviant drug users whom the police could quarantine.

The bureau maintained records of known addicts gathered from doctors' reports, local law enforcement agencies, and estimates based on surveillance of the traffic. Throughout the 1930s, Anslinger reported 50,000–60,000 addicts in the United States, a considerable reduction from the alleged 250,000–300,000 at the turn of the century before regulation. Older medical addicts appeared to be scattered across the country and throughout society. But the so-called wilful or criminal drug users were concentrated in the large cities where anonymity and confusion provided some cover for the illicit traffic. One major result of regulation was thus to identify the addict population with crime and illicit behavior and make it more dramatic at times of public concern.

As always in the drug debate, these figures were suspect. Despite Anslinger's consistent air of authority in reporting almost exact numbers, there was simply no way of knowing how many true opiate addicts or users of other drugs there were in the United States. The trend of the numbers for opiate addicts was surely downward on the whole. There were certainly fewer opium smokers and old-fashioned morphine addicts than before, though the number of heroin users probably increased somewhat. But there were doubtless more addicts than the Bureau of Narcotics reported.[22]

The image of the drug user as city street tough was not new but did not tell the entire story. Most towns had resident medical addicts, who regularly refilled their legitimate prescription to no one's consternation. Maintenance of elderly and hopeless cases was a well-known fact in both medical and police circles. The Narcotics Bureau sanctioned such procedures as long as no illicit traffic resulted.[23] The Keeley Institute received a steady stream of inquiries from potential drug patients, especially in small towns in the Midwest, who usually wanted a secret home treatment.[24] There was the occasional doctor who still dispensed opiates too freely, whether to bolster a failing practice or because he believed in them.[25] And physicians in towns as well as big cities knew there was an illicit traffic, since the users they would not treat obviously obtained drugs elsewhere.[26]

But these were not the addicts whose stories figured in the daily press or the bureau's annual reports. The public was not concerned about the woman who regularly took opiates to ward off migraine, or the trucker who controlled back pain with a daily dose of analgesic, or even the professional person with an old addiction who used just enough of a drug to seem normal to his neighbors and colleagues. They were true addicts, like their counterparts in the late nineteenth century, but did not represent crime, violence, or lassitude to the public mind.

Both the police and concerned citizens focused instead on the suppliers, peddlers, and addict element whose stereotypes figured in the discussion of drug use. This imagery involved first and foremost the small-time criminal or loafer who spent the day with people like himself, and who stole or gambled just enough to maintain his habit or stage an occasional spree. His friends, associates, and antagonists were mostly in the drug underworld, whether as fellow addicts or suppliers. They tended to be rootless, underemployed, their lives focused on drugs and each other, marginal in every way, and examples to critics of what drug use made of individuals. "It has been estimated that 80 percent of the present addiction occurs in the land of 'Hobohemia,' or in the underworld," an assistant surgeon general of the United States Public Health Service wrote in 1932.[27]

Other groups whose activities were equally suspect to the majority of citizens figured in the stereotypes of drug users in the 1920s and 1930s. Jazz musicians were a concern, especially if they worked on the mysterious and forbidden circuit of honkytonks and cabarets across the railroad tracks on the other side of respectability. By the 1930s, they figured publicly in the debate over marihuana but were also identified with cocaine and heroin.[28] They were clearly not respectable models, and their drifter image fortified the old notion that drugs cut the user off from society.

Forbidden drugs also attracted some of the "smart" sets during the 1920s and 1930s. Their favorite substances were cocaine and cannabis, but as in the late nineteenth century, opium smoking had its devotees among the chic and stylish. Once again, such drug use was often associated with forbidden sexual activity and prostitution.[29] There was also nonmedicinal use of drugs among some idle rich, artists, and movie stars.

Whatever their differences of status or occupation, the groups that continued to shape and fortify images of drug use in the interwar period were all divorced from conduct that society accepted or praised. They seemed unproductive, threatening to the cohesive power of family and home, using a false sense of individualism to escape responsibility, or even to mock the normal. This conduct was also now illegal, which enhanced its negative imagery in the public mind, and intensified the gray tawdriness that permeated the drug underworld. No one caught this atmosphere better than the novelist Raymond Chandler. "She wouldn't think about the Mexican and Negro slums stretched out on the dismal flats south of the old inter-urban tracks," he had a character say in *The Lady in the Lake* (1943). "Nor of the waterfront dives along the flat shore south of the cliffs, the sweaty little dance halls on the pike, the marihuana joints, the narrow fox faces watching over the tops of the newspapers in the far too quiet hotel lobbies, nor the pick-pockets and drifters and conmen and drunk rollers and pimps and queens of the board walk."[30]

The enforcers lived with other aspects of this melancholy world. They spent lives of watching and waiting, trying to discover how drugs flowed from one place or person to another, hoping to break the weak link in some chain of traffic. They used what human means came to hand and often acquired a sense of futility, however much they believed in their work. The people they dealt with reinforced their view of the drug world as a place of lost souls that must be quarantined from normal society. "But how weary I become of them," the narcotic agent Maurice Helbrant recalled of the informers he worked with, "of their meaningless lying, their continual sponging, their aptitude for getting into trouble at any hour of the day or night and calling up from a police station or some joint to get them out, their ubiquitous presence—they hang around your house, greet you in coming out in the morning, bob up anywhere, always looking for money or a job or (half the time) with some cock-and-bull story to tell you."[31]

Once in awhile, a muffled cry escaped from this netherworld. An anonymous addict wrote Postmaster General James A. Farley of his plight in 1934, as Anslinger solidified his position with the new Roosevelt administration. "Mr. Farley—Anslinger, shaking and trembling, knowing you are going to can him, is making a big noise recently (seeking publicity) pinching a lot of poor sick addicts," he wrote in a great scrawl on cheap notepaper. "And here is the sad part—a genuine tragedy—he conveys to society the impression that drug addicts are desperate criminals. Mr. Farley, drug addicts are the most harmless class of people in the country. A smart dick will tell you the same. Not a Narcotic Agent."[32] Of course, these views did not affect the public or alter Anslinger's determination to eliminate the drug traffic.

The gray imagery of the drug world resembled the explanations of the origins of drug use that psychologists and sociologists developed in the interwar period. The policeman and scholar had different solutions for the drug problem, but both began to see the drug user as an abnormal personality with character defects that drug use seemed to control. The movement away from physiological explanations of cause began at the end of the progressive period, when therapies based on removing opiates from the body and restoring normal functioning obviously failed. Researchers found no organic changes from opiate use that explained relapse or the failure of most treated patients to abstain for very long. It seemed clear that addiction and the urge to use drugs involved a desire or need for a drug experience as well as for a drug's actions.

Psychological explanations for drug use seemed logical in the 1920s, when they became popular in analyzing other human behavior. The approach now seemed subtle and complex rather than obscure and made sense given the failure of prior explanations based on body actions. And the new psychological categories of behavior enabled observers to see types rather than mere cases.

But the psychological models that reigned after the 1920s developed from earlier thinking about "nervous" people and environmental stresses in modern civilization. Late nineteenth-century analysts tended to see a hereditarian process at work in poor biological endowment of nervous energy. The new psychological thinkers were less literal. Such weaknesses in their view arose from faulty interpersonal relationships and poor ego development, for whose results drugs seemed to compensate. Social disapproval and now illegality reinforced the user's low self-image and sense of inadequacy. This in turn strengthened the tendency to use the drug experience to feel superior or normal, as the personality required. This process could occur in any social, economic, or class situation, depending on the individual's personal development. But most researchers tended to read backward from the cases at hand and identified this profile with the poor, uneducated, and marginal people who did not conform to majoritarian expectations.

Nearly every earlier research had emphasized some intangible causes for drug use, even while employing specific remedies. Mind was as important as brain or nerves. Dr. George E. Petty, who believed that toxemia caused addiction and was curable, agreed that some psychological forces were at work in the typical addict. He argued in 1913 that addicts were self-centered, immature in demanding gratification and avoiding distress, with "so little moral purpose, so little kindness, and so little care for anything but themselves that they are unwilling to suffer for even one moment." They were "usually out of harmony with themselves and everything surrounding them." The person society considered normal had little to fear from drug addiction. "The man with positive traits of character, fixed habits, and strong convictions as to what is right and wrong, and who has a keen sense of obligation to humanity, will, by the mere possession of these opinions and convictions, be protected from many of the snares and pitfalls that inevitably await those who are less fixed in their habits and convictions."[33]

Weakness had seemed at work in the addict personality in other ways. "The keynote of the psychology of morphinism is self-depreciation," Dr. Charles B. Pearson of Maryland wrote in 1918. "For out of this mental state arises the secretiveness, prevarication, seclusion, and the morphine or opium cowardice. The addict is secretive because he imagines that others have the same poor opinion of him that he has of himself."[34] The addict-memoirists of the late nineteenth century said much the same but blamed this reinforcing behavior on social disapproval rather than on the addict. Other observers agreed that drugs supplied something missing in the addictive personality. "The so-called 'inflated personality' and 'heroin hero' is no more than this—an inferior man who through the narcotic effect of one of these drugs has temporarily lost his sense of inferiority, together with the restlessness and discontent that go along with it," Surgeon General H. S. Cummings noted in 1925.[35]

Emphases within the general psychological model varied, but the new authorities agreed with earlier ones that the drug experience provided a sense of normality and fulfillment to people who felt inadequate.[36] Failure to understand the workings of these psychological needs led to disappointment with the low cure rates. "Bear this fact constantly in mind," Edward Huntington Williams warned in 1922 as the period of law enforcement began, "a drug addict 'cured' against his will is not really cured at all, no matter what method of treatment is used or how long he may be incarcerated."[37]

Psychological analysis strengthened a long-standing tendency to categorize addicts and drug users. The addict who remained respectable, with middle class status came to seem "otherwise normal," in such schemes. The user who engaged in crime was "delinquent." The one who rejected therapy and seemed to enjoy life in the drug world was "psychopathic." One of the complaints about law enforcement involved the refusal of police to differentiate between good and bad addicts, based on the social effects of their behavior. "In short, the Harrison Law penalizes all addicts as criminals and degenerates," Dr. Oscar Dowling wrote in 1925, "it does not even attempt to separate the wheat from the chaff."[38]

The deviance approach developed steadily during the interwar period. Dr. Lawrence Kolb of the Division of Mental Hygiene of the Public Health Service codified much of this thinking in a career in government service that began in 1909 and ended in 1944. He held that a normal person could not become addicted, since drugs satisfied needs only in abnormal personalities. The normal person who used opiates for pain, in this view, could withdraw satistac._.ily, while the addictive personality could not because it needed the drug effects for more than physical pain. "Opiates apparently do not produce mental pleasure in stable persons except a slight pleasure brought about in some cases by the reflex from relief of acute pain," he wrote in 1925. "In most unstable persons opiates produce mental pleasure during the early period of addiction. The degree of pleasure seems to depend upon the degree of instability."[39]

Nor did Kolb believe that addiction caused crime, a connection that underlay public support of law enforcement. "Habitual criminals are psychopaths, and psychopaths are abnormal individuals who, because of their abnormality, are especially liable to become addicts," he held again in 1925. "Addiction is only an incident in their delinquent careers, and the crimes they commit are not precipitated by the drugs they take."[40] Kolb at first supported strict law enforcement, combined with institutional care, simply to reduce the supply of drugs available to such personalities. He became the first medical director of the federal narcotic farm at Lexington, Kentucky, in 1935 and gradually turned away from law enforcement, chiefly because of its effects on addicts. In 1956 he recalled a scene that summarized the differences of approach in the generations of his childhood and maturity. The general store where he lived "had on its shelves a jar of eating opium, and a carton of laudanum vials — ten percent opium. A respectable woman in the neighborhood often came in to buy laudanum. She was a good housekeeper and the mother of two fine sons. Everybody was sorry about her laudanum habit, but no one viewed her as a sinner or menace to the community. We had not yet heard the word 'addict,' with its sinister, modern connotations."[41]

By the 1940s, the deviance explanation of the addict personality was dominant. In 1943 Dr. J. D. Reichard of the Lexington hospital summarized the viewpoint:

> We consider that basically a narcotic drug addict is an ill person who has accidentally been exposed to the use of a narcotic, has found this is a temporary answer to his difficulty and has then gone through a secondary social regression or degradation due to the fact that he has had to connive and deceive and lie, associate with members of the underworld and try to avoid, more or less unsuccessfully, arrest and conviction in order to maintain his dosage of drugs. We must never forget that if the poppy plant or marijuana had never been grown, if alcohol had never been manufactured and if various drugs used by other types of addicts had never been discovered or synthesized, these people would still be problems to someone. Addiction to drugs merely complicates and obscures the basic problem of somato-illness. When we can approach objectively the study and treatment of the basic personality defect, the prevention and cure of narcotic addiction will be simplified.[42]

Sociologists became the most notable critics of psychological models. Professor Alfred Lindesmith of Indiana University argued that the new classifications represented ways of both understanding and isolating the addict. He saw the new labels as restatements of older moralistic ideas about proper conduct and social responsibilities. "The modern, 'scientific' theory is, in short, merely a reflection and a rephrasing of old folk attitudes and is, in this sense, moralistic," he insisted in

1940. "It did not grow out of any body of tested evidence." He thought that society always had seen addicts as pariahs and that psychological explanations merely kept them outsiders. Lindesmith thought that addiction and drug use resulted more from chance, curiosity, peer pressure, and associations than any fundamental personality disorders. "There is no evidence to indicate that any personality type whatever in any part of the social hierarchy is immune to addiction," he noted.[43] Lindesmith went on to develop a reinforcement theory that explained addiction as basically a reaction complex against fear of withdrawal. His and similar sociological views attained popularity after World War II.

Addicts who knew nothing about clinical experiments and sophisticated speculations about drug use occasionally seemed to verify them in homelier terms. As in the past, the users often appeared to know more than the experts. " ... the drug can be cured from the body, but never from the mind," a federal narcotics prisoner wrote in 1939. "If the victim starts to use the drug while he is still in his youth, the drug grows within his body and brain cells, while he grows into manhood. The drug therefore, has become a part of his life, and when cut off from the same, a part of him is missing, that nature can never again restore, save through the drug. ... "[44] As another addict-memoirist said in the 1940s: " ... a drug addict can never come back, for though you can take it out of the body you cannot take it out of the mind."[45] That "mind" involved all the needs that spokesmen of psychological viewpoints saw drugs satisfying in the addictive personality.

All the new theories of causation grew out of past experience with the drug problem. Their subtleties and exactness increased over time, yet the suppositions of "normal" behavior and acceptable social roles remained fairly constant. The social and individual pressures on "normal" and "abnormal" personalities changed from generation to generation yet were always there in some form. History had its lessons and ironies, which a shrewd review of Thomas De Quincey's *Confessions* prefigured in this case in 1824. In its way it anticipated the next hundred years of speculation about why people used drugs and what kinds of persons were likely to do so. Social change, ambition, and normal human development inevitably placed every personality under strain, this reviewer said:

> The mind is thus incessantly harassed and pressed, like the garrison of a weak citadel besieged by a strong foe, to which it must finally surrender. Sympathy inflicts on us the sufferings of others, and makes misery contagious. Or if nothing external to the mind gives it trouble, it may possess within itself sufficient materials of misery; it regrets of the past;

or forebodings and despair of the future may settle upon it like a cloud, through which it can look at the world only as an undesirable place. Or mere vacancy, the pain of not being excited, is in itself an evil, that puts nimble and impatient spirits upon the pursuit of sensation.[46]

The interwar period was actually a time of considerable study of the drug question. Careful and detailed research on the pharmacology of opiates and other drugs, and of their actions in the body, went on in universities, under the auspices of private foundations, and in the U.S. Public Health Service and other scientific agencies. But this activity and the findings it produced seldom went beyond the highly specialized professionals involved. The mere complexity of the research, whether in pharmacology or psychology, made the subject arcane and remote to all except experts. It seemed far removed from the observable reality and inherited folk wisdom employed in forming attitudes toward social questions. The more experts thought they understood drug use, the more obscure their work seemed. This inevitably helped sustain the consensus for law enforcement, which was at least comprehensible and offered tangible results in the form of arrest statistics.

The most obvious method of handling the problem, publicly supported clinics, was the least acceptable to almost everyone in the equation. To the public this approach seemed to legitimize drug use. The AMA opposed clinics and any "ambulatory" treatment after 1924. Its investigating committees concluded that the experiment of 1919–21 demonstrated that addicts who received free drugs outside a controlled facility had no incentive to seek final cure. They also feared that clinics would spread drug use, especially among young people.[47] Few police authorities supported the idea, since it was an admission of failure and because the public did not favor it.

And throughout his long career, Anslinger flatly rejected a clinic system. As he wrote an inquirer in 1936, "whether or not the original intention of the earlier clinics was to attempt a cure of the so-called patients, it soon developed that the average clinic merely represented a supply depot for drug addicts."[48] In 1941 he compared such clinics to "Government stations to spread leprosy and smallpox."[49] By 1953 he still held that such a change in policy would repudiate enforcement in general, violate international treaties, encourage drug use, and further confuse understanding of the drug problem.[50] This attitude represented Anslinger's apparent personal beliefs, though he was clearly protecting his bureaucracy. He had never believed that leniency toward addicts was the correct policy, since the traffic would continue as long as they remained as a market. Clinic treatment would not prevent the development of new addicts and represented an abandonment of the long-held idea of permanent cure.

But the dominant psychological explanations of the causes of drug use and addiction naturally determined the nature of treatment. More and more experts within the professions studying the subject accepted the idea that "cure" consisted of freedom from drugs, with no guarantee of permanent abstinence. Aftercare that focused on analyzing the emotional problems of individual patients, and efforts to change their environments, thus became the most important aspect of treatment. This approach became another "magic bullet" aimed at curing addicts and preventing further addiction. It grew increasingly expensive, usually paid for with public funds. The recidivism rate was very high, no matter what therapy the experts employed or how much the typical addict seemed to want to stop using drugs.

Suggestions that the federal government view drug use as a public health problem and establish a systematic treatment program paralleled the growth of law enforcement.[51] This did not involve any great change of attitudes. Many clinicians wanted to study addicts and addictions, even while supporting law enforcement. And the narcotics violators posed special problems for prison custodians. They needed medical treatment that was not always available and were a standing threat to introduce or increase the drug traffic within federal prisons. By the mid-1920s, narcotics violators were the dominant element in federal penitentiaries, and the movement to build special facilities for them gained support in Congress. Imprisonment seemed appropriate for dealers and suppliers but not for users unless they were simply hard-core criminals.

The necessary legislation for two federal narcotic "farms" passed in 1929. The first opened in Lexington, Kentucky, in 1935, the second in Fort Worth, Texas, in 1938. The term "farm" indicated symbolically how much of the inherited antidrug consensus remained. Presumably, such facilities would take the addict out of the competitiveness, urban tensions, and crime that had caused his weak personality to succumb to drugs. The treatment regimen began with drugs and procedures to ease the distress of withdrawal. Long-term care focused on individual analysis, group therapies, outdoor work, job training, and restoration of normal health. Trained clinicians on the staffs carried out research on the causes and effects of drug use but found no cures. Security was strict, and for all the efforts at humane and individualized

United States Narcotic Farm, Lexington, Kentucky. Courtesy National Archives.

United States Narcotic Farm, Fort Worth, Texas. Courtesy National Archives.

treatment, the farms were modified prisons, complete with walls and bars.[52] The aura of law enforcement and social quarantine remained strong.

In due course, these institutions came under attack for being divorced from social change and for codifying outdated or narrow information, a common fate for all bureaucracies. By the 1960s their example yielded in states like New York, Massachusetts, and California to facilities and treatment programs that emphasized mobility for the patient, much like earlier approaches in the nineteenth century. And many private and even less formal regimens became popular.[53]

Research in the medical sciences on drug use, efforts to develop theories of causation and effect in psychology and sociology, and federal treatment centers did not weaken the national emphasis on law enforcement. State and local authorities cooperated well with federal agents, partly out of belief and partly because the narcotics agents had a potent reputation for overriding opposition. Enforcement enjoyed public and political support and benefited from the medical profession's general hostility or indifference toward drug users. There was little reason to seek further legislation during the interwar period. Administrative rulings closed most loopholes, and few of the parties in any narcotics case wanted to argue about the meaning of gray areas in the enforcement apparatus. The very lack of sharp public debate about drug use after about the late 1920s indicated a cohesive antidrug consensus. The problems of the Great Depression also turned public attention toward other, more pressing matters.

The major exception concerned cannabis, and a substance called "marihuana" in particular.[54] Some paint products, oils, and birdseeds still contained cannabis, but it had faded from public discussion as a drug after the late nineteenth century. It remained in the United States Pharmacopoeia from 1850 to 1942, and was in numerous household remedies ranging from mild tranquilizers to corn plasters.[55]

Many reformers had wanted to include it in the Harrison Act. Hamilton Wright wrote Bishop Brent in 1909 that legislation should cover "cocaine, Indian hemp, and other habitforming drugs, which will spurt in . . . and replace opium and morphine."[56] The New York *Times* had favored regulating it. "The inclusion of cannabis indica among the drugs to be sold only on prescription is only common sense," the paper held in the summer of 1914. "Devotees of hashish are now hardly numerous enough to count, but they are likely to increase as other narcotics become harder to obtain."[57] But the pharmaceutical and drug industries objected, and cannabis escaped inclusion in the Harrison Act, though state and local laws generally made it a prescription item. By

1916 the popular magazine *Survey* thought that failure to regulate chloral and cannabis was a major weakness in the new federal law, and both these drugs remained suspect, untouched only because their use was declining.[58]

Because of its effects on personality and associations with certain kinds of people, however, marihuana became an easy target for regulation. Cannabis had never won a firm identification in the public mind as a useful medicine. It was chiefly identified with suspect marginal groups such as artists and intellectuals in the nineteenth century, and jazz musicians, bohemians, and petty criminals in the twentieth. It continued its odyssey of such associations in the nation's Mexican and black communities in the 1930s and after.

Most commentators, beginning in the nineteenth century, incorrectly classed cannabis with narcotics and hallucinogens, making few distinctions about the differing effects of its various forms. The potent hashish preparations thus received more notoriety than did the mild tinctures used in medical practice. Marihuana smoking seemed another link in a chain that began a hundred years earlier in lurid reports of hashish effects from travellers to the Near East and the writings of Fitzhugh Ludlow. By the 1930s, the public tended to class together all drugs whose effects altered the user's observable personality or seemed to impair social functioning and productivity. To critics, marihuana clearly fell into this category.

Marihuana made little impact on the public mind until the 1930s. Early reports of its increasing use came from the South. Medical and police authorities thought it was especially popular in the Gulf ports, where it was easily obtainable from sailors who worked on shipping to and from South America and the Caribbean. It was identified with drifters, the underworld of petty crime and vice, and some marginal ethnic groups. Its popularity was supposedly liable to increase throughout the South, where the plant grew easily.[59]

By the early 1930s, state and local police authorities in the West also began to voice concerns about marihuana smoking among the Mexicans who worked in the fields. Its use allegedly caused violence among them, especially personal fighting, when they relaxed from back-breaking labor with a "high." But it supposedly was becoming attractive to Anglos, especially youngsters who had heard of marihuana's reputation for producing "thrills" and "kicks."[60] Anslinger insisted later that pressure on the national government from western and southern police authorities was the principal original impetus for federal laws.[61]

The Mexican imagery in the debate over marihuana use resembled that of the Chinese and opium smoking, and the black and cocaine in earlier generations.[62] It represented a predictable reaction against foreigners from a presumably backward country who were immigrating to the United States in increasing numbers. Their language, religion, and habits seemed threatening to spokesmen for the established culture, and their economic impact caused mixed reactions. They worked at jobs that Americans seldom wanted, but there was a growing fear that they would lower wages in general if left unchecked. In more subtle ways they also typified the poverty, ignorance, and alleged tendencies to disorder that Americans had long associated with drug use in marginal groups, and which they feared that drug use in the larger society would cause. The impact of the Mexicans' image also was strong because of their visibility, whether in the crowded barrios of California and Texas, or in the gangs that performed "stoop labor" in the western fields.[63]

Other ethnic groups figured in the debate. Black field hands supposedly used marihuana to relax from heavy labor in the cotton fields, canebrakes, and rice paddies of the South. In some urban settings, musicians, entertainers, and petty criminals in Harlem and other black communities allegedly used it freely. Puerto Ricans, East and West Indians, and other Caribbean nationalities entered the controversy and added to majoritarian fears that drug use helped create the unattractive conditions in which they lived.[64]

But while these were important points of emphasis for critics of marihuana use, broader fears about the drug's effects underlay public concern. Early studies of marihuana use among soldiers in the Canal Zone concluded that while it was not addictive, it reduced their efficiency and released some socially useful inhibitions. Prohibition seemed unnecessary, but it was not an attractive habit to encourage.[65] And marihuana quickly became identified with violence and unpredictable behavior. "Users of marihuana become stimulated as they inhale the drug and are likely to do anything," the New York *Times* noted in a report about the Denver area in 1934. "Most crimes of violence in this section, especially in country districts, are laid to users of the drug." The reporter also thought that marihuana was a "poisonous weed which maddens the senses and emaciates the body of the user...."[66] By 1937 as the discussion peaked and resulted in federal legislation, the newspaper spoke for much public opinion: "Its inhalation may produce criminal insanity and causes juvenile delinquency."[67] Opponents also thought that marihuana was an aphrodisiac, which seemed especially threatening given the people likely to use it.[68] But above all, marihuana appeared dangerous because its effects were unpredictable and produced an artificial personality detrimental to society and the user, an old theme in the drug debate. In some users it caused little or no effect, while in others it supposedly caused loss of control that critics equated with irrationality.[69]

Concern about marihuana's effects on young people became the chief focus of the discussion. Anslinger and other proponents of regulation ultimately used this fear skillfully, but it was always implicit in the developing concern. A writer in the *Michigan Municipal Review* in 1929 presaged much of the discussion to come, "Marahuana, the Mexican dope known as Indian hemp, or Loco, is being sold in large quantities around high schools in many localities," he noted. "This affords a peculiar thrill and is followed up until another addict to drugs is made and the helpless chap joins this gruesome procession that has only one end. This social drug is known as the murder weed."[70] Three years later in 1932 a public health writer emphasized similar points:

A new menace has arisen which affects particularly children of the school age. This is the use of marihuana, a weed employed by ten to thirty percent of the Mexicans for smoking. Of recent date, there has been an influx of this drug into New York where it is sold in the form of cigarettes, more reasonably procurable than any of the other habit-forming drugs. The danger to children is easily seen since most adolescents identify smoking with budding manhood and are likely to form this habit through associating it with ordinary smoking and the wearing of long trousers or long skirts.[71]

The image of adolescent users became potent in the discussion that resulted in regulation. They figured as hedonists, as sex-possessed, as senseless escapists from life's responsibilities, or as innocent victims of their immaturity and inexperience. They also appeared in lurid news reports of brutal murders and other crimes of violence, and of automobile accidents that marihuana use allegedly caused. Concern grew among parent groups, educators, and religious circles that the next generation faced serious threats from marihuana use.

Marihuana also grew nearly everywhere, was easy to use, and difficult to monitor. This reinforced fears that its use was spreading to elements of society that had not employed drugs before, and would become uncontrollable.[72] Few experts thought marihuana addictive, though it might cause dependence among users who liked the experiences it produced. Critics attacked its alleged relation to violence and personality changes. They also depicted it as a stepping-stone to other truly addictive drugs.

The drive for federal control of marihuana peaked in the mid-1930s and resulted in the Marihuana Tax Act of 1937. By that time some twenty-four states regulated the substance and as with so many previous drug laws, this one seemed to be an addition to existing regulation rather than an innovation. The Bureau of Narcotics was somewhat ambivalent throughout the controversy. Anslinger apparently dreaded the process of trying to control the production and use of such a common plant as marihuana. He also feared that prolonged discussion of the subject might cause many people to experiment with it out of curiosity. He seemed to respond more to pressure for legislation that came from local and state authorities than to seek it himself. But once it became clear that other elements of the federal government, especially Congress and the Treasury Department, wanted something to satisfy constituent pressure, Anslinger spoke for control. He employed his formidable powers of persuasion with the press, politicians and citizen groups to favor regulation. And he skillfully used the occasion to create support for a Uniform State Narcotic Law that interested him and the bureau more than did marihuana control.[73]

There was some equal ambivalence in the medical community. The *JAMA* voiced skepticism about the need for federal regulation. It thought that while doctors seldom prescribed cannabis, they should have the right to do so without paying taxes or keeping more records for narcotic agents to monitor. Federal regulation of other drugs had not produced any cures to date or stopped the drug traffic, and the *Journal* suggested that marihuana be left to local control and an education campaign.[74] Dr. William C. Woodward, who spoke for the AMA at congressional hearings on the proposed legislation, faced hostile congressmen to say much the same. He especially opposed further regulation of medical practice.[75]

This did not imply any approval of marihuana use. There was little careful experimental evidence about either its physiological or psychological effects. Medical and scientific experts, whose work did not figure much in the debate over regulation, did not generally believe marihuana addictive or especially harmful to the body. But it was clearly dangerous to some users, had the potential to cause dependence, and had uncertain psychological effects.[76] The medical profession's spokesmen dreaded further federal regulation, doubted that marihuana use was a serious social problem, and doubtless hoped it would not develop beyond being a fad. But they did not hold that it was harmless, either to the user or society.

A significant body of research on marihuana developed after regulation. It had no immediate effect on official policy, partly because the war interrupted the discussion. The Narcotics Bureau also ruthlessly refuted any deviations from its official viewpoint. These studies retained considerable ambivalence toward marihuana use. Dr. Walter Bromberg, a psychiatrist at Bellevue Hospital in New York City, produced some of the earliest authoritative studies on marihuana's effects. He held that it was not addictive or linked to irrationality and violence. But his conclusions on marihuana's less tangible effects at least paralleled the general ideas that sustained regulation. The confirmed marihuana user sought to "recapture over and over again the ecstatic, elated state into which the drug lifts him," he wrote in 1934. "The addiction to cannabis is a sensual addiction: it is in the service of the hedonistic elements of the personality."[77] He repeated much the same in 1939:

> The most that one can say on the basis of ascertainable facts is that prolonged use of marihuana constitutes a 'sensual' addiction, in that the user wishes to experience again and again the ecstatic sensations and feelings which the drug produces. Unlike addiction to morphine, which is biochemically as well as psychologically determined, prolonged use of marihuana is essentially in the service of the hedonistic elements of the personality.[78]

Other researchers in the 1940s generally supported the view that marihuana was not addictive, did not produce tolerance, and was not linked to insanity. But they left the impression that it could cause dependence in some personality types, that it released some inhibitions, especially relating to sex, and lowered efficiency.[79]

Anslinger became a strong supporter of regulation after 1937. "Those of us who have followed this problem closely from day to day feel that the marihuana evil can no longer be temporized with," he wrote shortly after the act went into effect, "but that it must be subjected to the same rigid method of control as the traffic in other dangerous drugs."[80] He doubtless believed that marihuana use was socially threatening. But in years to come, he also refused to yield on regulating it lest this weaken the consensus on law enforcement.

The drive for federal regulation originated with special interest groups in law enforcement and politics, but the public accepted the ideas about marihuana that set the parameters on debate for the next forty years. In this view, marihuana was unpredictable in effects, but it could produce a state of abnormal personality. It also reduced productivity and efficiency. It was escapist, and especially attractive to impressionable young people, and was a stepping-stone to other drugs. One of the major effects of legal regulation of drugs after 1914 was to make every substance that subsequently became suspect prove itself by the company it kept. Marihuana seemed to keep the company of the established drug underworld and marginal groups that society disliked or feared.

The debate subsided as quickly as it arose. The Bureau of Narcotics was not interested in drawing attention to marihuana through sudden and harsh enforcement, and the problem faded. "I saw no future in special work on marihuana for the present," Maurice Helbrant recalled on the eve of World War II. "When some brilliant scientist isolates the narcotic in marihuana and we have 'marihuanine' in pill or powder form on the market, then will be the time to watch out."[81]

At the end of the 1930s, the Bureau of Narcotics seemed to have the drug problem well in hand. The web of law enforcement involved local as well as federal authorities, and the international traffic appeared to be low and stabilized. As Helbrant recalled, there was a sense of dwindling importance around the drug question. The same names and kinds of smuggling activities appeared year after year in the government's official reports and newspaper stories. To the casual observer the hope of finally stopping supplies and ending the production of new addicts seemed about to come true. Helbrant and other insiders thought it time to seek more money and manpower and end the problem once and for all.[82]

The outbreak of war in 1941 strengthened the hope of finally ending drug use. It now seemed possible to stop the international traffic and control domestic distribution in the name of the war effort. The Treasury Department stockpiled enough opiates to fulfill normal needs during the projected war years, including maintenance of registered addicts, and tightened its surveillance of pharmaceutical houses.[83]

If anything, law enforcement became harsher than ever, since illicit drug production and use were now unpatriotic as well as illegal. A spokesman for the U.S. Attorney's office in Boston typified official thinking in holding that the drug problem was "primarily—I might say almost wholly—a law-enforcement matter, and resolves itself into one of control of narcotic addiction through control of illicit narcotic traffic. The medical aspects are merely incidental and supplementary." Only prevention, in this view, would solve the drug problem, and the wayward addict who rejected treatment must face a drugless world. "Relapses are most frequent when drugs are most accessible."[84]

Throughout the war, federal and state agents monitored the traffic and paid close attention to potential new trouble spots such as the congested towns around war plants and military bases. The floating populations there had money and the need for leisure or recreation that might involve drugs. Opiate use in such circumstances was unusual, and alcohol remained the nation's drug of choice for relaxation or release. But new terms such as "goofball" began to enter the language, as use of barbiturates and amphetamines spread among an increasing number and variety of people seeking stimulation or rest.[85]

The war years were bleak for addicts. Most continued to buy from suppliers whose prices skyrocketed in the name of the risks they took. The number of thefts of drugs from bonded warehouses, drugstores, and doctors' offices increased. Milk sugar and other dilutants were the dominant ingredients of the heroin that was available. Some addicts turned to patent nostrums that contained small amounts of opiates, such as cough syrups with codeine, or boiled down paregoric. The Bureau of Narcotics reported a steady decrease in the number of addicts, and popular magazines like *Time* saw this process as a final, unwitting cure regimen for the nation's hardcore addicts.[86] The law enforcement system took some cautious pride in the decrease of drug-related crime. But few observers noted that much of this apparent change merely reflected the presence in the armed forces of young men, the population element most likely to use drugs or commit crimes.

Throughout the conflict various commentators hoped that the postwar settlement would somehow deal a death blow to the international traffic. The new United Nations established agencies modeled on those of the League of Nations to monitor the traffic. Anslinger and others urged special attention to countries that cultivated the opium poppy. Whatever the outcome of political and social change in the new world order, drug control must remain high on the list of international concerns. This seemed especially necessary in relation to Japan, which in Anslinger's opinion had staged many drug Pearl Harbors on the United States before the start of actual hostilities in 1941.[87] The New York *Times* condemned Japan in 1944 as "one of the world's great traffickers in drugs."[88] Japanese war criminals faced specific charges of encouraging the drug traffic among conquered peoples. "Of all the indictments against Japan," the paper said in 1946, "that of the use of opium and its derivative, heroin, as deliberate government policy to corrode the minds of conquered peoples, and of all Japan's enemies, is perhaps the most damning."[89] The American occupation government immediately banned opium, cocaine, and cannabis after 1945 and Americans helped successive Japanese governments control barbiturates and amphetamines.[90]

The feared epidemic of drug use among GIs in Japan and the Orient did not materialize, and the home front in the drug war seemed calm as Americans turned to demobilization and the resumption of normality both as individuals and a nation. Some experts within the scientific and law enforcement worlds expected a sharp upturn in drug use with peace, but this was not a major public concern in the late 1940s.[91] In some ways, the Bureau of Narcotics was a victim of its own propaganda and apparent success. Congress was not disposed to increase its budget, and any new rise in drug use would pose serious problems for law enforcers. "Our funds are so low that we couldn't even send an agent across the border from El Paso unless he walks and doesn't spend any money for gasoline," Anslinger complained privately in 1947.[92] But at the same time, he expected the international traffic to grow, focused once again on poppy production in the Near East and Asia.[93]

The situation changed in the early 1950s with a scare that sharpened all the old images and fears about drug use. The country's major cities, especially New York, were the focus of news reporting of heroin use. The discussion became national in scope and generated fears that drug use was once again suddenly threatening to spread throughout society.[94] *Newsweek* turned from believing in 1948 that the drug issue was dead to warning in late 1950 that it had revived in fearsome forms. Throughout 1951 it was one of many widely read publications that reported on the use of heroin among urban young people, especially blacks and Puerto Ricans. In the fall of 1951, it held that teenagers were "turning their arms and legs into pincushions."[95] Even Anslinger, who disliked admitting any upswing in the drug problem, noted privately in August 1951 that "We are having some upsurge in the drug traffic today...."[96]

Once again the nature of the users was influential in forming or solidifying public attitudes. As in the progressive period, the addict population was changing. The typical addict of the preceding generation, who was the product of illegality and law enforcement was disappearing. The new addicts were predominantly black, young males from urban ghettos, especially in the Northeast.[97] They supposedly stole to finance their habits, often lived in tough street gangs, and had no apparent desire to enter mainstream society.

This pattern of drug use was alarming enough, but more and more reports indicated that teenagers of all kinds were experimenting with a variety of substances. Drug use appeared to reflect a growing rebelliousness among young people, especially in cities, but potentially everywhere.[98] And some kind of broad social changes that drug use only represented also seemed at work. The reigning typology of the drug addict as abnormal began to weaken. "The most terrifying thing about this bewitching of the youthful to parents and social workers who are worried about the rapid spread of addiction is that it happens to 'normal' and average children," the New York *Times* reported in a 1951 series of reports on drug use among ordinary young people.[99] It was easy enough to blame this on organized crime or pushers, the "Typhoid Marys" of the drug world,[100] but their clientele seemed to be changing. "Hard pressed to create a market, peddlers have left the slums and invaded middle-class schools and neighborhoods," a popular science magazine, *Science Digest,* suggested in 1952.[101] Once again, drugs seemed ready to undermine the majority's values, as typified in its young people. The press reports and the numbers of alleged new users were greatly exaggerated, but the sharp public response revealed again the power of the antidrug consensus.

This concern about heroin addiction widened into public realization that some elements of society were using an increasing array of drugs for escape or pleasure or because suddenly it was the thing to do in their circles. Marihuana, and to a lesser extent, cocaine were common in such exotic locales as the movie colony of Hollywood, New York City's smart sets, and the bohemias of Greenwich Village and North Beach, San Francisco. This was tolerable as long as use did not spread outside the informal red-light districts that society accorded such groups. In the American popular mind, the arts and thought always lived across the railroad tracks. But drugs also became identified with the spirit of rebellion typified in a new breed of social critics, exemplified in the "beatnik."[102]

Many people had warned in the 1930s that marihuana was a drug with a future, a prediction that seemed ready to come true as the 1950s closed.[103] Public disapproval of it seemed as great as in the 1930s. The one nontechnical study of its effects, the so-called "Mayor's Report," or "LaGuardia Report" done in New York City on the eve of the war and published in 1944, concluded in general that marihuana's dangers were greatly exaggerated. It did not connect marihuana to violence, crime or insanity, or find it addictive or a stepping-stone to heroin. On the whole, most users seemed to use it for momentary escape and to produce reverie. Marihuana might lessen inhibitions but seldom caused unusual actions. But the report did identify its use with blacks, Puerto Ricans, and the drug underworld in general.[104]

These findings changed few minds at the time. The *JAMA* rejected them as unscientific and dangerous to the law enforcement consensus. During the scare of the 1950s, most spokesmen continued to see marihuana use as a prelude to heroin addiction. Anslinger and the enforcement establishment strongly opposed debating the subject and held to the existing line. "Whereas the opiates can be a blessing when properly used, *marihuana has no therapeutic value*," he insisted in a 1953 book on the drug problem, "and its use therefore is always an abuse and vice."[105] Marihuana remained a part of the forbidden drug world.

The most immediate result of this new spasm of concern in the 1950s was increased regulation in familiar patterns. State and local authorities cooperated with the Narcotics Bureau. Congress passed the Boggs Act of 1951 and the Narcotic Control Act of 1956, which provided lengthy mandatory sentences for drug traffickers, and permitted the death penalty in some cases. Narcotics agents were allowed to carry firearms. Several highly publicized congressional investigations of organized crime further allied the drug traffic with sinister elements in society.[106] On the surface, the consensus against drug use and for enforcement seemed stronger than ever.

But other forces were at work beneath these appearances that indicated some changing attitudes. This was apparent within the medical professions. The prestigious New York Academy of Medicine sponsored two conferences on drug use among adolescents in 1951 and 1952, and generally recommended a return to medical control of the problem. There was even talk during the decade of a modified and carefully controlled clinic experiment. The National Institutes of Health staged a symposium on the broad problem of addiction and abuse in 1958. And reigning psychological ideas on the causes of addiction and drug use began to weaken. The events of the 1950s demonstrated that some drug experiences appealed to people who seemed normal. They took drugs by chance, to please associates, to be sociable, and for mere pleasure or relaxation. The delinquency model that had reigned since the 1920s might still explain some drug users but was clearly not the final word.[107] It was also obvious that a generation of law enforcement had failed to eliminate the problem and that the country faced another episodic upswing in drug use that law could not manage.[108]

Some specialists within the health professions began to agree with Lawrence Kolb. "The opinion of informed physicians should take precedence over that of law enforcement officers, who in this country, are too often carried away by enthusiasm for putting people in prison, and who deceive themselves as well as the public about the nature and seriousness of drug addiction," he wrote in 1956.[109] New state treatment programs for addicts began to seem more humane and forward-looking than the federal enforcement system. And jail for the new juvenile and social users seemed inappropriate, even to a public that feared drug use. This was especially true as more and more offenders came from respectable backgrounds. Other approaches appeared to be in order.

The 1950s was an important transitional period in public policy toward drug use. It opened with a scare that reinforced the law enforcement approach, but closed with a vague yet tangible feeling that something new was in order, especially since the user population was changing. By the dawn of the 1960s, the drug issue was developing a multiple constituency again, similar to the one of the progressive era. The medical profession began to assert its prerogatives in both research and treatment. Some people in the psychology, social work, public health, and sociology disciplines began to devote more energy and a broad social viewpoint to the problem. This concern was in order, for American society faced a time when drug use and all it represented would come to the center of national life.

A NEW PROBLEM

THE TRANSFER OF POLITICAL LEADERSHIP from President Eisenhower to President Kennedy in 1961 symbolized a desire for change that permeated American society. The 1940s and 1950s were decades of consolidation and caution. But from the first the 1960s seemed oriented toward innovation and experimentation, whether in economics, technology, or social relationships.

This was as true of the sciences and professions that studied the drug question as of those that prepared the nation for a revolution in technology that put men on the moon and made computers household gadgets. Most of the medical and social science professions had developed enough expertise and confidence to seem on the cutting edge of a new wave of modernization in both material and intellectual matters. And addicts profited, at the beginning of the decade at least, from a new belief that human problems were soluble and that the marginal elements of society deserved fresh attention. Many physicians, medical scientists, lawyers and social theorists now wanted to correct the impression that they were uninterested in the drug addict's plight.[1]

These groups focused on new approaches to treatment. This might win some support from a public that was naturally concerned with tangible results to real problems. It might also help the addict and potential drug user, and produce new research. Above all, the heavy reliance on simple law enforcement would likely yield only to some alternative that appeared to ameliorate the drug problem.

A variety of therapies came under discussion. For the first time since the progressive era there was some interest in a clinic system. The

British policy of maintaining known opiate addicts as regular patients of physicians was also well known. This approach accepted the fact that many addicts could not practice abstinence but could function reasonably well in society under maintenance. The system seemed to work well in Britain, which had a very low rate of addiction and no history of harsh police control of drugs, and it was both inexpensive to the public and humane for the addict.[2]

Yet despite considerable discussion, the idea of such individual maintenance or public clinics won few adherents in the United States. Critics believed that such an arrangement would merely legitimize the drug use and inevitably create new addicts. It also seemed morally wrong to write off addicts or abandon the idea of rehabilitation.[3] There was little public support for spending tax dollars on clinics, which seemed ironic given the escalating costs of law enforcement, but which also showed the power of inherited moralism and the fear of even seeming to weaken on the question of prohibiting heroin.

After a White House Conference on Narcotics and Drug Abuse in 1962, which took generally more open, medically oriented views of the subject, the AMA seemed to soften its stand against maintenance. But this was more apparent than real. Its statements of 1963 still held that maintenance was acceptable only in treating withdrawal, for the hopelessly addicted, or as part of a legitimate effort at final abstinence. At most, it suggested a carefully controlled experiment with a clinic but did not see this as the solution to the heroin problem.[4]

Something resembling a modest clinic system did develop involving the substance called methadone. German chemists made this synthetic opiate during the war and christened it "Dolophine" in honor of Adolph Hitler. It was known in some American medical and psychiatric circles by the late 1940s. Doctors at the Lexington and Fort Worth facilities used it to ease patients' withdrawal in the 1950s. By 1964 Doctors Vincent Dole and Marie Nyswander had launched a significant pilot program at Rockefeller University in New York City of substituting methadone for heroin. In the next few years nearly every city had one or more clinics that dispensed the drug in the name of treatment, a semantic license that gained some public support and kept such operations within the law.[5]

The enthusiasm for methadone grew, as it seemed to answer many social as well as medical problems. It was addictive but taken in stabilized maintenance doses blocked withdrawal distress. This presumably freed the addict from constant anxiety about drug supplies and permitted him to begin sorting out the root causes of his troubles. In social terms, methadone seemed to promise that the addict could hold a job, rear a family, and function as a citizen while seeking long-term therapy that resulted in abstinence. In short, it promised to make the heroin addict normal, the inherited ideal of all treatment. Supporters of methadone emphasized this aspect of the therapy in seeking public support and funding.

These programs also had many advantages to policy-makers. They were cheap, relatively easy to administer and removed far more addicts from street life than did either incarceration or psychological therapies based on small groups. Methadone was also identified with medical and scientific expertise and promised more immediate effects than psychological or sociological approaches.

But the methadone treatment always had critics. Its apparent acceptability stemmed from the public's hope that it would stop the crime wave that addicts allegedly caused, especially in large cities. This did not amount to support for methadone unless it did lead to permanent cures. Many critics saw methadone maintenance as limited and unimaginative, merely controlling the overt symptoms of drug addiction rather than focusing on primary causes. Its use amounted to exchanging an unpopular addiction for one that was more socially acceptable. By the 1970s, many black activists attacked methadone as simply another way the white majority controlled ethnic minorities. Methadone did not seem involved in upward mobility. And its use was voluntary and did not affect addicts who preferred the drug experience to "normal" living. This increasingly left the majority of society puzzled and critical, as the ideal of final abstinence once more receded under the impact of events.[6] By the late 1970s, methadone programs were under attack as another offensive that had failed in the war against drug use.

Other people turned away from such technical answers to programs that were suspect to the established medical and social science disciplines. The most influential of these were treatment arrangements in the hands of volunteers and patients rather than experts or warders. They were typically located in old houses or other converted buildings instead of hospitals or prisonlike facilities. The former addicts who lived in them were usually under the influence of a charismatic leader. They supported each other in the struggle against drug use, especially heroin, and tried to develop a program focused on personal responsibilities and group allegiance. They were frankly hostile to the formalities and bureaucracies of medicine, psychiatry, and social work, which seemed to them as repressive and stagnant as law enforcement. The participants in these programs engaged in "rap sessions," a term that soon gained widespread currency in the nondrug world, and in similar practices that differed sharply from controlled clinical approaches in the hands of experts.

The most famous of these facilities was Synanon, which a recovered alcoholic named Charles Dederich founded in Santa Monica, California, in 1958.[7] Such approaches gained considerable public appeal in the late 1960s and early 1970s. They seemed both humane and realistic about what addicts must do in order to function in the existing society. They were also a welcome contrast to the complex, impersonal, lavishly funded approaches that did not seem to produce the final cure that the public still associated with all therapies.But Synanon-like programs were also popular in some measure because they recapitulated many American values and ideals. In their special context they emphasized self-help, the work ethic, individualism, and acceptance of the inherited ideals of productivity, realism, and rationality.

But as time passed, it became increasingly clear that addicts in these programs had in fact entered an insulated world. It might be a microcosm of society's hopes and values, but its therapies helped most addicts only through dependence on group loyalties that remained separated from the competitiveness and risks of the larger world. In the end, cure rates for these approaches were not significantly higher than for other approaches.

At the same time, some official policies seemed to soften in favor of the addict, even as law enforcement against suppliers continued. This was especially true in the wealthy populous states with well publicized drug problems, such as New York, Massachusetts, Illinois, and California, which spent huge sums on drug rehabilitation programs tailored to avoid the appearance of punishment or incarceration even while treating addicts in special facilities. The federal government helped pay for these and also poured large sums into basic research on drug actions, as scientists continued to seek to unravel the mechanisms of addiction. Other researchers looked for substances that would negate the effects of addictive drugs. Mental health experts conducted expensive experiments to refine the ideas in personality typology. And the harsh legal penalties, so common in the previous generation, often yielded to some kind of treatment focused on psychology and medicine rather than punishment.

These and other approaches helped make the 1960s seem more "humane" and "reformist" in relation to the opiate addict than the 1950s were. But their final results were often ironic repetitions of previous history. The increasing complexity of laws and regulations, for instance, inevitably reinforced the popular idea that addiction was baffling and contagious. Medical science appeared caught in an endless search for some substance or body mechanism that explained it, but which might never become clear. Therapies based on psychology seemed interminable and often unproductive, another kind of life sentence whose costs the public thought onerous. The sociological explanation that addiction developed from poverty, slum living, and discrimination seemed logical, until opiate addiction and a broad range of drug use appeared in the nation's affluent suburbs. And the new treatment centers remained segregated from society, however cheerful their appearance, or well-meaning and modern their staffs. This was equally true of the widely touted halfway houses and other informal facilities. Politicians, community leaders, and reformers applauded their work but were usually glad that they were not in their own neighborhoods.

As the 1960s began the attention of both the public and drug experts remained focused on heroin. Because of its identification with dependence, its social associations, and alleged relationship to street crime, it remained the most feared of drugs. The sense that its use was increasing among some groups in the preceding decade was roughly true, but this still seemed confined to marginal elements of society. The stereotyped addict was still a black male teenager who lived in an urban slum, an analogous white delinquent, or some other person separated from the social mainstream.

This pattern changed as the 1960s developed and white middle-class young people experimented with many drugs, including heroin. This widely discussed apparent change in the user's developing profile caused great public concern and prompted support for both tighter law enforcement and new treatment approaches.

The war against heroin also became part of the struggle for civil rights. It became increasingly popular to believe that racism, poverty, and alienation among blacks caused drug use. These social forces did not "cause" heroin addiction as a virus caused a cold. But they were part of a larger social milieu which made susceptible people likely to use drugs. That use in turn seemed both more inevitable and understandable than in affluent white society. Many of the decade's social programs were aimed at treating the addict and at eliminating the environment that allegedly caused drug use.

The effort to solve the drug mystery also benefited from other dramatic events and broader social concerns. Intense public fear of and resentment at rising crime, especially muggings and burglaries focused attention on drug users, particularly heroin addicts. Whether or not drug addicts caused a disproportionate amount of crime, the public always thought so.[8] By the 1960s, the junkie-burglar-mugger image paralleled the mobster-supplier image in the public consciousness. After 1969, the Nixon administration increased expenditures on the crime problem, which resulted in using some funds on drug prevention and treatment programs.

The idea that heroin use was widespread among American servicemen in Viet Nam also had some ironically beneficial effects on the drug problem, at least momentarily. As the war in Southeast Asia dragged on amid bitter controversy, more and more servicemen revealed the disdain for authority that characterized antiwar protesters at home. Alcohol retained its ancient appeal as a relaxant among the troops and sailors, but marihuana use quickly became an aspect of military life. Enterprising South Vietnamese soon began to row-crop marihuana and developed a sizeable cottage industry and distribution system for the GI market.[9]

The Army's heavy-handed crackdown on marihuana use seemed to turn many soldiers to heroin, which was easily procured and often cheap. By the spring of 1971, the press began to report a major heroin problem in Viet Nam. As many as 10 or 15 percent of the enlisted men were allegedly using heroin; some sources reported as much as 25 percent, or about 60,000 men.[10]

Public opinion now fed on several fears. As at so many times in the past, it seemed that evil foreigners, Asiatics in this case, were corrupting innocent American youth. It also appeared likely that a horde of addicts would return from combat. Prison was inappropriate for these veterans, and the public supported special rehabilitation programs for the returning men. As with other historical scares about addicted servicemen, only a small percentage of Viet Nam veterans were in fact heavy heroin users, though they were clearly more familiar with other drugs such as marihuana than were predecessors in earlier wars.[11]

At about the same time, the Nixon administration stepped up efforts to stop or lessen the international opium traffic. With support from Congress and the public, it adopted stringent measures against opiates, marihuana, and cocaine from Latin America, Asia, and the Near East. It even compensated poppy growers in Turkey who agreed not to plant an annual crop. These and other enforcement actions had a roller-coaster effect on statistics, since they could not be sustained. It proved impossible either to seal the nation's borders or to compel foreigners to stop supplying a lucrative market in the United States. The annual reports on heroin use at least resembled these efforts, rising one year and falling another. The rate of addiction did seem to decline or at least stabilize from time to time in the 1970s as more potential users became aware of the drug's dangers. But a sudden apparent upsurge of heroin use was quite likely to follow any official pronouncements that its use was declining.[12]

Concern about other drugs paralleled public fear of heroin. Cocaine emerged as a drug of experimentation in the late 1960s and 1970s. Despite its fascinations for many people, the public still related it to irrationality and dissipation. In 1973 the National Commission on Marihuana and Drug Abuse, which took a lenient view of marihuana smoking, remained hostile to cocaine. It sought to "reduce legitimate cocaine production in this country (including import of coca leaves for purposes of extracting cocaine) to the minimum quantities needed for domestic research and medical uses. If no unique therapeutic use of the drug remains, the government should eliminate manufacture altogether. In addition, the United States should work through diplomatic channels to persuade other countries not to manufacture cocaine for export."[13]

The debate over cocaine's dangers continued into the 1970s. As in the past, few experts thought it addictive, though like any other drug, it could produce psychological dependence. Its prolonged use also had some adverse physical effects. But its importance in the broader context of public concern about drugs lay elsewhere. Where once it had seemed allied to crime, especially among blacks, it now figured on the college campus, in the intellectual salon, and at the discotheque. It was increasingly identified with members of the middle class, in search of sexual release or abandon, a "high" for pleasure's sake, and escapism.[14] Critics feared that its use would affect inherited values, and also that it might be the entering wedge for a new wave of general drug use among the educated, young, middle-class.

The increasing use of drugs that were once generally solely identified with medicine won growing public attention in the 1960s and 1970s. Chief among these were amphetamines and barbiturates, and new chemicals with similar actions. Amphetamines gained some notoriety in the late 1930s and during World War II as "stay awake" compounds designed to help users through sudden demands on time and energy. Soldiers on all sides in the conflict used them to remain alert on watch or patrol. They soon became popular with people seeking to lose weight, since they depressed the appetite, to study for examinations or work overtime, or merely to appear bright and active when tired.

These substances were identified with medical practice and the physician, and did not seem dangerous or suspect until the public realized that billions of doses were in general use every year. By the mid-1960s, they had entered the drug black market and were known as "uppers" among users seeking a high which they often described in sexual terms. As usual, attention focused on young people, especially the alternately fascinating and threatening drop-outs and hippies who lived in such forbidden territory as the Haight-Ashbury district of San Francisco.

Once amphetamines lost their identification with medicine, society increasingly allied them with unwelcome changes of personality that resembled paranoia, with escapism, and with an abnormal and dangerous artificial personality. In many ways, they gained a reputation similar to that of cocaine at the turn of the century for causing irrational and often violent behavior when used in large doses. "Freaking out" became a popular term to describe the results of overdoses. Amphetamines were liable to cause dependence and adversely affected many functions of the body as well as the mind. Even proponents of drug use to explore the mind quickly condemned them as dangerous to the individual as well as society, and for making drug experiences in general suspect. "Let's issue a general declaration to all the underground community, *contra speedamos ex cathedra*," the famous beatnik poet Allen Ginsberg told the Los Angeles *Free Press* in 1965. "Speed is antisocial, paranoid making, it's a drag, bad for your body, bad for your mind, generally speaking, in the long run uncreative and it's a plague in the whole dope industry. All the nice gentle dope fiends are getting screwed up by the real horror monster Frankenstein speed freaks who are going around stealing and bad mouthing everybody."[15]

Barbiturates and similar compounds that had the opposite effect from amphetamines drew a similar response. These substances dated from the beginning of the century but had gained significant use only by the 1930s. Like amphetamines, they were identified with medicine and the physician but always had the potential for abuse in the popular imagination. Barbiturates could produce sleep and rest but also created a sense of tensionless well-being, or "low," and could mask or control psychological problems. They were liable to cause dependence, were harmful to the body, and as depressants were potentially deadly. The nonmedical user also lost efficiency and alertness and used them to avoid personal or social problems. In many ways they resembled the chloral hydrate and bromides that were so popular in the late nineteenth century. All of this led many experts and the AMA to recommend regulation of them as early as the 1930s.[16]

By the 1960s, doctors prescribed both barbiturates and amphetamines routinely. Respectable users employed a barbiturate to produce sleep and an amphetamine to restore at least the appearance of vigor and alertness. Their use was especially widespread among women. Both substances were easy to manufacture and distribute outside legitimate channels and thus had dual constituencies. By the 1970s, many cautionary voices had warned against the overuse of both barbiturates and amphetamines. Doctors grew more cautious about prescribing them without attention to a patient's basic anxieties. And other users learned from experience that both substances were indeed dangerous.

The use of "tranquilizers" grew equally. These substances first won attention in the fight against mental illness and helped sedate or control persons with emotional problems. By the post–World War II years they were becoming fashionable in treating mild depression, anxiety, and dissatisfaction that had no apparent organic basis. As with so many similar products in the late nineteenth century, their use attested to a sense of intensified social change, alterations of values, and vague discontent with life's rewards or directions. They were heavily used among middle-class women. Like barbiturates, they thus resembled chloral hydrate and earlier hypnotics. And experts also warned that they and similar compounds offered false security against distress. "Many of us are often unwilling to endure mild discomfort if there is a drug available to subdue the distress," the National Commission on Marihuana and Drug Abuse," noted in 1973. "More and more people are using drugs as if they were the only possible solution to the inevitable vicissitudes of life."[17] This echoed the views of George M. Beard and other students of "American nervousness" in the 1880s and 1890s.

Tranquilizers answered many immediate problems. For the patient they produced some sense of equilibrium and normality with ease. They enabled the doctor to manage these vague but distressing problems quickly, cheaply, and effectively, for the moment at least. "Only a small number of people can get psychiatric help," a Florida doctor noted in a 1957 *Time* report on the subject, "so a lot of emotional problems are thrown back to the family physician; he turns to tranquilizers that he might not use if he had more time." A Beverly Hills, California, psychiatrist even suggested that "the government subsidize slot machines for tranquilizers on every corner."[18]

In the 1950s, products like "Miltown" became household words for seeming to produce confidence against anxiety, calm in the midst of chaos, and relaxation in the face of demands on psychic energy. By the 1970s, "Valium" had become the most widely used drug in history. As with so many drugs in prior generations, there was a minimum of caution and a maximum of expectation from everyone involved.

All these substances caused ambivalent reactions in the public. Opinion might sympathize with the harried housewife and mother who took barbiturates to sleep, amphetamines to "get going," and tranquilizers to "cope" with the day's activities. But it frowned on the high school student who experimented with them. And class differential played its part. The harassed executive or worker could employ all of these, at least in periods of stress, without arousing much criticism. After all, in the popular view he was pursuing or fulfilling the American dream. Help was in order, at least if the doctor said so. But the rock entertainer, "hippie," black adolescent, or other member of a marginal and unrespectable group who used these substances was an "abuser." If a doctor prescribed them, they were legitimate. If one took them to avoid responsibilities, hide personal problems, or escape from society they were illegitimate. In one case they were "medication," in the other "dope."

By the late 1960s, there was a growing fear that American society was saturated with addictive or dangerous drugs. The chemical and pharmaceutical industries poured out an endless stream of new discoveries and refinements of old products that threatened to produce socially controversial side effects if used outside of medical practice. Commentators began to discuss "drug abuse" as much as addiction, seeing the former as any nonmedicinal use of substances that altered behavior or mood from what society thought was normal. As in the late nineteenth century, the discussion quickly focused on the effects of these drugs on the individual personality and on social mores, expectations, and fears. The country's poor sense of history, especially about this social issue, made drug abuse seem a new problem. In fact, the substances and potential users had changed more than the images and anxieties in the debate.

The consensus against heroin remained powerful, and concern over increasing use of chemicals for nonmedicinal reasons was also important. But by the mid-Sixties, public attention focused especially on several substances that seemed to threaten general values and social stability. Chief among these was marihuana.

Interest in it had subsided after its regulation in the late 1930s, but had never quite disappeared from public debate. World War II overrode the fairly comprehensive "Mayor's Report" on its use in New York City in the early 1940s. But psychiatrist Walter Bromberg, who was among the first to study marihuana scientifically in the early 1930s, noted in 1945 that it had a peculiar notoriety, whatever its actual level of use. Commissioner Anslinger worried about it, but marihuana seemed safely locked into the antidrug consensus in the 1950s, though it did appear in discussions of the heroin scare during that decade. As the 1960s opened, its reputation remained ambivalent. Some experts saw it as habit-forming and as a stepping-stone to more dangerous drugs. A few others thought it relatively harmless and warned that no matter what anyone believed, its use would increase among a new generation unfamiliar with past controversy about it and attuned to experimentation.[19]

Critics of marihuana still thought it was potentially harmful to the user's personality, either through causing loss of mastery or dependence. The images of irrationality and violence inherited from the 1930s were still strong. But its relationship to other drugs, and the social results of its use also caused concern. Critics feared that it led to heroin use and was also especially attractive to young people. In this view, marihuana smoking was the first of a series of falling dominoes that led the user into a life centered on drugs. Both users and experts disagreed, holding that only a few people went on to opiates or chemicals as a result of smoking marihuana, or even became compulsive cannabis users. Occasional users had little fear about either its physiological or psychological results. At most, in this alternative view, people who experimented with one drug tended to experiment with others but did not become truly dependent in any great numbers. The ladder was thus a better symbol than the domino when analyzing the relationship of various drugs, and the user could climb either up or down.

But as so often in the past, the public did not differentiate much in the effects of various drugs and tended to lump together the experiences they produced. Widespread concern remained about the long-term social effects of marihuana smoking. People feared the loss of individualism, production, efficiency, and social responsibility among marihuana users. After surveying public opinion, the National Commission on Marihuana and Drug Abuse noted how much of the antidrug consensus remained in relation to marihuana. "Use of the drug is linked with idleness, lack of motivation, hedonism and sexual promiscuity," the body noted in its report of 1972. "Many see the drug as fostering a counter-culture which conflicts with basic moral precepts as well as with the operating functions of our society. The 'dropping out' or rejection of the established value system is viewed with alarm. Marihuana becomes more than a drug; it becomes a symbol of the rejection of cherished values."[20]

This opposition did not prevent marihuana use from increasing dramatically in the 1960s and 1970s, especially on college campuses, and then throughout society. It was a natural product, which made it seem more normal and less dangerous than chemicals. It also benefited from a generation of familiarity with cigarette smoking. And it gained some cachet through association with the artistic and intellectual rebels of the 1950s. The generation that came of age in the 1960s was more self-assured and skeptical of received wisdom than its predecessors. It was

A pro-marihuana demonstration in San Francisco, 1964. Courtesy United Press
International.

eager to defy convention in order to establish an identity. Marihuana
use gained momentum through identification with an individualism
based on desire for pleasure and self-exploration rather than on accepting and fulfilling reigning ideals. Marihuana's adherents were also often
militant in proclaiming its virtues as a way of relaxing from or escaping
the restrictions and ambitions that supposedly had made America too
rich and powerful. All of this reinforced the older generation's bewilderment and hostility: how had improved education and affluence led to
less caution about drug use?

Defiance and new definitions of freedom had their place in explaining increased marihuana use. But many commentators offered
broader social explanations as the decade of the 1960s unfolded in
domestic and foreign turmoil. The entire system of inherited American
values seemed on the wane. The new generation simply did not believe
in them and had the leisure time and money to indulge this disbelief
through drug use, especially marihuana. Young people also appeared to

be more present-minded than ever, less certain about future security, often alienated from the community values that had sustained their fathers through depression and war.[21] And lighting up a "joint" was an easy way to summarize these many generational disagreements and ambivalences.

By the late 1960s, marihuana use had swept through American society. Its ease of cultivation made it almost impossible to suppress. To its proponents, a stand of marihuana in the countryside, or in a pot in the kitchen window, was as comforting as homemade wine was to many older people. Commissioner Anslinger's old fear of having to control marihuana production had come true. But most supplies came from Latin America, especially Colombia and Mexico. Despite considerable action, law enforcers watched helplessly as a multibillion dollar business developed, with special impacts on the ports of the South.[22]

This naturally affected both public support for law enforcement and its operations. Support for legal action retained a great deal of strength. One survey in 1969 revealed that 42 percent of American parents would report their own children to the police for using illicit drugs.[23] This applied chiefly to heroin and some chemicals, but even in 1972 the consensus against marihuana was substantial. The National Commission on Marihuana and Drug Abuse reported in that year that about one-fourth of the public favored abandoning controls of marihuana, while another fourth favored enforcing strict penalties against it. But about one-half wanted to enforce laws against dealing in marihuana, without making the user a criminal.[24]

The laws also had obvious loopholes when it came to strict enforcement. No police force could apprehend anything like a significant number of users and soon used selective enforcement, often to further other ambitions. A tacit distinction between private and public use developed out of realism about enforcement's limitations. Respectable users were not likely to face prosecution for smoking marihuana in their homes. But known or suspected criminals or deviants were likely to face arrest for possessing even a small amount of marihuana. As one anonymous observer noted wryly in the 1960s: "In California, it is illegal to smoke marihuana unless you have your hair cut at least once a month."[25]

The obvious inability to enforce antimarihuana laws short of police action that would threaten individual privacy and constitutional liberties gradually led to both formal and informal modification of them in some states. The National Commission on Marihuana and Drug Abuse recommended in 1972 that the laws be relaxed but favored discouraging marihuana use, while further intensive research on its long-term effects went forward. In this view only compulsive use posed any threat to society or to the individual. The body suggested making the use or possession of small amounts of marihuana a misdemeanor at most.[26]

These views developed into the idea of "decriminalization," which Oregon adopted in 1973. Ohio, Alaska, Colorado, Maine, California, Minnesota, Mississippi, North Carolina, New York, and Nebraska followed suit in the 1970s, with variants of lenient laws against the possession or use of small amounts of marihuana. This policy did not represent the abandonment of enforcement or acceptance of marihuana use. It was at most a recognition of the limits of law enforcement. Legalization, or the absence of regulation, would have to await further changes of public opinion, whether they grew from approval or resignation.

The use of some other drugs seemed especially threatening to reigning social values in the 1960s and after. As in the mid-nineteenth century a small but articulate body of spokesmen saw some drug experiences not as an escapism or hedonism, but as means of expanding individual consciousness and of intensifying experience. In many ways they resembled earlier devotees of hashish and opium in holding that the world of observable reality was not satisfying enough for the modern psyche, especially for creative people. Such minds could perceive realities beyond the mundane with the help of some drugs. These substances tended to intensify perceptions and to rearrange mental processes so that users thought they perceived connections and relationships among experiences that were more meaningful, imaginative, and satisfying than those of ordinary life. Users tended to see such "trips" or experiences as expansive and creative. Critics usually perceived them as flights into the irrational.

In the 1950s, a few experimenters such as the writer Aldous Huxley reported on the magical effects of peyote and mescal, derived from cactuses, which in their view helped them expand their consciousness and better understand the self and world.[27] These substances were familiar to some southwestern Indians, who used them in religious rites. Government agents had attempted for decades to stop the practice, since it seemed to threaten the Indians' relationship to larger society. To white critics, peyotism also appeared to be a reversion to uncivilized practices, wholly out of place in modern times. Far from being creative or imaginative, it seemed a flight from rationality.

In the two decades that followed, a long procession of gurus, mystics, and intellectuals preached the gospel of expanding consciousness with "hallucinogens," whether they were natural or chemical in origin. This in turn became a major and much discussed aspect of the

rejection of materialism and social control that produced a counterculture allegedly based on concern for the inner rather than the outer
world.[28]

LSD attracted more public attention and concern than any other
hallucinogen. In 1943 Dr. Albert Hofmann of the Sandoz Laboratories in
Basel noted strange symptoms after being around a new derivative of
ergot, d-lysergic acid diethylamide. He then ingested a small amount of
LSD-25, the chemical's shorthand name, and noted that it produced
dizziness, distorted but intensified perception, and a sense of being
disconnected from reality.

LSD gained some familiarity in the medical and psychiatric
worlds after the war because it could reproduce states in subjects that
seemed to resemble paranoia and schizophrenia. By 1960–62, Harvard
psychologist Timothy Leary and a circle of colleagues were experimenting with LSD and other hallucinogens such as psylocibin. Scientists at
the Lexington hospital studied LSD's effects, though the compound's
actual usefulness as a medicine remained somewhat uncertain.[29]

As with so many drugs in the past, LSD moved beyond the
medical community's control. In 1965 two investigators reported to the
AMA that LSD was easily available on the black market. Its price
varied, as did its form. A gelatin capsule of it in powder form cost from
two to ten dollars in Harlem. A teaspoon of the diluted liquid was about
thirty-five dollars. Users usually took this on sugar cubes. In the Boston
area LSD was called "crackers" because users put it on animal crackers. In New York City it was often called "coffee" because it was
available at the coffee-houses that intellectuals, artists, and bohemians
frequented.[30]

By the late 1960s, "dropping acid," or using LSD became a
familiar term. The substance especially frightened mainstream society
because its use seemed a wilful rejection of rationality, order, and
predictability. Its psychic effects varied greatly in individuals, often
causing "bad trips" that seemed to border on mental illness. Its
physiological effects were also uncertain but to critics at least seemed
very dangerous. Overuse allegedly caused chromosome damage, which
might threaten future generations. This remained unproved but helped
mark LSD as potentially dangerous to both the minds and bodies of
some users.

Despite a great deal of often lurid reporting, LSD was not in fact
widely used on a regular basis outside of a few elements dedicated to
drug experiences. The number of college students who used it and
similar hallucinogens regularly was small, and the substances quickly
earned reputations as dangerous.[31] But the controversy and publicity

around LSD use resembled that around heroin, and it became a feared drug to nonusers, which strengthened their demand for regulating hallucinogens.

An endless stream of reported experiments with various substances reinforced the public's bewilderment during the 1960s and into the 1970s. There was a scare about adolescents who sniffed glue, and even gasoline, for a momentary high, much as earlier generations had used ether or chloroform. Some members of the counterculture who emphasized natural living praised the use of plant drugs, while condemning chemicals. And medical chemistry steadily produced new discoveries and refinements of older products that were open to what the public called abuse.[32]

The changing nature of the kinds of users was also striking. Many substances, especially marihuana, were clearly popular with a wide range of people who did not fit the inherited ideas about drug users. The delinquency models might still help explain heroin use but were obviously inadequate to demonstrate why people experimented with or adopted the use of other substances. Affluent professionals and business people were as likely to use marihuana, cocaine, or even LSD, as were the thrill-seeking, ignorant youngsters or petty thieves of legend. Factory workers and truck drivers employed marihuana, amphetamines, and barbiturates to help tolerate boring and repetitive labor.[33]

But young users remained the chief targets of public concern. Youngsters of all social status were using drugs allegedly to relieve boredom, escape social problems, control anxieties about relationships with peers or parents, or to reject the world they were meant to inherit.[34] But a simple desire for pleasure was also obvious, and drug use became a stereotyped part of relaxed sexual conduct. To the older generation, the most vivid example of this rejection of convention was the rock concert, with its emphasis on overt and suggested sexual action, abandonment to momentary pleasure, and use of drugs to relax inhibitions.

Proponents of drug use were also opposed to the war in Viet Nam and to American interventionist foreign policy in general. The young man or woman who removed his or her clothes at an antiwar rally, or scattered flowers before the advancing national guard, or lay down in front of police cars likely also praised the use of marihuana or other drugs to weaken the conformity and control he or she attacked in the name of peace. To many people drug use was thus unpatriotic as well as dangerous to social values.

Above all, the popular mind associated drugs with the counterculture that openly flouted the nation's history, ambitions, and alleged ideals. The very term "drug trip" indicated the user's desire to go

A "smoke-in" protesting marihuana laws in front of the Connecticut state capitol, 1973. Courtesy United Press International.

somewhere else than America. The public imagination equated the "crash pad" with the old opium den for its filth, transience, and passivity. The college campus often seemed to resemble the old-fashioned red-light district, where anything went as long as it did not cross the tracks into town. And the hippie became the racial image of the 1960s drug debate, representing the passivity, and unproductivity that so many people still equated with drugs. The identification of many drugs, especially the hallucinogens but also marihuana, with mystical eastern religions reawakened the old stereotypes of passivity and weakness long associated with those cultures.

The relationships of drug use to disorder and attacks on accepted social values tended to reinforce the antidrug consensus momentarily. But as drug use spread to new elements of society during the 1960s and 1970s, and as law enforcement seemed hopeless, policies and opinions changed under the impact of events. Government at all levels became more oriented to medical care for the opiate addict, and for research into the effects of other drugs that seemed liable at least to pose health hazards or cause dependence. In general, the public slowly began to make distinctions about the effects of drugs, especially marihuana. A division between "soft" and "hard" drugs, essentially between those that produced true dependence and those that did not, became current.

While general attitudes changed under the pressure of events and the failures of older policies, other voices in the debate took on the tones of caution and maturity. As with so many human and social problems, participants in the drug drama learned chiefly from experience. Many black spokesmen condemned heroin use as a major stumbling block to changing the black's status. To them it was indeed counterproductive, isolated the user from mainstream society and its benefits, and reinforced adverse images about black life.[35] Many leaders of the 1960s rebellions who had been cavalier or confident about some drug use began to warn against the ill effects of some substances a decade later. These opened no doors to utopia after all. A stoned society was not necessarily more humane or secure than a straight one. And many people benefited from tragic personal examples, whether the boy or girl next door, or a famous personality such as the rock star Janis Joplin.

By the late 1970s, yet another drug scare had passed through American society, recapitulating with appropriate variations the themes that had shaped the discussion of drug use throughout American history. The informed public still believed there was a drug problem. But it generally favored medical and psychiatric attention for the heroin addict, prevention of indiscriminate drug use through education that the young would believe, research, and law enforcement against drug suppliers. It disapproved of marihuana use but believed it would increase. A certain weariness informed this eclectic approach, based on the realization that many people would not or could not avoid suspect drugs, and that still others would always find some drug experience attractive.[36]

As the 1980s opened, the old consensus against drug experiences that ran counter to accepted social norms seemed weakened. The use of so-called soft drugs was greater than ever, and each oncoming generation seemed to have to learn their story. Yet public interest and anxiety was high. Large numbers of parents remained convinced that various drugs threatened their children and supported political and legal action against their use. The law enforcement apparatus still identified a great deal of drug use with crime and deviance. Experts in the medical and psychological sciences warned that the preceding generation was too sanguine about the effects of many drugs on both the mind and body.

By the same token, many users of drugs developed some maturity. Amphetamines and barbiturates became suspect, LSD was clearly dangerous to many psyches. Even devotees of "soft" drugs such as marihuana gained a sense of caution. It might not be addictive, but like any psycho-active substance it could cause dependence in some users. And in physiological terms, it made no more sense to inhale burning cannabis than burning tobacco. Marihuana was probably less harmful than alcohol, yet both substances answered needs in users that might be met more safely some other way. Occasional use thus generally developed as an acceptable norm among those so inclined, while compulsive or habitual use became increasingly suspect. Decriminalization was a classic compromise between the desire to prohibit and the understanding that large numbers of people would not obey such a law. It retained the trappings of society's disapproval while recognizing social change.

The consensus against other more "dangerous" drugs remained strong. The public still feared and opposed those that caused true addiction, that adversely affected free will and efficiency, and that turned the personality away from observable reality more than momentarily. The public also supported medical and psychological treatment for true addicts but retained an ideal of final abstinence. There was little support for simply maintaining those who could not or would not stop using drugs. There was also an uneasy sense that the future would bring substances that required social control. Medical research steadily enlarged and refined the range of mood-altering compounds. Many of these would bear the relationship to heroin or amphetamines that jet aircraft bore to canvas biplanes. Law enforcement retained its role not merely against current suppliers of feared drugs such as heroin, but as a necessary system for the future.

The controversy over drug use and its effects on the individual and society thus went on. It remained as important in American life for what it represented as for the numbers or kinds of users involved. For a hundred years many people had pursued the drug genie to obtain escape from problems, harmony, or expanded consciousness. Still others had tried to eliminate the genie they considered a force for irrationality, enslavement, decadence, or rejection of responsibility. Only one thing was clear: the genie remained loose.

NOTES

1—GOD'S OWN MEDICINE

1. Oliver Wendell Holmes, "Currents and Counter-Currents in Medical Sciences," *Medical Essays* (Boston: Houghton, Mifflin, 1892), pp. 202–203.

2. Shadrach Ricketson, "Experiments on the Cultivation of the Poppy-Plant, and the Method of Preparing Opium, Etc.," *Medical Repository,* ser. 2, 1, no. 3 (1800): 407–411.

3. H. Wilkins, "Observations on the Extraction of Opium from the Poppy," *Philadelphia Medical Museum: Medical and Philosophical Register* 6, no. 1 (1809): 55–56; and Milton Anthony, "Observations on the Cultivation of the Poppy and the Formation of Opium," ibid., n.s. 1, no. 3 (1810), pp. 142–46.

4. James Thacher, *The American New Dispensatory* (Boston: T. B. Wait, 1810), pp. 454–57; "English Opium," *Boston Medical Intelligencer* 2 (October 5, 1824): 88, and ibid., 3 (July 12, 1825): 40.

5. "Virginia Opium," *Boston Medical and Surgical Journal* 76 (May 23, 1867): 344; *American Journal of Pharmacy* 40 (January 1868): 77, and ibid., 40 (November 1868): 513–16; Charles E. Terry and Mildred Pellens, *The Opium Problem* (New York: Bureau of Social Hygiene, 1928), p. 7, n6.

6. "American Opium Cultivation," *Medical and Surgical Reporter* 15 (July 21, 1866): 79; "California Opium," ibid., 30 (May 23, 1874): 485; "Culture of Opium in California," *Pacific Medical and Surgical Journal* 9 (December 1866): 264–65.

7. Edward M. Brecher, *Licit and Illicit Drugs* (Boston: Little, Brown, 1972), p. 4; "Native Opium of the United States," *Medical Repository,* ser. 3, 1 (August, September, October 1809): 192–94; "Domestic Opium," *New England Journal of Medicine and Surgery* 1 (July 1812): 315; F. E. Oliver, "The Use and Abuse of Opium," in Massachusetts State Board of Health, *Third Annual Report* (Boston: Wright and Potter, 1872), p. 166.

169

8. John Redman Coxe, *The American Dispensatory,* 9th ed. (Philadelphia: Carey and Lea, 1831), p. 521. An early list of the preparations and uses of opium is in George W. Carpenter, "Observations and Experiments on the Pharmaceutical Preparations and Constituent Principles of Opium," *Philadelphia Journal of the Medical and Physical Sciences,* n.s. 5, [14], no. 10 (1827): 239–53.

9. "Opium in Dysenteric Cholera," *Boston Medical and Surgical Journal* 1 (January 20, 1829): 776–78; David A. Hoffman, "Opium in a Case of Epidemic Dysentery," *Ohio Medical and Surgical Journal* 4 (May 1852): 383–84.

10. James Ewell, *The Medical Companion,* 3rd ed. (Philadelphia: Anderson and Meehan, 1816), p. 287; "Minute Doses of Morphine in the Treatment of Typhoid Fever," *New Orleans Medical and Surgical Journal* 9 (July 1852): 95–96; W. S. Sinn, "Eight Cases," *American Medical Monthly,* 2 (December 1854): 453–54; Moore Hoit, "On the Use of Opium in Yellow Fever," *Virginia Medical Journal* 7 (August 1856): 118–22; "Opium in Therapeutics," *Pacific Medical and Surgical Journal,* n. s. 1 (June 1867), pp. 38–39.

11. John Armstrong, "Some Observations on the Utility of Opium in Certain Inflammatory Disorders," *American Medical Recorder* 7 (October 1824): 783–90; Wright Post, "Some Observations on the Use of Anodynes and Opium in the Treatment of Inflammatory Affections," *New York Medical and Physical Journal,* n.s. 1 (April 1829), pp. 81–83; W. H. Ranking, "On the Use of Opium in Inflammation," *Southern Medical and Surgical Journal,* n.s. 3 (December 1847), pp. 737–39; A. S. Hudson, "Opium: Its Influence in Febrile, Inflammatory and Other Diseases," *Chicago Medical Journal* 3 (January 1860): 27–48.

12. "Opium Treatment of Rheumatism," *Southern Medical and Surgical Journal,* n.s. 2 (July 1846), p. 440; "Hypodermic Injections," *Chicago Medical Journal* 4 (April 1861): 238. Alonzo Calkins, *Opium and the Opium Appetite* (Philadelphia: Lippincott, 1871), p. 80, notes in passing that "Neuralgia has been the scape-goat for a multitude of opium sins."

13. "Opium in Pneumonia," *American Medical Monthly* 14 (September 1860): 213; "Opium in Diabetes Mellitus," *New Orleans Medical and Surgical Journal* 23 (October 1870): 800.

14. J. W. Montross, "Case of Convulsions," *Medical Repository,* ser. 2, 5 (August, September, October 1807): 149–53; "Opium in Uterine Hemorrhage," *New England Journal of Medicine and Surgery* 4 (October 1815): 397; "Dangers of Opium in Delirium Tremens," *Maryland Medical and Surgical Journal* 2 (January 1842): 372–78; "Nervous Headaches Cured by the Inoculation of Morphia," *Southern Medical and Surgical Journal* 1 (March 1838): 514; "Morphine in the Reduction of Hernia," *Western Journal of Medicine and Surgery,* ser. 3, no. 2 (October 1848), p. 363.

15. "Dr. Graves' Prescription of Opium in Cerebral Excitement," *Southern Medical and Surgical Journal,* n.s. 2 (December 1846), p. 762; "Large Doses of Opium and Its Salts in Cases of Insanity," *American Medical Monthly* 8 (October 1857): 264; "Monthly Summary of Foreign Medical Literature," ibid., 15 (January 1861): 63. Two among many early sources noting opium's use in nervousness and mental illness are: George Young, *A Treatise on Opium Formulated Upon Practical Observation* (London: A. Millar, 1753), pp. 106–108, 113–14; and Ewell, *Medical Companion,* pp. 324–26.

16. Nathaniel Chapman, *Elements of Therapeutics and Materia Medica,* 2 vols. (Philadelphia: Carey and Lea, 1821), 2:201. See also Richard Reece, *The*

Medical Guide (Philadelphia: B. B. Hopkins Co., 1808), p. 38, and Thomas White Ruble, *The American Medical Guide for the Use of Families* (Richmond, Ky.: E. Harris, 1810), p. 35.

17. Samuel Crumpe, *An Inquiry Into the Nature and Properties of Opium* (London: G. G. and J. Robinson, 1793), pp. 184–95. The quotation is from "Narcotics in Inflammation," *Boston Medical Intelligencer* 4 (July 11, 1826): 69–70. See also Ruble, *American Medical Guide*, p. 30, and John Eberle, *A Treatise of the Materia Medica*, 2 vols. (Philadelphia: Webster, 1822), 2:3–4, 9–10.

18. "The Curiosities of Longevity," *Scribner's Monthly* 11 (November 1875): 32–42. See also "On the Use of Opium," *Boston Medical and Surgical Journal* 6 (April 18, 1832): 156–57; "A Long-lived Opium Eater," *Pacific Medical and Surgical Journal*, n.s. 2 (June 1868), p. 41; J. B. Mattison, "An Extraordinary Case of Opium Inebriety," *Medical Record* 12 (April 14, 1877): 239–40; and George Eugene Pettey, *The Narcotic Drug Diseases and Allied Ailments* (Philadelphia: F. A. Davis Co., 1913), pp. 138–39.

19. Neal D. Rowell, "A Case of Poisoning by Opium," *Western Medical and Physical Journal* 1 (May 1827): 92–95; "Large Doses of Opium," *Western Lancet* 13 (April 1852): 262–63; "The Muriate of Opium," *Virginia Medical Journal* 6 (May 1856): 420. The quotation is from John McNulty, "Notes of Eight Cases," *American Medical Monthly* 9 (March 1858): 186–91.

20. John Jones, *The Mysteries of Opium Revealed* (London: Richard Smith, 1700), pp. 31–33.

21. "Destructive Practices," *Boston Medical Intelligencer* 1 (June 1823): 19.

22. John Sprott, "Effects of Morphine not Mentioned by Medical Writers," *New Orleans Medical and Surgical Journal* 22 (July 1869): 506.

23. Jones, *Mysteries of Opium Revealed*, p. 245.

24. Ruble, *American Medical Guide*, pp. 34–35.

25. Eberle, *A Treatise of the Materia Medica*, 2:34.

26. "The Opium Habit," *Medical and Surgical Reporter* 20 (May 8, 1869): 364.

27. See Glenn Sonnedecker, "Emergence of the Concept of Opiate Addiction," *Journal Mondiale Pharmacie* 6 (September–December, 1962): 275–90, and David F. Musto, *The American Disease: Origins of Narcotic Control* (New Haven: Yale University Press, 1973), pp. 73–74.

28. Valentine Seaman, "Case of the Deleterious Effects of Opium Remedied by the Excitement of Pain," *Medical Repository*, ser. 2, 3, no. 2 (1800): 150–51; Charles A. Lee, "Case of Poisoning by Laudanum," *New York Medical and Physical Journal* 7 (October, November, December 1828): 518–20; James C. Cross, "An Essay on Poisoning by Opium," *Transylvania Journal of Medicine and the Associate Sciences* 1 (November 1828): 453–84; J. Newton Smith, "Case of Poisoning by Opium," ibid., 9 (October, November, December 1836): 722–23; A. B. Whitney, "Opium vs. Belladona," *Eclectic Medical Journal of Pennsylvania* 7 (January 1869): 17–20.

29. Thacher, *American New Dispensatory*, p. 178.

30. The medical literature is filled with suicide cases; see John Dawson, "Two Cases of Poisoning," *Ohio Medical and Surgical Journal* 3 (July 1, 1851): 252–27; William C. Rogers, "A Case of Poisoning from Opium," *American*

Medical Monthly 12 (August 1859): 104–107; James T. Neuman, "Opium and Belladona," *Chicago Medical Journal* 24 (November 1867): 529–32; W. C. Bellamy, "Is Belladona an Antidote to Opium?" *Atlanta Medical and Surgical Journal*, n.s. 8 (December 1867), pp. 425–29; J. H. Smith, "A Case of Morphia Poisoning," *Medical News* 40 (March 25, 1882): 318.

31. Jones, *Mysteries of Opium Revealed*, pp. 19–30; Althea Hayter, *Opium and the Romantic Imagination* (Berkeley: University of California Press, 1968), pp. 24–26.

32. "Confessions of an English Opium-Eater," *North American Review* 18 (January 1824): 92.

33. "Opium Eating," *Boston Medical and Surgical Journal* 9 (September 4, 1833): 66–67.

34. "Use of Opium," *Western Lancet* 1 (November 1842): 328.

35. "Opium Eating in Siam," *Boston Medical and Surgical Journal* 16 (April 26, 1837): 193–94.

36. *Medical Examiner*, n.s. 6 (June 1850), pp. 346–48. See Nathan Allen, *The Opium Trade* (Boston: John P. Jewett, 1850).

37. "Opium Eater," *Boston Medical Intelligencer* 2 (June 1, 1824): 13.

38. "Opium Eating," *Boston Medical and Surgical Journal* 18 (March 28, 1838): 128–29.

39. Allen, *The Opium Trade*, pp. 24–25.

2—THE THERAPEUTIC REVOLUTION

1. Glenn Sonnedecker, "Contribution of the Pharmaceutical Profession Toward Controlling the Quality of Drugs in the Nineteenth Century," in John B. Blake, ed. *Safeguarding the Public Health: Historical Aspects of Medicinal Drug Control* (Baltimore: Johns Hopkins University Press, 1970, pp. 97–111.

2. "Hypodermic Treatment of Syphilis with Mercury," *Pacific Medical and Surgical Journal*, n.s. 3 (October 1869), pp. 207–212.

3. "Foreign Papers, Etc.," *American Medical Recorder* 1 (January 1818): 37–52; "New Medicines," *New York Medical and Physical Journal* 6 (October, November, December 1827): 699–701; "Nature, Effects, and Modes of Prescribing What Are Called the New Medicines," *Boston Medical and Surgical Journal* 2 (May 5, 1829): 185–86.

4. T. B. Townshend, "Neuralgia Treated by Enormous Doses of Sulphate of Morphia," *Ohio Medical and Surgical Journal* 15 (January 1, 1863): 87–90; Horace B. Day, *The Opium Habit, With Suggestions as to the Remedy* (New York: Harper and Bros., 1868), p. 212; H. H. Kane, *The Hypodermic Injection of Morphia* (New York: C. L. Bermingham, 1880), pp. 309–312; H. H. Kane, *Drugs That Enslave* (Philadelphia: P. Blakiston, 1881), p. 206; J. B. Mattison, "The Prevention of Opium Addiction," *Louisville Medical News* 17 (February 23, 1884): 113–15.

5. "Intemperate Use of Chloroform," *Southern Medical and Surgical Journal*, n.s. 7 (May 1851), pp. 313–14.

6. Henry M. Lyman, *Artificial Anaesthesia and Anaesthetics* (New York: William Wood, 1881), pp. 5, 136ff.

7. Frederick H. Hubbard, *The Opium Habit and Alcoholism* (New York: A. S. Barnes, 1881), pp. 237ff; J. E. Clark, "The Chloroform Habit," *Detroit Lancet*, n.s. 9 (December 1884), pp. 254–56; A. G. Browning, "A New Habit," *Medical Record* 27 (April 25, 1885): 452–545; "Chloroform Inebriety," *Quarterly Journal of Inebriety* 7 (April 1885): 97–101; Thomas D. Crothers, *Morphinism and Narco-Manias From Other Drugs* (Philadelphia: W. B. Saunders, 1902), pp. 293–302, 322–26; New York *Times*, January 16, 1911. The quotation is from A. G. Browning, "The Chloroform Habit," *Louisville Monthly Journal of Medicine and Surgery* 18 (January 1912): 232–37.

8. "Hydrate of Chloral," *St. Louis Medical and Surgical Journal*, n.s. 6 (November 10, 1869), pp. 561–63; "Hydrate of Chloral," *Pacific Medical and Surgical Journal*, n.s. 3 (May 1870), p. 569; C. A. Stivers, "Hydrate of Chloral in Delirium Tremens," ibid., n.s. 3 (May 1870), pp. 559–60. The quotation is from "Dangers of Chloral Hydrate," ibid., n.s. 4 (November 1870), p. 276. See also Thomas C. Butler, "The Introduction of Chloral Hydrate into Medical Practice," *Bulletin of the History of Medicine* 44 (1970): 168–72.

9. "Chloral," *New Orleans Medical and Surgical Journal* 23 (January 1870): 147–48; D. F. Lincoln, "Hydrate of Chloral," *Medical Archives* 4 (February 1870): 90–100; N. N. Canady, "Chloral," *Indiana Journal of Medicine* 2 (December 1871): 341–52.

10. C. H. Hughes, "Chloral Hydrate," *Medical Archives* 7 (December 1871): 577–80. See also "Chloral, The New Anaesthetic," *Pacific Medical and Surgical Journal*, n.s. 3 (December 1869), pp. 324–25, and J. B. Andrews, "The Physiological Action and Therapeutic Use of Chloral," *American Journal of Insanity* 28 (July 1871): 35–36.

11. Alban S. Payne, "Hydrate of Chloral," *Southern Medical Record* 4 (December 1874): 685.

12. "Chloral Hydrate," *Medical Summary* 3 (April 1881): 40.

13. D. D. Bramble, "Hydrate of Chloral," *Transactions of the . . . Ohio State Medical Society* 26 (1871): 151–91.

14. Carlos F. McDonald, "Hydrate of Chloral," *St. Louis Clinical Record* 4 (July 1877): 81–84.

15. Thomas Kennard, "Hydrate of Chloral," *Medical Archives* 6 (May 1871): 135–40.

16. J. H. Etheridge, "Lectures on Chloral Hydrate," *Chicago Medical Journal* 29 (September 1872): 521–27.

17. J. B. Mattison, "Chloral Inebriety," Medical Society of the County of Kings, Brooklyn, *Proceedings* 4 (April 15, 1879): 65–77, and his *Chloral Inebriety* (New York: H. T. Cornett, 1879).

18. W. B. Meany, "Chloral Inebriation," *Louisville Medical News* 1 (February 26, 1876): 103; Oliver, "The Use and Abuse of Opium," 166n; Crothers, *Morphinism*, pp. 288–89; William Allen Pusey, *A Doctor of the 1870's and 1880's* (Springfield, Ill.: Charles C. Thomas, 1932), p. 98; Kane, *Drugs That Enslave*, p. 150.

19. William Rosser Cobbe, *Doctor Judas: A Portrayal of the Opium Habit* (Chicago: S. C. Griggs, 1895), p. 135.

20. G. Archie Stockwell, "Erythroxylon Coca," *Boston Medical and Surgical Journal* 96 (April 5, 1877): 402.

21. William O. Moore, "The Physiological and Therapeutical Effects of Coca Leaf and Its Alkaloid," *New York Medical Journal* 41 (January 3, 1885): 19–22; J. D. Whittaker, "Cocaine in the Treatment of the Opium Habit," *Medical News* 47 (August 8, 1885): 148; "Cocaine," *Chambers Journal* 3 (March 6, 1886): 145–47; "The Decline of Cocaine," *Medical and Surgical Reporter* 54 (April 3, 1886): 446.

22. William A. Hammond, "Coca," *Transactions of the Medical Society of Virginia* (November 1887), pp. 212–26.

23. Angelo Mariani, *Coca Erythroxylon (Vin Mariani), Its Uses in the Treatment of Disease,* 4th ed. (Paris and New York: Mariani Co., 1886), pp. iii, 19–20; William H. Helfand, "Vin Mariani," *Pharmacy in History* 22 (1980): 11–19; W. Golden Mortimer, *History of Coca: The 'Divine' Plant of the Incas* (New York: Vail, 1901), pp. 492, 507; George Andrews and David Solomon, eds., *The Coca Leaf and Cocaine Papers* (New York: Harcourt, Brace, 1975), pp. 16–17; Brecher, *Licit and Illicit Drugs,* p. 271; David Musto, "A Study in Cocaine, Sherlock Holmes, and Sigmund Freud," *JAMA* 204 (April 1, 1968): 125–30. One of many contemporary reports on experimenting with coca to improve performance among athletes is E. R. Palmer, "Coca in Fatigue," *American Practitioner* 31 (January 1885): 258–60.

24. E. R. Palmer, "The Opium Habit: A Possible Antidote," *Louisville Medical News* 9 (May 29, 1880): 258–60.

25. Robert Byck, ed., *Cocaine Papers by Sigmund Freud* (New York: Stonehill, 1974), p. 133.

26. B. F. Kittrell, "Cocaine," *Transactions of the Mississippi State Medical Association* 19 (1886): 67–73.

27. See Willard H. Morse, *New Therapeutic Agents* (Detroit: George S. Davis, 1882), pp. 18–19. Hammond, "Coca," has interesting references to sexual disorders, and a British authority made the point in William Martindale, *Coca, Cocaine and Its Salts* (London: H. K. Lewis, 1886), pp. 49–51, 58–65.

28. The Parke-Davis catalog is in Byck, *Cocaine Papers,* p. 144. See also George Le Forger, "Coca in the Opium Habit," *Therapeutic Gazette,* n.s. 3 (December 25, 1882): 458; *Quarterly Journal of Inebriety* 7 (January 1885): 48.

29. "Antidote to the Opium Habit," *Medical Tribune* 6 (March 15, 1890): 49; Mortimer, *History of Coca,* p. 507.

30. D. H. McDonald, "Concerning Coca," *Louisville Medical News* 10 (July 17, 1880): 28, has the quotation; see also Morse, *New Therapeutic Agents,* pp. 18–19, and J. B. Mattison, "Cocaine Dosage and Cocaine Addiction," *Lancet* 1 (May 21, 1887): 1024–26.

31. "The Cocaine Habit," *Kansas City Medical Record* 3 (February 1886): 71; Judson B. Andrews, "Report of Two Cases of Morphia and Cocaine Habit," *Transactions of the New York State Medical Association* 3 (1886): 68–77; "A Doctor Dies From the Cocaine Habit," *American Lancet* 13 (March 1889): 107–108.

32. "The Cocaine Habit," *Kansas City Medical Record* 3 (February 1886): 71.

33. Hammond, "Coca," pp. 220–25, and the same author's "Cocaine and the So-called Cocaine Habit," *New York Medical Journal* 44 (December 4, 1886): 637–39.

34. J. H. Hughes, "The Autobiography of a Drug Fiend," *Medical Review of Reviews* 22 (January 1916): 42.

35. An early report, focusing on the work of one Dr. O'Shaughnessy who reported on experiences in India, is "Indian Hemp," *Western Lancet* 3 (May 1844): 32–36.

36. Richard J. Bonnie and Charles H. Whitebread II, *The Marihuana Conviction* (Charlottesville: University Press of Virginia, 1974), p. 4; "The Indian Hemp," *Medical Examiner* 6 (May 13, 1843): 108; W. G. G. Willson, "Success of the Cannabis Indica in the Treatment of Tetanus," *New Orleans Medical Journal* 2 (July 1845): 156–61; W. H. Gantt, "Indian Hemp as a Remedy in Tetanus," *St. Louis Medical and Surgical Journal* 9 (May 1850): 209–211; "Indian Hemp," ibid., 18 (November 1860): 524–28; "Indian Hemp," *Eclectic Medical Journal of Pennsylvania* 1 (September, October 1863): 159.

37. "Cannabis Sativa a Cure for Gleet," ibid., 2 (July, August 1864): 127; "Treatment of Chorea by the Use of Cannabis Indica," *Medical Examiner*, n.s. 1 (September 1845), pp. 568–70; S. A. McWilliams, "Cannabis Indica in Strychnine Poisoning," *Medical Archives* 3 (January 1869): 60–61.

38. Robert Andrews, "Cannabis Indica," *Boston Medical and Surgical Journal* 61 (September 22, 1859): 173–78; "On Indian Hemp, Particularly in Relation to Its Properties of Producing Sleep," *Ohio Medical and Surgical Journal* 14 (January 1, 1862): 32–34; "Indian Hemp," *Eclectic Medical Journal of Pennsylvania* 5 (September, October 1867): 236.

39. J. B. Mattison, "Cannabis Indica as an Anodyne and Hypnotic," *New Orleans Medical and Surgical Journal*, n.s. 19 (November 1891), pp. 333–39.

40. "Cannabis in Insanity," *Pacific Medical and Surgical Journal*, n.s. 1 (December 1867), p. 333; John C. Peters, "Hysteria," *Virginia Medical Monthly* 4 (December 1877): 654; "Cannabis Indica," *Chicago Medical Times* 25 (November 1893): 418–19. The quotation is from George M. Beard, *A Practical Treatise on Nervous Exhaustion (Neurasthenia)*, 3rd ed. (New York: E. B. Treat, 1894), pp. 191–'3.

41. "Indian Hemp," *Western Lancet* 4 (May 1845): 42.

42. "Cannabis Indica," *An Ephemeris of Materia Medica, Pharmacy, Therapeutics and Collateral Information* 3 (April 1892): 1290–91.

43. George B. Wood and Franklin Bache, eds, *The Dispensatory of the United States of America*, 9th ed. (Philadelphia: J. B. Lippincott, 1851), pp. 310–311; G. S. D. Anderson, "Remarks on the Remedial Virtues of Cannabis Indica, or Indian Hemp," *Western Journal of Medicine and Surgery* 4 (December 1855): 427; Edward Parrish, "Notes on the Narcotics," *Chicago Medical Journal* 4 (October, November 1861): 617–21.

44. Horatio C. Wood, Jr., "On the Medical Activity of the Hemp Plant, as Grown in North America," *Proceedings of the American Philosophical Society* 11 (November 19, 1869): 226–32.

45. James G. Wiltshire, "Personal Experience in the Effect of Cannabis Indica," *Southern Clinic* 1 (June 1879): 331–36. See also Wood and Bache,

Dispensatory, pp. 310–311, and George Bacon Wood, *A Treatise on Therapeutics and Pharmacology, or Materia Medica,* 2 vols. (Philadelphia: J. B. Lippincott, 1856), 1:779–84.

46. Kane, *Drugs That Enslave,* p. 218.

47. "Narcotics," *North American Review* 95 (October 1862): 274–315.

48. "Effects of Cannabis Indica," *Medical Age* 3 (March 10, 1885): 107.

49. Henry W. Sawtelle, "Notes Relative to the Effects of Cannabis Indica," *New Orleans Medical and Surgical Journal,* n.s. 29 (June 1897), pp. 671–74.

50. Mattison, "Cannabis Indica," pp. 333–39. Fitzhugh Ludlow had noted this much earlier in his *The Hasheesh Eater* (New York: Harper and Bros., 1857), p. 102.

51. Wood, *Treatise on Therapeutics,* 1:779–84.

52. John Bell, "On the Haschisch, or Cannabis Indica," *Boston Medical and Surgical Journal* 56 (April 16, 1857): 209–216.

53. "Haschisch Candy," ibid., 75 (November 22, 1866): 349; Hubbard, *The Opium Habit and Alcoholism,* pp. 256–57; "The Opium, Chloral and Haschisch Habits," *The American* 3 (January 7, 1882): 201; Kane, *Drugs That Enslave,* pp. 206ff; H. A. Hare, "Clinical and Physiological Notes on the Action of Cannabis Indica," *Therapeutic Gazette* 11 (1887): 225–28.

54. Two good contemporary studies of the development of hypodermic medication are S. W. Caldwell, "Hypodermic Medication," *Mississippi Valley Medical Monthly* 5 (February 1885): 49–63, and D. I. Macht, "The History of Intravenous and Subcutaneous Administration of Drugs," *JAMA* 66 (March 18, 1916): 856–60. The basic historical treatments are: John B. Blake, "Mr. Ferguson's Hypodermic Syringe," *Journal of the History of Medicine* 15 (October 1960): 337–41, and Norman Howard-Jones, "Origins of Hypodermic Medication," *Scientific American* 224 (January 1971): 96–102.

55. "Ward on Opiate Frictions," *New York Medical and Philosophical Journal and Review* 2, no. 2 (1810): 197–204.

56. William Blecher, "Observations on the Application of Opium," *American Medical Recorder* 8 (October 1825): 833–34; "Case of Death Caused by the External Application of Opium," ibid., 14 (July 1828): 168–69.

57. See Crumpe, *Opium,* pp. 27–30; "Acetate of Morphia," *Boston Medical Intelligencer* 4 (August 25, 1826): 107–108; "Cases of Rheumatism Treated by the Local Use of Acetate of Morphia," *Transylvania Journal of Medicine* 6 (April, May, June 1833): 37–38; "Endermic Therapeutics," *Medical Magazine* 1 (March 1833): 550.

58. "Injection of Medicinal Substances into the Veins," *New England Journal of Medicine and Surgery* 9 (January 1820): 7–10; "Injection of Opium in the Veins," *American Medical Recorder* 7 (July 1824): 632–34. The army doctor's case is in J. M. Steiner, "On the Injection of Stimulants Into the Veins," *Medical Examiner,* n.s. 5 (November 1849): 644–47.

59. Kane, *Hypodermic Injection of Morphia,* pp. 13ff; T. Curtis Smith, "Hypodermic Medication," *Kansas City Medical Journal* 2 (April 1872): 73–84, and ibid., 2 (June 1872): 151–62; Edward Warren, "A Lecture on the Subcutaneous Injection of Morphia," *Medical and Surgical Reporter* 16 (February 9, 1867): 101; Macht, "History of Intravenous and Subcutaneous Admin-

istration of Drugs," *passim;* S. W. Caldwell, "Hypodermatic Medication," *Mississippi Valley Medical Monthly* 5 (February 1885): 60; Benjamin Woodward, "Hypodermic Injections," *Kansas City Medical Journal* 1 (June 1871): 171–75.

60. "Hypodermic Injections," *Eclectic Medical Journal of Pennsylvania* 5 (January, February 1867): 34; J. S. Burns, "Medication by Hypodermic Injection," *Nashville Journal of Medicine and Surgery*, ser. 2, 14 (August 1874): 80–92; "Hypodermic Medication," *Ohio Medical Recorder* 1 (October 1876): 215–17.

61. "Hypodermic Medication," *Pacific Medical and Surgical Journal* 7 (1864): 275–76.

62. J. C. Bishop, "Hypodermic Medication," *Southern Medical Record* 4 (June 1874): 315–33.

63. "A Non-professional View of the Hypodermic Treatment," *Pacific Medical and Surgical Journal*, n.s. 3 (February, 1870), p. 420.

64. H. C. Smith, "Hypodermic Injections," *Medical and Surgical Reporter* 21 (November 20, 1869): 326–27.

65. *Pacific Medical and Surgical Journal*, n.s. 3 (April 1870), pp. 514–15.

66. Antoine Ruppaner, *Hypodermic Injections in the Treatment of Neuralgia, Rheumatism, Gout and Other Diseases* (Boston: Burnham, 1865), p. 13.

67. W. A. Greene, "Hypodermic Administration of Medicinal Agents," *Atlanta Medical and Surgical Journal* 8 (May 1867): 97.

68. [Henry Gibbons], "Notes on the Hypodermic Treatment of Diseases," *Pacific Medical and Surgical Journal* 9 (October 1866): 183–84.

69. C. J. Douglas, "Morphine in General Practice," *New York Medical Journal* 97 (April 26, 1913): 882.

70. J. I. Rooker, "The Indiscriminate Use of Hypodermic Medication," *Transactions of the Indiana State Medical Society* 20 (1877): 89–90.

71. "A Point on the Therapeutics of Opium," *Indiana Medical Journal* 1 (April 15, 1883): 558–60.

72. D. W. Cathell, *Book on the Physician Himself, and Things That Concern His Reputation and Success* (Philadalphia: F. A. Davis, 1902), pp. 255–56.

73. [Charles S. Briggs], "Hypodermic Medication," *Nashville Journal of Medicine and Surgery*, ser. 2, 18 (August 1876): 90–92; "Habit of Taking Opium-Inordinate Use of the Hypodermic Syringe," *Medical Record* 11 (August 26, 1876): 572; "Hypodermic Use of Morphia," *Medical and Surgical Reporter* 41 (November 15, 1879).

74. See John A. O'Donnell and Judith P. Jones, "The Diffusion of the Intravenous Techniques Among Narcotic Addicts," in John C. Ball and Carl D. Chambers, eds. *The Epidemiology of Opiate Addiction in the United States* (Springfield, Ill.: Charles C. Thomas, 1970), pp. 147–64.

75. Kane, *Hypodermic Injection of Morphia*, pp. 281–82. Ever since the introduction of hypodermic medication, authorities have noted the needle's attraction for the self-medicated or addicted. An addict noted in 1876 that morphine was better by needle than by mouth. "It is more pleasant, ethereal, and less gross, I may say," and referred to "its immediate and exhilarating effect or influence"; see *Opium Eating: An Autobiographical Sketch*, p. 71. A proces-

sion of later writers noted this attraction. Edward C. Mann, "On the Treatment of the Disease of Inebriety" *Brooklyn Medical Journal* 1 (April 1888): 305–306, noted that "Patients also seem to feel a pleasure in making the punctures, and use generally concentrated solutions which are painless." B. F. Ward, "Opium," *Journal of the Mississippi State Medical Association* 9 (July 1904): 106–118, reported addicted patients who preferred to wait for a hypodermic than take morphine orally. E. W. Fell, "The Social Aspects of Morphine Addiction," *Institution Quarterly* 15 (December 1925): 103–108, believed that some addicts needed the hypodermic ritual more than opiates. John A. Hawkins, a Virginia physician who dealt with numerous addicts, thought that many of them developed a "spike habit" that was independent of a need for drugs; see his *Opium Addicts and Addiction* (Boston: Bruce Humphries, 1937), pp. 137–38. A narcotic agent, Maurice Helbrant, held in the 1930s that many addicts took injections with plain water, simply to enjoy the needle ritual; see Maurice Helbrant, *Narcotic Agent* (New York: Vanguard Press, 1941), pp. 28–29. Modern authorities identify this with sexual needs and symbolisms; see Richard Ashley, *Heroin: The Myths and the Facts* (New York: St. Martins, 1972), pp. 78–79, 93.

76. Kane, *Hypodermic Injection of Morphia*, pp. 276–78, has the quotation. See also Henry Gibbons, "Letheomania," *Pacific Medical and Surgical Journal*, n.s. 3 (April 1870), pp. 481–95; H. Y. Evans, "The Hypodermic Use of Morphia," *Medical Archives* 7 (October 1871): 181–84; "Morphinism," *Chicago Medical Journal and Examiner* 35 (November 1877): 536–38; S. W. Caldwell, "Hypodermatic Medication," *Mississippi Valley Medical Monthly* 5 (February 1885): 62–63; "Hypodermic Use of Morphine," *Cincinnati Lancet-Clinic*, n.s. 22 (February 9, 1889), p. 179; P. C. Remondino, "The Hypodermic Syringe and Our Morphine Habitues," *Medical Sentinel* 4 (January 1896): 4–7.

77. Kane, *Hypodermic Injection of Morphia*, pp. 189, 268, 277.

78. H. L. Harrington, "Hypodermic Use of Morphia," *Chicago Medical Journal and Examiner* 37 (July 1878): 73–75.

79. "The Morphine Habit, *New York Medical Journal* 22 (August 1875): 209; New York *Tribune*, December 26, 1878.

80. Quoted in Howard-Jones, "Origins of Hypodermic Medication." See also J. C. Wilson, "The Causes and Prevention of the Opium Habit and Kindred Affections," *Medical and Surgical Reporter* 59 (November 24, 1888): 646–47; New York *Tribune*, March 6, 1892.

81. "Popularity of Hypodermic Syringe," *Chicago Medical Journal and Examiner* 45 (December 1882): 668–69, quoting a story from the New York *Sun*.

82. See the illustrations in Fred L. Israel, ed, *1897 Sears Roebuck Catalogue* (New York: Chelsea House, 1968), p. 32.

83. J. G. Sewall, "Opium Eating and Hypodermic Injection," *Boston Medical and Surgical Journal*, n.s. 5 (June 2, 1870), pp. 422.

84. All the prefaces are reprinted in Roberts Bartholow, *A Manual of Hypodermatic Medication,* 5th ed. (Philadelphia: J. B. Lippincott, 1891).

85. "More Than a Modicum of Truth," *Medical Age* 12 (June 25, 1894): 376. For early cautions against opiate addiction, see: J. B. Mattison, "The Impending Danger," *Medical Record* 11 (January 22, 1876): 69–71; A. A. Lyon, "The Opium Habit," *Southern Medical Record* 6 (April 1876): 202–203; Kane, *Hypodermic Injection of Morphia*, p. 208, and the warnings sounded in a review

of Kane's book, "Review: The Hypodermic Injection of Morphia," *Chicago Medical Review* 1 (March 5, 1880): 119–20; William H. Jones, "The Reckless Injection of Morphine Hypodermically," *Cincinnati Lancet-Clinic,* n.s. 18 (February 12, 1887): 195–96.

3—THE HABITUÉS: THE NINETEENTH CENTURY

1. Alonzo Calkins, "Opium and Its Victims," *Galaxy* 4 (May 1867): 34; "General Facts About the Use of Opium in This Country," *Quarterly Journal of Inebriety* 2 (September 1878): 215; "The Opium Habit," *Medical Herald* 1 (May 1879): 41; Martin I. Wilbert, "Drug Intoxication: An Economic Waste and a Menace to Public Health," *American Journal of Pharmacy* 87 (March 1915): 137.

2. Day, *The Opium Habit,* p. 7; Beard, *Stimulants and Narcotics,* p. 19; New York *Times,* January 6, 1878; "General Facts About the Use of Opium in This Country," p. 215; Crothers, *Drug Habits and Their Treatment,* p. 61; H. P. Hynson, "Report of the Committee on Acquirement of the Drug Habit," *American Journal of Pharmacy* 74 (November 1902): 551; Martin I. Wilbert, "The Number and Kind of Drug Addicts," *Public Health Reports* 30, no. 2 (August 6, 1915): 2289–94.

3. Hugh C. Weir, "The American Opium Peril," *Putnam's Magazine* 7 (December 1909): 329–36.

4. "The Problem of the Drug Addict," *American Medicine* 23 (December 1917): 794; Charles F. Stokes, "The Military, Industrial, and Public Health Features of Narcotic Addiction," *JAMA* 70 (March 16, 1918): 766–68.

5. U.S. Treasury Department, *Traffic in Narcotic Drugs: Report of the Special Committee of Investigation Appointed March 25, 1918, by the Secretary of the Treasury* (Washington: GPO, 1919).

6. New York *Times,* April 13, 1919.

7. See Cornelius F. Collins, "The Drug Evil and the Drug Law," New York City, Department of Health, *Monthly Bulletin* 9 (January 1919): 2; and S. A. Knopf, "The One Million Drug Addicts in the United States," *Medical Journal and Record* 119 (February 6, 1924): 135–39.

8. See H. H. Drysdale, "Some of the Effects of the Harrison Narcotic Law in Cleveland," *Cleveland Medical Journal* 14 (May 1915): 353–64; Alexander Lambert, "The Underlying Causes of the Narcotic Habit," *Journal of the Medical Society of New Jersey* 17 (January 1920): 1–5; Williams, *Opiate Addiction,* p. xxiii; Lawrence Kolb, "The Prevalence and Trends of Drug Addiction in the United States and the Factors Influencing It," U.S. Treasury Department, *Public Health Service Reports* 39, no. 21 (May 23, 1924): 1193–1202.

9. J. B. Mattison, "Narcotic Abuse and the Public Weal," *Medical News* 82 (April 4, 1903): 638 was an early statement of this view. See also David T. Courtwright, "Opiate Addiction in America, 1800–1940," (Ph.D. diss., Rice University, 1979), p. 35.

10. Terry and Pellens, *The Opium Problem,* pp. 1–2.

11. C. S. S. to Editor, *Boston Medical Surgical Journal* 63 (November 15, 1860): 325.

12. New York *Times,* July 8, 1879.

13. "The Consumption of Opium in the United States," *Medical and Surgical Reporter* 44 (April 16, 1881): 438–39.

14. *Opium Eating: An Autobiographical Sketch by An Habituate* (Philadelphia: Claxton, Remsen and Haffelfinger, 1876), p. 113.

15. W. D. Wilhite, "The Opium Habit: A Narrative of Personal Experience," *St. Louis Clinic Record* 9 (April 1881): 39.

16. Cobbe, *Doctor Judas*, p. 168.

17. Henry G. Cole, *Confessions of An American Opium Eater: From Bondage to Freedom* (Boston: J. H. Earle, 1895), p. 201.

18. New York *Times*, December 30, 1877.

19. Holmes, "Currents and Counter-Currents," pp. 200–201; Calkins, *Opium and the Opium Appetite*, pp. 40–41; Oliver, "The Use and Abuse of Opium," p. 168; O. Marshall, "The Opium Habit in Michigan," Michigan State Board of Health, *Annual Report* 6 (1878): 61–73; J. M. Hull, "The Opium Habit," State Board of Health of the State of Iowa, *Third Biennial Report* (Des Moines: George E. Roberts, 1885), pp. 535–45; Lucius P. Brown, "Enforcement of the Tennessee Anti-Narcotic Law," *American Journal of Public Health* 5 (April 1915): 323–33; Thomas S. Blair, "The Relation of Drug Addiction to Industry," *Journal of Industrial Hygiene* 1 (October 1919): 284–96 and the same author, "The Dope Doctor and Other City Cousins of the Moonshiner," *Survey* 44 (April 3, 1920): 16–20; Sara Graham-Mulhall, "Experiences in Narcotic Drug Control in the State of New York," *New York Medical Journal* 113 (January 15, 1921): 106–111; John A. O'Donnell, *Narcotics Addicts in Kentucky* (Washington: GPO, 1969).

20. Alfred R. Lindesmith, *Opiate Addiction* (Bloomington, Ind.: Principia Press, 1947), p. 187; Duane A. Smith, *Rocky Mountain Mining Camps* (Bloomington, Ind.: Indiana University Press, 1967), pp. 222, 231, 239; Barbara Sicherman, "The Quest for Mental Health in America, 1880–1917," (Ph.D. diss., Columbia University, 1967), p. 36.

21. Cobbe, *Doctor Judas*, p. 173.

22. See Collins, "The Drug Evil and the Drug Law," pp. 4ff; Graham-Mulhall, "Experiences in Narcotic Drug Control," p. 106; Pearce Bailey, "The Drug Habit in the United States," *New Republic* 26 (March 16, 1921), pp. 67–69; Terry and Pellens, *The Opium Problem*, p. 39. The quotation is from Williams, *Opiate Addiction*, p. 46.

23. New York *Times*, March 2, 1877.

24. New York *Tribune*, July 10, 1877.

25. "The Opium Habit," *Medical and Surgical Reporter* 38 (January 12, 1878): 40.

26. Basil M. Wooley, *The Opium Habit and Its Cure* (Atlanta: Atlanta Constitution Press, 1879), and *The Opium and Whiskey Habits and Their Cure* (Atlanta: Franklin Publishing and Printing Co., 1888).

27. Leslie E. Keeley, *The Morphine Eater* (Dwight, Ill: C. L. Palmer, 1881), p. 17, and his *An Essay Upon the Morphine and Opium Habit* (Dwight, Ill.: Keeley Co., 1882), p. 3.

28. "The Opium Habit," *Virginia Medical Monthly* 4 (March 1878): 841–42; T. J. Happel, "The Opium Curse and a Preventative," *Memphis Lancet* 2

(March 1899): 130; J. J. McCarthy, "How the Drug Habit Grips the Unwary," *Pearson's Magazine* 24 (1910): 169–76.

29. Cobbe, *Doctor Judas*, pp. 172–73.

30. Brown, "Enforcement of the Tennessee Anti-Narcotic Law"; Kolb, "Prevalence and Trends of Drug Addiction"; James Harvey Young, *The Toadstool Millionaires* (Princeton: Princeton University Press, 1961), pp. 98–99.

31. New York *Times*, December 30, 1877; and Calkins, *Opium and the Opium Appetite*, pp. 162ff; Charles W. Earle, "The Opium Habit: A Statistical and Clinical Lecture," *Chicago Medical Review* 2 (1880): 422–46; Perry M. Lichtenstein, "Narcotic Addiction," *New York Medical Journal* 100 (November 14, 1914): 964–65.

32. "General Facts About the Use of Opium in This Country," p. 216.

33. J. D. Roberts, "Opium Habit in the Negro," *North Carolina Medical Journal* 16 (October 1885): 206–207. The following query from a physician in Anniston, Alabama, is also interesting: "Is there a case on record of a fullblooded Negro dying during the inhalation of chloroform? I have asked many physicians this question, and have been invariably informed that they knew of none." See "Negroes and Chloroform," *Medical and Surgical Reporter* 59 (September 29, 1888): 414. The author apparently is suggesting that blacks' nervous systems were not sufficiently refined to be susceptible to chloroform overdose.

34. Courtwright, "Opiate Addiction in the United States, 1800–1940," p. 57; Carl D. Chambers and Arthur D. Moffett, "Negro Opiate Addiction," in John C. Bell and Carl D. Chambers, eds., *The Epidemiology of Opiate Addiction in the United States* (Springfield, Ill: Charles C. Thomas, 1970), pp. 178–201; Brecher, *Licit and Illicit Drugs*, pp. 18–19.

35. "Editorial: Four Hundred Opium Dens in San Francisco," *Pacific Medical and Surgical Journal* 23 (April 1881): 523; "Amount of Opium Used in the United States," ibid., 24 (August 1881): 138; Kane, *Opium Smoking*, p. 8; "Opium Smoking in America," *Medical Record* 19 (October 22, 1881): 475; "Opium 'Joints' in the Black Hills," *Chambers's Journal* (October 13, 1888), pp. 654–55; John W. Robertson, "The Morphin Habit," *Medical News* 73 (August 27, 1898): 257; Henry O. Whiteside, "The Drug Habit in Nineteenth-Century Colorado," *Colorado Magazine* 55 (Winter 1978): 46–68.

36. Kane, *Opium Smoking in America and China*, pp. 4–5 and the same author's "A Hashish-House in New York," *Harper's Monthly* 67 (November 1883): 944–49; "The Increase of the Opium Habit," *Medical and Surgical Reporter* 52 (January 17, 1885): 86–87; Charles W. Earle, "Opium Smoking in Chicago," *Chicago Medical Journal and Examiner* 52 (February 1886): 104–112; W. H. Atkinson, "Death From Opium Smoking, *Description* of Smoker's Layout, Etc.," *Virginia Medical Semi-Monthly* 1 (December 11, 1896): 472–74; New York *Times*, August 2, 1908.

37. [Dr. Armand], "The Therapeutic Employment of the Fumes of Opium," *Chicago Medical Journal* 26 (March 1, 1869): 129–33.

38. Kane, *Opium Smoking in America and China*, p. 156; "Chinese Opium Smoking," *Chicago Medical Review* 4 (October 5, 1881): 448–50; J. B. Mattison, "A Case of Opium Smoking," *Medical Times* 16 (December 12, 1885): 199.

39. H. H. Kane, "A Case of Opium Smoking and Morphine Taking," *St. Louis Clinical Record* 8 (June 1881): 81–84; see also J. B. Mattison, "The Genesis of Opium Addiction," *Detroit Lancet,* n.s. 7 (January 1884), pp. 303–305.

40. Cobbe, *Doctor Judas,* pp. 124–32; Cole, *Confessions of An American Opium Eater,* pp. 229–30.

41. Hubbard, *The Opium Habit and Alcoholism,* p. 147.

42. See the long article on opium dens and smoking in San Francisco in New York *Tribune,* June 19, 1881, and a similar report for Eureka, Nevada in New York *Times,* July 29, 1877; and Kane, *Opium Smoking in America and China,* pp. 11–12, 61, 71–72; Atkinson, "Death From Opium Smoking, Description of Smoker's Layout, Etc.," pp. 472–74; Winslow Anderson, "The Opium Habit in San Francisco," *Medical and Surgical Reporter* 57 (December 10, 1887): 784–85.

43. W. S. Whitwell, "The Opium Habit," *Pacific Medical and Surgical Journal* 30 (June 1887): 321–28.

44. Lindesmith, *Opiate Addiction,* pp. 115, 187–88.

45. New York *Tribune,* June 19, 1881. See also "The Use of Opium," *Pacific Medical and Surgical Reporter* 34 (March 18, 1876): 236; New York *Times,* July 29, 1877; George H. Fitch, "A Night in Chinatown," *Cosmopolitan* 2 (January 1887): 349–58; Whitwell, "The Opium Habit," pp. 321–28.

46. Kane, *Opium Smoking in America and China,* pp. 2–3.

47. See Edward Miller, "Remarks on the Cholera, or Bilious Diarrhea of Infants," *Medical Respository* 1, no. 1 (1797): 58–65, for typical advice of the old school that suggests combining opium and calomel. "Laudanum," *Boston Medical and Surgical Journal* 10 (April 23, 1834): 174–75, is an early warning against dosing infants with opiated compounds.

48. For England, see: "The Factory System," *Quarterly Review* 57 (December 1836): 422; London *Times,* July 17, 1840, and January 30, 1845; "Consumption of Opium," *Virginia Medical Journal* 9 (July 1857): 85, which reports on growing use of opiates in English "factory towns"; and Mordecai Cubbitt Cooke, *The Seven Sisters of Sleep* (London: J. Blackwood, 1860), pp. 199–200.

49. George W. Winterburn, "A Seductive Drug," *Medical Tribune* 4 (December 1882): 510; see also Enos Stevens, "Opium," *Boston Medical and Surgical Journal* 41 (September 12, 1849): 119–21; W. L. McMillen, "Remarkable Recovery from Poisoning by Opium," *Ohio Medical and Surgical Journal* 10 (May 1, 1858): 388–90; Thomas Pollard, "Use of Opium in Children," *Atlanta Medical and Surgical Journal* 4 (November 1858): 129–34; "Narcotics," *North American Review* 95 (October 1862): 302; Calkins, *Opium and the Opium Appetite,* p. 49; New York *Times,* January 6, 1878; C. A. Bryce, "A Case of Opium Poisoning with 'Dr. Bull's Cough Syrup,'" *Southern Clinic* 2 (June 1880): 399; Marshall, "The Opium Habit in Michigan," pp. 63–73.

50. Winterburn, "A Seductive Drug," p. 511.

51. Louis Fischer, "The Opium Habit in Children," *Medical Record* 45 (February 17, 1894): 197.

52. Cobbe, *Doctor Judas,* p. 123; and Day, *The Opium Habit,* p. 199; F. Baldwin Morris, *The Panorama of a Life, and Experience in Associating and*

Battling With Opium and Alcoholic Stimulants (Philadelphia: G. W. Ward, 1878), pp. 86ff.

53. D. W. Nolan, "The Opium Habit," *Catholic World* 33 (September 1881): 835; see also Marshall, "The Opium Habit in Michigan," pp. 63–73; Hull, "The Opium Habit," pp. 539ff; and F. M. Hamlin, "The Opium Habit," *Medical and Surgical Reporter* 51 (February 14, 1885): 221.

54. "Opium Eating," *Boston Medical and Surgical Journal* 9 (September 4, 1833): 66–67; John Q. Winfield, "A Case of Opium Habit," *Virginia Medical Monthly* 7 (December 1880): 701–702; Ira Russell, "Opium Inebriety," *Medico-Legal Journal* 5 (September 1887): 144–45.

55. *Medical and Surgical Journal* 20 (June 26, 1869): 484.

56. Morris, *Panorama of a Life*, pp. 85ff; New York *Times*, November 17, 1878; New York *Tribune*, December 26, 1878, and April 13, 1890.

57. "The Medical Abuse of Opium," *Medical Age* 12 (October 25, 1894): 631; and A. T. Schertzer, "Excessive Opium Eating," *Boston Medical and Surgical Journal*," n.s. 5 (January 20, 1870), p. 56.

58. J. B. Mattison, "Opium Habituation," *Medical Record* 16 (October 4, 1879): 332–33; and New York *Tribune*, September 4, 1881; Hubbard, *The Opium Habit and Alcoholism*, p. 17; H. P. C. Wilson, "The Indiscriminate Use of Opiates in the Pelvic Diseases of Women," *North American Practitioner* 3 (January 1891): 9–13.

59. Ruppaner, *Hypodermic Injections*, passim; D. M. Forman, "Hypodermic Injections," *Cincinnati Medical News*, n.s. 4 (April 1875): 159–61; F. M. Hamlin, "The Opium Habit," *Medical Gazette* 9 (September 9, 1882): 427.

60. Beard, *Stimulants and Narcotics*, p. 51; and Thomas D. Crothers, "Inebriety in America—Some Historical Facts," *New England Medical Monthly* 3 (February 1884): 209; S. Weir Mitchell, *Doctor and Patient*, 5th ed. (Philadelphia: Lippincott, 1904), p. 83.

61. See John S. Haller and Robin M. Haller, *The Physician and Sexuality in Victorian America* (Urbana, Ill.: University of Illinois Press, 1974), p. 25.

62. Wilson, "The Indiscriminate Use of Opiates," pp. 9–13; and Terry and Pellens, *The Opium Problem*, p. 61, citing a work of 1832 concerning opiates and women; Calkins, *Opium and the Opium Appetite*, pp. 45–46, 286; Joseph Parrish, "Opium Intoxication," *Medical and Surgical Reporter* 39 (November 15, 1873): 343; "The Opium Habit," *Toledo Medical and Surgical Journal* 4 (March 1880): 99–100.

63. T. J. Happel, "The Opium Curse and Its Prevention," *Medical and Surgical Reporter* (Philadelphia) 72 (May 25, 1895): 731.

64. New York *Times*, August 28, 1882, reporting out of the Philadelphia *Times* on a plush smoking parlor for genteel women. H. S. Duncan, "The Morphia Habit," *Nashville Journal of Medicine and Surgery*, n.s. 35 (June 1885), pp. 246–48, comments on boredom. J. T. Wittaker, "Cocaine for the Opium Habit," *Medical and Surgical Reporter* 53 (August 15, 1885): 177 quotes a doctor who had society women ask him for cocaine shots "to make them lively and talkative." Sara Graham-Mulhall, *Opium: The Demon Flower* (New York: Harold Vinal, 1926), pp. 62–63, is a late date for connecting opiates with rich and idle women. Walter L. Cuskey, et al., "Survey of Opiate Addiction Among

Females in the United States Between 1850 and 1970," *Public Health Reviews* 1 (1972): 6–39, makes obvious comparisons between nineteenth-century women using opiates and chloral, and bored housewives a century later using tranquilizers.

65. New York *Tribune*, September 4, 1881.

66. J. B. Mattison, "The Modern and Humane Treatment of the Morphine Disease," *Medical Record* 44 (December 23, 1893): 804; and the same author's "Opium Addiction Among Medical Men," ibid., 23 (June 9, 1883): 621–23; C. E. Patterson, "The Morphine Habit and Its Cure," *Medical Brief* 25 (July 1897): 1041; C. C. Stockard, "Some Cases of the Drug Habit," *Atlanta Medical and Surgical Journal*, n.s. 15 (April 1898), pp. 80–85; "Morphinism Among Physicians," *Quarterly Journal of Inebriety* 22 (January 1900): 98–100; W. D. Partlow, "Alcoholism and Drug Addiction Among Physicians of Alabama," *Transactions of the Medical Association of the State of Alabama* (1914), pp. 685–91; Crothers, *Morphinism*, p. 30.

67. *Bulletin of Pharmacy* 11 (June 1897): 244, and "Morphine Habit," *Chicago Medical Observer* 1 (July 1898): 189, summarize a report from Europe that 40 percent of male addicts were doctors, with high rates among physician families.

68. Mitchell, *Doctor and Patient*, pp. 98–99. The following touch on drugs among doctors' families: Wilson, "Causes and Prevention of the Opium Habit," pp. 505–506; J. B. Mattison, "Morphinism Among Women," *Atlantic Medical Weekly* 5 (June 20, 1896): 389–92; C. B. Burr, "Concerning Morphine Addiction and Its Treatment," *Quarterly Journal of Inebriety* 28 (Winter 1906): 168–74; W. C. Ashworth, "The Increasing Frequency of the Use of Narcotic Drugs by Members of the Medical Profession, and the Probable Reasons For It," *Charlotte Medical Journal* 61 (May 1910): 305–306.

69. C. L. Hudgins, "A Physician's Experience," *Banner of Gold* 14 (April 1899): 56; Mattison, "Morphinism in Medical Men," pp. 186–88.

70. W. F. Waugh, "Spirit and Drug Taking Among Medical Students," *Journal of Inebriety* 33 (Autumn 1911): 100–107.

71. Mattison, "Opium Addiction Among Medical Men"; and S. Grover Burnett, "The Relation of Medicine to Morphinism: A Clinical Deduction From 100 Cases," *Oklahoma Medical News-Journal* 16 (June 1908): 469–76; Crothers, *The Disease of Inebriety*, p. 357; Pettey, *Narcotic Drug Diseases*, pp. 24–25.

72. Cathell, *Book on the Physician*, pp. 118–19. Cobbe, *Doctor Judas*, pp. 189–90 remarked on the addiction rate among overworked country doctors. Hudgins, "A Physician's Experience," p. 56, made the same point from experience. Daniel Frederick MacMartin, *Thirty Years in Hell; or, the Confessions of a Drug Fiend* (Topeka, Kan.: Capper Printing Co., 1921), pp. 113–14 was one among many addict-memoirists who mentioned the number of addicted physicians he encountered in the underground.

73. C. B. Pearson, "The Treatment of Morphinism," *Medical Times* 42 (August 1914): 245–46.

74. New York *Sun*, May 19, 1915, has a typical case of a scrip doctor in the period of regulation's beginnings, who lost an excellent practice because of drug use. Windsor C. Cutting, "Morphine Addiction for 62 Years," *Stanford Medical Bulletin* 1 (August 1942): 39–41 has a fascinating case of the opposite kind, the

story of a distinguished anonymous physician who functioned normally in practice with little or no physical and emotional ill-effects despite a sixty-two-year addiction to morphine.

75. Kane, *The Hypodermic Injection of Morphia*, pp. 272ff, suggests as of 1880 that "Persons of decidedly nervous temperament" should be culled out of medical practice. The quotation is from Curran Pope, "The Treatment of the Morphine Habit," *Cincinnati Lancet-Clinic*, n.s. 53 (December 3, 1904): 564. Robert T. Edes, "Addiction of Physicians to Morphine and Liquor," *JAMA* 46 (January 6, 1906): 57 disputes the reported high rates of addiction among doctors, but puts them with the "brain-working classes" likely to use drugs.

76. For material on the continuing problem of physician-addicts at later dates, see: J. DeWitt Fox, "Narcotic Addiction Among Physicians," *Journal of the Michigan State Medical Society* 56 (February 1957): 214–26; Lois Hoffman, "Coming: A Plan for Helping Doctor-Addicts," *Medical Economics* 35 (April 14, 1958): 105–123; "Narcotics Addiction a Hazard to Physicians," *Science Digest* 48 (December 1960): 50–51; Frederick Lemere, "Alcohol and Drug Addiction in Physicians," *Northwest Medicine* 64 (March 1965): 196–98; and Herbert C. Modlin, "The Medical Profession Addict," in John G. Cull and Richard E. Hardy, eds., *Types of Drug Abusers and Their Abuse* (Springfield, Ill.: Charles C. Thomas, 1974), pp. 3–15.

77. Calkins, *Opium and the Opium Appetite*, p. 104. See also Day, *The Opium Habit*, p. 7, and three early news reports on drug use among the so-called higher classes in New York *Times*, December 30, 1877, January 6, 1878, and November 19, 1882.

78. E. C. Mann, "On the Use of Cocaine in the Opium Habit," *Alienist and Neurologist* 7 (January 1886): 51–57; and Hull, "The Opium Habit," p. 537. There is a fine burst of purple prose on this score in D. W. Nolan, "The Opium Habit," *Catholic World* 33 (September 1881): 827: "Opium-eating, unlike the use of alcoholic stimulants, is an aristocratic vice and prevails more extensively among the wealthy and educated classes than among those of inferior social position; but no class is exempt from its blighting influence. The merchant, lawyer, and physician are to be found among the host who sacrifice the choicest treasures of life at the shrine of Opium. The slaves of Alcohol may be clothed in rags, but vassals of the monarch who sits enthroned on the poppy are generally found dressed in purple and fine linen."

79. Crothers, *Morphinism*, pp. 44–45.

80. See Henry Smith Williams, *Drug Addicts Are Human Beings* (Washington: Shaw, 1938), p. 15.

81. Cobbe, *Doctor Judas*, p. 307.

82. All the early studies of drug use and users offer some evidence on age, and generally agree that most users in general, and addicts to opiates in particular, in the late nineteenth century were in the mid-years. See Calkins, *Opium and the Opium Appetite*, pp. 162ff; "General Facts About the Use of Opium in This Country," p. 215; L. D. Mason, "Statistical Profile of Two Hundred and Fifty-two Cases of Inebriety," *Quarterly Journal of Inebriety* 4 (April 1881): 67–89, which deals mainly with alcoholics, but has some information on drug users; Earle, "The Opium Habit," p. 443; Kane, *Drugs That Enslave*, pp. 24–25; Hull, "The Opium Habit," pp. 539ff.

4—SOCIETY AND THE HABITUÉS

1. Mattison, "Impending Danger," p. 71. There is an interesting evolutionary analogy in "Opium Mania," *Quarterly Journal of Inebriety* 3 (December 1878): 48: "There are those who, by reason of a perverted system, founded far back, it may be, in ancestral disease, take to this drug, after having once felt its effects, as an aquatic animal seeks water."

2. "Heredity," *Quarterly Journal of Inebriety* 2 (September 1878): 208; B. N. Comings, "Mental Strain and Heredity as Causes of Inebriety," ibid., 3 (March 1879): 78–88; Crothers, *Morphinism and Narcomanias,* pp. 56ff; Thomas D. Crothers, *The Drug Habits and Their Treatment* (Chicago: G. P. Engelhard, 1902), pp. 62–63; Mark H. Haller, *Eugenics: Hereditarian Attitudes in American Thought* (New Brunswick: Rutgers University Press, 1963), pp. 30–31; Nathan G. Hale, Jr., *Freud and the Americans* (New York: Oxford University Press, 1971), pp. 52, 56, 63–64; Charles E. Rosenberg, "The Bitter Fruit: Heredity, Disease, and Social Thought in Nineteenth Century America," *Perspectives in American History* 8 (1974): 189–235. Pusey, *A Doctor of the 1870s,* pp. 85–86, has the interesting views of a contemporary practitioner.

3. Cobbe, *Doctor Judas,* pp. 170–71.

4. "The Hash-heesh Eater," *The Knickerbocker* 51 (February 1858): 197–98.

5. Calkins, *Opium and the Opium Appetite,* p. 57.

6. *Opium Eating: An Autobiographical Sketch,* p. 112.

7. "Narcotics," *North American Review* 95 (October 1862): 415.

8. Edward P. Thwing, "American Life as Related to Inebriety," *Quarterly Journal of Inebriety* 10 (January 1888): 43–50.

9. Kane, *Drugs That Enslave,* p. 17; and Beard, *Stimulants and Narcotics,* pp. 38–39; "Inebriety and Allied Nervous Diseases in America," *Quarterly Journal of Inebriety* 4 (January 1880): 31–34.

10. "Abstracts and Reviews," ibid., 5 (October 1883): 261. The author is probably referring to the fashion for analyzing "hysteria."

11. Thwing, "American Life as Related to Inebriety," pp. 43–50.

12. See "Abuse of Chloral Hydrate," *Quarterly Journal of Inebriety* 4 (January 1880): 53–54; Hubbard, *The Opium Habit,* pp. 202ff; J. B. Mattison, "The Genesis of Opium Addiction," *Detroit Lancet,* n.s. 7 (January 1884), pp. 303–305; Virgil G. Eaton, "How the Opium-Habit is Acquired," *Popular Science Monthly* 33 (September 1888): 663–67; Elias Wildman, "Morphine Habit and Treatment," *Memphis Medical Monthly,* 9 (January 1889): 56–59; Mitchell; *Doctor and Patient,* p. 94; Smith Ely Jelliffee, "Hypnotics, Analgesics and Resultant Drug Addictions," *JAMA* 40 (February 28, 1903): 571–72; Eberle, "Robert of the Committee on the Acquirement of the Drug Habit," p. 479; Alexander Lambert, "Indiscriminate Drug Taking" *New York Medical Journal* 95 (February 17, 1912): 314; Towns, "Drugs and the Drug User," p. 47.

13. Fitzhugh Ludlow, "What Shall They Do To Be Saved?" *Harper's Monthly* 8 (August 1867): 377–87.

14. Comings, "Mental Strain and Heredity," p. 86. See also M. M. W., "Stimulants and Stimulation," *Eclectic Medical Journal of Pennsylvania* 7

(May 1869): 234–36; Oliver, "Use and Abuse of Opium," p. 169; Kane, *Opium Smoking in America and China*, p. 72, and his *Drugs That Enslave*, p. 17.

15. Cole, *Confessions of An American Opium Eater*, pp. 7–8.

16. Charles H. Bass, "Why Are We Not a Healthy People?" *Atlanta Medical and Surgical Journal* 5 (December 1859): 197–207.

17. Beard, *American Nervousness*, pp. 101–192, and his *Practical Treatise on Nervous Exhaustion*, pp. 31–32; "Inebriety and Allied Diseases in America," *Quarterly Journal of Inebriety* 4 (January 1880): 32; "The Opium, Chloral and Hashisch Habits," *The American* 3 (January 7, 1882): 200–201.

18. Beard, *American Nervousness*, pp. 120–21.

19. W. Xavier Sudduth, "The Psychology of Narcotism," *JAMA* 27 (October 10, 1896): 798.

20. Crumpe, *Opium*, p. 48.

21. Coxe, *American Dispensatory*, pp. 510–29; John W. DeForest, "The Hasheesh Eater," *Putnam's Magazine* 8 (September 1856): 233–39; "Narcotics," *North American Review* 95 (October 1862): 396; Calkins, *Opium and the Opium Appetite*, p. 390; "Editorial: The Effects of the Habitual Use of Opium," *Cincinnati Lancet-Clinic*, n.s. 29 (December 3, 1892), pp. 771–72.

22. Kane, *Drugs That Enslave*, p. 23; and New York *Tribune;* March 5, 1890; Cobbe, *Doctor Judas*, p. 128; Curran Pope, "The Treatment of the Morphine Habit," *Cincinnati Lancet-Clinic*, n.s. 53 (December 3, 1904), p. 567; J. Howe Adams, "Morphinomania and Kindred Habits," *Medical Times* 35 (January 1907): 13–16.

23. "The Opium Trade," *Boston Medical and Surgical Journal* 42 (May 1, 1850): 277.

24. New York *Times*, March 12, 1911.

25. "Monthly Periscope: Opium Eating," *Buffalo Medical Journal* 9 (December 1853): 432–33; and Day, *The Opium Habit*, pp. 220–21.

26. Marshall, "The Opium Habit in Michigan," pp. 63–73.

27. Kane, *Opium Smoking in America and China*, p. 80.

28. Allen, *Opium Trade*, p. 25.

29. "Opium and Alcohol," *Boston Medical and Surgical Journal* 49 (November 23, 1853): 345.

30. Joseph Parrish, "Opium Intoxication," *Medical and Surgical Reporter* 39 (November 22, 1873): 363.

31. "Opium Eating," *Lippincott's Magazine* 1 (April 1868): 409; and *Opium Eating: An Autobiographical Sketch*, pp. 90–91; New York *Times*, December 30, 1877; Cobbe, *Doctor Judas*, pp. 31–32, 68.

32. *Opium Eating: An Autobiographical Sketch*, p. 121.

33. Kane, *Opium Smoking in America and China*, pp. 68–69.

34. New York *Times*, July 14, 1889.

35. Cobbe, *Doctor Judas*, pp. 162–64.

36. Ludlow, *The Hasheesh Eater*, p. 362; and Calkins, "Opium and Its Victims," p. 30.

37. S. W. Gould, "The Opium Habit," *Medical and Surgical Reporter* 38 (June 22, 1878): 496–97.

38. Cobbe, *Doctor Judas*, p. 68.

39. Hubbard, *The Opium Habit and Alcoholism*, p. 18.

40. *Opium Eating: An Autobiographical Sketch*, pp. 58–59; Cobbe, *Doctor Judas*, p. 40.

41. Cathell, *Book on the Physician*, p. 255.

42. Cole, *Confessions of An American Opium Eater*, p. 196.

43. Cobbe, *Doctor Judas*, pp. 17ff; J. H. Hughes, "The Autobiography of a Drug Fiend," *Medical Review of Reviews* 22 (January 1916): 28; MacMartin, *Thirty Years in Hell*, pp. 9–10; D. C. Van Slyke, *The Wail of a Drug Addict* (Grand Rapids: W. B. Eerdmans, 1945), p. 12.

44. "Monthly Periscope: Opium Eating," pp. 432–33.

45. *Opium Eating: An Autobiographical Sketch*, pp. 70–71, 131–50. De Quincey fascinated the literary addicts of the 1850s and after; for more reactions to his story see: "Confessions of an English Opium-Eater," *The Knickerbocker* 18 (October 1841): 352–53; "Monthly Periscope: Opium Eating," pp. 432–33; Day, *The Opium Habit*, p. 16; George Parsons Lathrop, "Some Aspects of De Quincey," *Atlantic Monthly* 40 (November 1877): 569–84; Nolan, "The Opium Habit," p. 831; Leslie E. Keeley, *An Essay Upon the Morphine and Opium Habit* (Dwight, Ill.: Author, 1882), p. 2; Cole, *Confessions of An American Opium Eater*, p. 6; Cobbe, *Doctor Judas*, pp. 12, 71ff, 104–105; Pettey, *The Narcotic Drug Diseases*, p. 1; Graham-Mulhall, *Opium*, pp. 76ff.

46. Cobbe, *Doctor Judas*, pp. 71–72.

47. "Literary Notices," *Harper's Monthly* 15 (November 1857): 834–35 has the quotation; see also "Editor's Easy Chair," ibid., 42 (December 1870): 139–40; Louis J. Bragman, "A Minor De Quincey," *Medical Journal and Record* 22 (January 7, 1925); and Oriana Josseau Kalant, "Ludlow on Cannabis: A Modern Look at a Nineteenth Century Drug Experience," *International Journal of the Addictions* 6 (June 1971): 314.

48. The first quotation is from Ludlow, *The Hasheesh Eater*, p. 64, the second from ibid., p. 149. See also Allen, *Opium Trade*, pp. 23–25; "The Vision of Hasheesh," *Putnam's Monthly* 3 (April 1854): 402–408; Bayard Taylor, *The Lands of the Saracen: Pictures of Palestine, Asia Minor, Sicily, and Spain: or the Lands of the Saracen* (New York: Putnam's, 1855), pp. 133–48.

49. Ludlow, *The Hasheesh Eater*, pp. 362–63; and Calkins, "Opium and Its Victims," p. 35.

50. "Opium Eating," *Lippincott's Magazine* 1 (April 1868): 404.

51. Day, *The Opium Habit*, p. 216. See also Jones, *The Mysteries of Opium Revealed*, pp. 322–25; "Opium and Alcohol," *Boston Medical and Surgical Journal* 49 (November 23, 1853): 341; Wood, *Treatise on Therapeutics*, 1:718; New York *Times*, December 30, 1877; Nolan, "The Opium Habit," p. 827. Cobbe wrote in *Doctor Judas*, p. 301: "The fact of opium slavery is fairly good evidence of intelligence; for it would seem that those who are stolid, those who are commonplace, and those who are stupid have no affinity for the drug."

52. "Narcotics," *North American Review* 95 (October 1862): 391.

53. J. H. Hughes, "Autobiography of a Drug Fiend: Part III," *Medical Review of Reviews* 22 (March 1916): 186. The British authority Francis Anstie had some interesting observations on what caused the states associated with

alcohol, chloroform, and hashish in particular. He thought that inebriation from these drugs "consists in the destruction of the capacity of the brain for retaining or recalling moral and prudential impressions, and also for any kind of continuous intellectual labor; and that the apparent *excitement* of the emotions and desires is, in truth, but the unveiling of the lower part of our nature, which is more or less ready in each of us, to spring into action when the customary checks are removed." He agreed that the visions and dreams associated with opiates and belladonna were "various antecedent impressions" that revived when the drugs released inhibitions. See his *Stimulants and Narcotics* (London: Macmillan, 1864), pp. 173–81. Similar views are in *Opium Eating: An Autobiographical Sketch,* p. 30, and Kane, *Drugs That Enslave,* p. 49. The idea that some drug experiences create new ideas or powers in the user, or enable the consciousness to see new things, remains popular.

54. Cobbe, *Doctor Judas,* pp. 83–84.

55. Ibid., pp. 143, and 106–107; see also Calkins, *Opium and the Opium Appetite,* pp. 324, 326n, 328–30; Kane, *Drugs That Enslave,* pp. 208–209, and his *Opium Smoking in America and China,* pp. 8, 14, 52, 81, 93, 131–32.

56. Jones, *The Mysteries of Opium Revealed,* pp. 17–18 suggests that opium "excites venery, applied to the Perinaeum." B. Woodward, "Action of Opium on the Genito-Urinary Organs," *Boston Medical and Surgical Journal* 65 (September 26, 1861): 157–58, reports that "I could give the cases of several men for whom I have prescribed opium, to enable them to overcome their lustful propensities, and always with benefit, as it held the desire in abeyance, and enabled them to bring their moral powers to bear." "Remarks on the Opium Habit," *Medical and Surgical Reporter* 37 (December 1, 1877): 436–37, notes that opiates may excite sexuality at first, but rapidly become anaphrodisiac. "Opium Habit and Impotency," *Medical and Surgical Reporter* 62 (June 28, 1890): 751, is a typical case history of a middle-class, professional male addict impotent as a result of large doses of opiates. Addict memoirs agree that opiates depressed or eliminated the sex drive, but Hawkins, *Opium Addicts and Addictions,* pp. 88–89, comments on a man he treated for opiate addiction who was apparently a sexual athlete, which if true, illustrated again the great variation of effects in users. Calkins, *Opium and the Opium Appetite,* p. 165, is one of numerous sources allying opiate use and prostitution, though few such commentators ever made clear whether they thought prostitutes used opiates to enhance the sexual drive, or to numb themselves in their work.

57. *Opium Eating: An Autobiographical Sketch,* pp. 79–81.

58. Cobbe, *Doctor Judas,* pp. 70–71.

59. "Opium Eating," *Lippincott's Magazine* 1 (April 1868): 406; and Layard, "Morphine," p. 698; C. H. Hughes, "The Opium Habit (Chronic Meconism or Papaverism)," St. Louis Medical Society of Missouri, *Proceedings* 1 (August 1878): 79–90; Butler, *Textbook of Materia Medica,* p. 435; Pettey, *The Narcotic Drug Diseases,* p. 21; Williams, *Opiate Addiction,* p. 165.

60. Calkins, *Opium and the Opium Appetite,* p. 80.

61. New York *Tribune,* December 26, 1878.

62. "Tricks of Opium Habitues," *Cincinnati Lancet-Clinic,* n.s. 10 (February 10, 1883), p. 144; Cole, *Confessions of An American Opium Eater,* p. 56; G. H. Lehmann, "The Treatment of the Morphine Habit in General Practice," *At-*

lanta Journal-Record of Medicine 10 (October 1908): 365–71; Williams, *Opiate Addiction*, p. 167; Hawkins, *Opium Addicts and Addiction*, pp. 30–31; Van Slyke, *Wail of a Drug Addict*, p. 34.

63. "The Opium Habit," *Kansas City Medical Record* 1 (April 1884): 162–63.

64. Calkins, *Opium and the Opium Appetite*, pp. 59ff, 75ff, 385–86.

65. Cole, *Confessions of An American Opium Eater*, p. 42.

66. William F. Waugh, "The Opiate Habit," *Medical Record* 74 (December 26, 1908): 1086–88. This prompted an interesting response from the Rev. Frederic Rowland Martin of Albany, ibid., 75 (January 9, 1909): 69, objecting to the impression that all such scholarly or refined and withdrawn people might be addicted. He also thought that many people controlled nervousness with opiates and were better members of society for it. And he attacked Waugh's notion that "'producing' is the great end of human life," holding that true reflection and thought, apart from addiction, were equally valuable.

67. Thomas D. Crothers, "Inebriety From Bad Surroundings," *Medical and Surgical Reporter* 50 (April 26, 1884): 517–20.

68. Crothers, *Morphinism and Narcomanias*, pp. 204–205.

69. See Wooley, *The Opium Habit and Its Cure*, p. 3.

70. C. B. Pearson, "The Prognosis of Morphinism," *Western Medical Times* 28 (August 1918): 43–49.

71. C. H. Hughes, "The Opium Psycho-Neurosis; Chronic Meconism or Papaverism," *Alienist and Neurologist* 5 (January 1884): 133. The fear that alcohol was destroying innocent families was a potent factor in the temperance movement. See Norman H. Clark, *Deliver Us From Evil* (New York: Norton, 1976), pp. 42–43.

72. Calkins, *Opium and the Opium Appetite*, pp. 75ff.

73. Earle, "Opium Smoking in Chicago," p. 112.

74. David Starr Jordan, "Drugs and Character," *The Independent* 52 (May 3, 1900): 1050–53.

75. Charles C. Cranmer, "The Use and Abuse of Opium," *Medical and Surgical Reporter* 33 (November 6, 1875): 378.

76. Cobbe, *Doctor Judas*, p. 69.

77. This is well stated in *Opium Eating: An Autobiographical Sketch*, p. 122.

78. Cobbe, *Doctor Judas*, p. 52. See also Morris, *Panorama of a Life*, p. iii; MacMartin, *Thirty Years in Hell*, pp. 41–42; Pettey, *Narcotic Drug Diseases*, p. 307. Van Slyke, *Wail of An Addict*, p. 36, has a good summary of this fear and its accompanying remorse from an addict of the 1920s or 1930s, speaking after taking a shot of morphine: "Do you see that stuff? Well, let me tell you something! Because of it I have never had a home! I have never had a wife or children! I have had no friends! I have been an outcast having to slink down alleys; afraid of police; the stigma of a 'hop head' on me. I have no clothes, many times I have had nothing to eat, I have slept in box cars with a newspaper for a covering, and all because of this stuff. It's taken every cent I could scrape together, all I can get by hook or crook goes for this—and . . . now the habit is so big I can't get enough dope to satisfy it. I am in misery all the time. I know not what to do—I have tried time and again to quit, but it's no use, it's got me!"

Lindesmith, *Opiate Addiction*, pp. 6–7, 115, reports the same general feeling of ostracism and blighted life among addicts in the post–World War II years. This sense may have changed, since the character of the addict population has altered after the 1960s. Many addicts still desire respectability and integration into society, but many others are indifferent or defiant, seeing the drug experience as merely an alternate and viable life style.

79. Day, *The Opium Habit*, pp. 6, 76; Hubbard, *The Opium Habit and Alcoholism*, p. 6; *Opium Eating: An Autobiographical Sketch*, pp. 67, 83–85; J. B. Mattison, "The Curability of Opium Addiction," *Quarterly Journal of Inebriety* 5 (October 1883): 252–57; Hull, "The Opium Habit," pp. 543–44; Cobbe, *Doctor Judas*, pp. 46ff; Morris, *Panorama of a Life*, p. 77.

5—CURES AND TREATMENTS

1. "Opium Eating," *Boston Medical and Surgical Journal* 9 (September 4, 1833): 66–67.

2. *Opium Eating: An Autobiographical Sketch*, p. 91.

3. "Opium Eating" *Medical and Surgical Reporter* 22 (January 29, 1870): 104; "The Opium Habit," ibid., 25 (September 9, 1871): 242; George R. Cooke, "Opium and Morphine Habit," *Medical Brief* 8 (February 1880): 55; E. H. Pritchett, "Opium Habit," ibid., 9 (January 1881): 13; H. M. D., "Opium or Morphine Habits," ibid., 13 (April 1885): 169; V. S. Deaton, "[Therapeutics of Opium]," *Ohio Medical Recorder* 5 (September 1880): 162–63; Day, *The Opium Habit*, pp. 60–61.

4. Beard, *Stimulants and Narcotics*, p. iii; F. R. Boyd, "Treatment of the Morphine Habit," *Medical Review* 31 (January 26, 1895): 64.

5. Cobbe, *Doctor Judas*, p. 8.

6. Hubbard, *Opium Habit and Alcoholism*, p. iv; H. E. Smith, "The Nature and Treatment of the Opium Habit," *Atlanta Medical and Surgical Journal*, n.s. 6 (September 1889), pp. 398–410.

7. Young, *The Toadstool Millionaires*, pp. 39–41, 97, 101.

8. J. B. Mattison, "'Opium Antidotes' and Their Vendors," *JAMA* 7 (November 20, 1886): 568–70.

9. There is illustrative material on Collins and Wooley in Haller and Haller, *The Physician and Sexuality*, pp. 298–300.

10. "Collins' Remedy for the Opium Habit," *Cincinnati Medical News*, n.s. 2 (May 1873), p. 235; [J. B. Mattison], "Opium Antidotes," *Medical Record* 12 (May 19, 1877): 319; "Opium Cures," *Northwestern Lancet* 6 (December 1, 1886): 91–92; W. S. Watson, "On the Evil of Opium Eating," *JAMA* 14 (May 10, 1890): 671–74; *Sears Catalogue for 1897*, drug insert, pp. 32–33.

11. Benton J. Hon, "Coca in Opium-Habit," *Louisville Medical News* 10 (August 7, 1880): 63; and J. H. Hughes, "The Autobiography of a Drug Fiend," *Medical Review of Reviews* 22 (February 1916): 105–120, which has a good account of the addict underworld of scrip doctors and cures.

12. Hull, "The Opium Habit," pp. 538–39; and "Morphine Habit," *American Druggist* 15 (October 1886): 199; Samuel Hopkins Adams, *Great American Frauds* (New York: P. F. Collier and Son, 1906), pp. 112–22.

13. E. B. Partin, "Opium Habit," *Medical Brief* 14 (August 1886): 362–63; J. B. Mattison, "A Tale of the Poppy and Its Moral," *Atlantic Medical Weekly* 5 (April 11, 1896): 228–30.

14. Edwin W. Knowles, "Narcotic Addiction and Its Treatment," *Colorado Medicine* 8 (August 1911): 286; "The Problem of Narcotic Drug Addiction," *American Medicine*, n.s. 14 (April 1919), pp. 189–92.

15. New York *Times*, December 30, 1877.

16. Hubbard, *The Opium Habit and Alcoholism*, p. iv.

17. W. D. Ronaldson, "Treatment of Opium and Alcohol Habitues," *Dunglison's College and Clinical Record* 5 (1884): 190–92; and Curran Pope, "The Treatment of the Morphine Habit," *Cincinnati Lancet-Clinic*, n.s. 53 (December 3, 1904), p. 568.

18. J. B. Mattison, *The Treatment of Opium Addiction* (New York: G. P. Putnam's Sons, 1885), p. 2; and the same author's "Morphinism in the Young," *Atlantic Medical Weekly* 5 (March 14, 1896): 165–67.

19. J. B. Mattison, "The Curability of Opium Addiction," *Quarterly Journal of Inebriety*, 5 (October 1883): 257.

20. Eberle, *A Treatise of the Materia Medica*, 2:11.

21. Williams, *Opiate Addiction*, p. 6.

22. James Coulter Layard, "Morphine," *Atlantic Monthly* 33 (June 1874): 709–710; Kane, *Drugs That Enslave*, p. 19; Cobbe, *Doctor Judas*, pp. 204–205; R. C. Cabot, "Pain Allaying Drugs as Used and Abused," *Good Housekeeping* 53 (July 1911): 57–60; Ernest S. Bishop, "The Narcotic Addict, the Physician and the Law," *Medical Times* 44 (May 1916): 145–50; Pettey, *Narcotic Drug Diseases*, p. 6.

23. Charles B. Towns, "Drugs and the Drug User," *Survey* 37 (October 14, 1916): 47–49.

24. *Opium Eating: An Autobiographical Sketch*, pp. 64–65, 118.

25. Ludlow, "What Shall They Do to be Saved?" pp. 377–87.

26. Frank McRae, "The Opium Habit," *St. Louis Courier of Medicine* 9 (April 1883): 319–22.

27. J. B. Mattison, "The Modern and Humane Treatment of the Morphine Disease," *Medical Record* 44 (December 23, 1893): 804–806 is a convenient summary of the basic approaches.

28. J. C. Wilson, "The Morphia Habit," *College and Clinical Record* 9 (May 1888): 107.

29. The English edition of Levinstein's book is *Morbid Craving for Morphia* (London: Smith, Elder, 1878); see also "The Sudden Checking of Opium Eating," *Medical and Surgical Reporter* 36 (January 6, 1877): 17; W. O'Daniel, "Cure of Opium Habit," *Atlanta Medical and Surgical Journal* 16 (February 1879): 643–44.

30. J. B. Mattison, "Successful Management of an Opium Habit," *Medical Record* 10 (April 3, 1875): 249–51.

31. JCL [James Coulter Layard] to Editor, New York *Times*, September 27, 1878.

32. Hughes, "The Experiences of an Opium Eater During the Withdrawal of the Drug," pp. 26–35; and Stephen Lett, "The Opium Habit and Its Treatment," *Canadian Practitioner* 9 (October 1884): 301–307.

33. J. B. Mattison, "A Personal Narrative of Opium Addiction," *Medical Gazette* 10 (July 7, 1883): 316; Morton, "An Experience With Opium," pp. 334–39. The notion of punishing addicts with withdrawal had a long life; for an example of that view, which the author changed, in the 1930s, see Hawkins, *Opium and Opium Addicts*, pp. 36–37.

34. For an early recommendation of gradualism, see Wood, *A Treatise on Therapeutics*, 1:735. See also "The Morphine Habit and Its Treatment," *Cincinnati Lancet-Clinic*, n.s. 9 (July 22, 1882): 109; E. W. Mitchell, "Treatment of Morphia Mania," ibid., n.s. 27 (December 12, 1891), pp. 759–62; McRae, "The Opium Habit," pp. 319–23; John S. Marshall, "The Opium Habit," *Medical and Surgical Reporter* 51 (December 13, 1884): 695; I. A. Loveland, "Opium Habit," *Medical Brief* 14 (May 1886): 225; "What is the Proper Treatment of Morphino-Mania?" *Southern California Practitioner* 3 (January 1888): 19; Editorial, "On The Treatment of the Morphine Habit," *Medical Age* 7 (April 10, 1889): 157.

35. "Coca in the Opium Habit," *Louisville Medical News* 9 (June 12, 1880): 290. See also J. G. Core, "The Coca in Opium-Habit," ibid., 10 (July 3, 1880): 2; J. D. Irwin, "A Case of the Opium Habit Treated With Coca," *St. Louis Clinical Record* 7 (October 1880): 199–200; A. N. Read, "Morphinism and Alcoholism Treated With Cocaine," *Gaillard's Medical Journal* 42 (April 1886): 369; E. C. Mann, "On the Use of Cocaine in the Opium Habit," *Alienist and Neurologist* 7 (January 1886): 51–57; "Cocaine in the Morphine Habit," *American Practitioner* 32 (December 1885): 378; "Cocaine in the Opium Habit," *An Ephemeris of Materia Medica, Pharmacy, Therapeutics and Collateral Information* 2 (March 1885): 763–64, the Squibb drug company publication; Albrecht Erlenmeyer, *On the Treatment of the Morphine Habit* (Detroit: G. S. Davis, 1889), p. xiii; F. A. Overall, "Cocaine in Alcohol and Opium Habit," *Medical Summary* 13 (August 1891): 147–48, and ibid., 13 (November 1891): 231–32.

36. J. B. Mattison, "Chloral Inebriety," *Proceedings of the Medical Society of the County of Kings* 4 (April 15, 1879): 75; Pope, "The Treatment of the Morphine Habit," p. 571; John M. White, "Opium Habit," *Medical and Surgical Reporter* 46 (January 14, 1882): 53–54; "Cannabis Indica in the Opium Habit," *Medical News* 46 (April 4, 1885): 376. For use of cannabis in treating opiate addiction at later dates, see: John A. Snowden, "Home Treatment and Cure of Opium and Morphine Addicts," *Kentucky Medical Journal* 15 (March 1, 1917): 127, and "Marihuana Found Useful in Certain Mental Ills," *Science News Letter* 41 (May 30, 1942): 341–42.

37. E. H. M. Sell, "The Opium Habit: Its Successful Treatment by the *Avena sativa*," *Medical Gazette* 9 (April 22, 1882): 186–90; J. W. Putnam, "A Case of Opium Habit," *Buffalo Medical and Surgical Journal* 23 (December 1883): 223–25; J. B. Mattison, "*Avena sativa* in the Treatment of Opium Addiction," *Medical Bulletin* 7 (October 1885): 308–314; "Scotch Oats Essence," *Medical World* 6 (June 1888): 236.

38. "A New Remedy for the Opium Habit," *Medical Age* 16 (May 25, 1898): 304; W. W. Winthrop, "Further Particulars Concerning the Plant Husa as a Cure for the Opium Habit," *New York Medical Journal* 67 (June 25, 1898): 906–907.

39. W. H. Lindenburger, "Treatment of the Opium Habit by Codeine," *Medical News* 42 (August 22, 1885): 219.

40. "Hypnotism and the Treatment of the Morphin Habit," *American Medicine* 3 (May 31, 1902): 922.

41. Ernest S. Bishop, "Some Fundamental Considerations of the Problem of Drug Addiction," *American Medicine* 21 (November 1915): 807–815.

42. James Johnston, "Treatment of the Morphine Habit," *Daniels' Texas Medical Journal* 7 (March 1892): 321–24.

43. William F. Waugh, "The Morphine Habit—Home Treatment," *Medical Brief* 23 (October 1895): 1185. See also Day, *The Opium Habit*, p. 285; New York *Times*, January 6, 1878; Crothers, *Morphinism and Narcomanias*, pp. 141ff, 192; Charles J. Douglas, "Cocainism," *Medical News* 85 (July 16, 1904): 116; *Bulletin of Pharmacy* 18 (April 1904): 174; Pettey, *Narcotic Drug Diseases*, p. 140. Of course, there were critics of the emerging sanitarium system, who either believed that the treatments involved were ineffective, however well intentioned, or that sanitarium proprietors simply created a market they could satisfy. Opponents of the disease theory also objected to yet another medical subspecialty. For typical comments along this line see N. E. Brill, "Ethics of Opium Habitues," *Medical and Surgical Reporter* 59 (September 29, 1888): 414, and Charles W. Earle, "The Responsibilities and Duties of the Medical Profession Regarding Alcoholic and Opium Inebriety," Illinois Medical Society, *Transactions* 39 (1889): 56–74.

44. "The Opium Habit," *Medical and Surgical Reporter* 25 (September 9, 1871): 242; Mattison, "Opium Intoxication," pp. 3–4; New York *Times*, September 27, 1878, T. S. Bell, "The Opium Cure," *Louisville Medical News* 11 (January 29, 1881): 56; Hughes, "Experiences of an Opium Eater During the Withdrawal of the Drug," pp. 26–35; Crothers, *Drug Habits and Their Treatment*, p. 5; A. J. Pressey, "Static-Electricity in the Treatment of Morphinism," *Quarterly Journal of Inebriety* 25 (April 1903): 151–55; D. M. L. Newbury, "A New Method of Treating the Drug Habit," *California Medical and Surgical Reporter* 3 (April 1907): 178–79; W. S. Robinson, "A Few Suggestions on How to Cure the Drug Habit," *Oklahoma Medical News-Journal* 18 (April 1910): 101–102.

45. "The Opium Habit," *Medical and Surgical Reporter* 25 (September 2, 1871): 242; Stanford E. Chaille, "The Opium Habit and 'Opium-Mania Cures,'" *New Orleans Medical and Surgical Journal*, n.s. 3 (May 1876), pp. 767–75; J. B. Mattison, "Clinical Notes on Opium Addiction," *Proceedings of the Medical Society of the County of Kings* 7 (February 1883): 256–62, and his "The Curability of Opium Addiction," ibid., 8 (July 1883): 119–24; J. D. Griffith, "The Opium Habit," *Medical and Surgical Reporter* 51 (December 15, 1884): 569; C. C. Stockard, "A Few Points in the Treatment of Morphinism," *Atlanta Medical and Surgical Journal*, n.s. 13 (September 1896), pp. 444–45.

46. Cole, *Confessions of an American Opium Eater*, pp. 107ff; Cobbe, *Doctor Judas*, p. 157.

47. Calkins, *Opium and the Opium Appetite*, pp. 237, 248 notes the new asylums. George F. Foote, *Inebriety and Opium Eating: In Both Cases a Disease* (Portland, Maine: Tucker, 1877), is an interesting early pamphlet from some kind of cure doctor, who says that he began treating inebriates without restraints and in pastoral terms in 1848. There is a typical picture of a sanitarium and an advertisement for its procedures in *Quarterly Journal of Inebriety* 2 (September 1878), advertising section, pp. 12–14. L. F. Kebler, *Habit Forming Agents*, U. S. Department of Agriculture, Bulletin 393 (Washington: GPO, 1910), p. 3, notes the number of sanitaria. Arnold Jaffe, "Addiction Reform in

the Progressive Era: Scientific and Social Responses to Drug Dependence in the United States, 1870–1930," (Ph.D. diss., University of Kentucky, 1976), also contains much helpful information on sanitaria and the development of the disease theory of addiction.

48. New York *Times*, March 28, 1904.

49. J. H. Kellogg, "A New and Successful Method of Treatment for the Opium Habit and Other Forms of Drug Addiction," *Modern Medicine and Bacteriological Review* 7 (June 1898): 125–32, and ibid., 7 (July 1898): 151–57, and his "The Treatment of Drug Addiction," *Quarterly Journal of Inebriety* 25 (January 1903): 30–43.

50. Keeley gave some biographical information in his publications, which include *The Opium Habit: Its Proper Method of Treatment and Cure Without Suffering and Inconvenience* (Dwight: Keeley Co., 1880); *An Essay Upon the Morphine and Opium Habit* (Dwight: Keeley Co., 1882); *A Popular Treatise on Drunkenness and the Opium Habit and Their Successful Treatment With Double Chloride of Gold, the Only Cure* (Dwight: Keeley Co., 1890); "My Gold Cure," *North American Review* 153 (December 1891): 759–61; "Inebriety and Insanity," *Arena* 8 (August 1893): 328–37; *Drunkenness and Heredity and the Inebriety of Childhood* (Chicago: Banner of Gold, 1893); *The Non-Heredity of Inebriety* (Chicago: S. C. Griggs, 1896); and two pamphlets in the National Library of Medicine, *Drunkenness, a Curable Disease* (n.p., n.d.), and *Inebriety is a Disease* (n.p., n.d.). Similar information is in The Keeley League, *Report of the Proceedings of the Second General Convention Held at Dwight, Illinois, September 13, 14, 15, 1892* (Pittsburgh: J. M. Kelly, 1892), p. 342. The Chicago *Tribune* obituary notice of February 22, 1900, presumably reflecting a long acquaintance with Keeley and his friends, repeats familiar information. So does "The Author of 'Gold-Cure' Treatment Dead," *Medical Record* 57 (March 3, 1900): 372. The basic reference biography is in the *Dictionary of American Biography*, 1963 edition, 5, pt. 1, pp. 280–81. Fred B. Hargreaves, *Gold as a Cure for Drunkenness: Being an Account of the Double Chloride of Gold Discovery Recently Made by Dr. L. E. Keeley, of Dwight, Ills.* (n.p., n.d.), a pamphlet in the National Library of Medicine, is by an early associate of Keeley's. who later broke with him, and contains some biographical material. The sketch of Keeley, which friends or family presumably checked and paid for in *National Cyclopedia of American Biography* (New York: James T. White and Co., 1936), 25:335–36, diverges from the biographical information Keeley gave about himself and which was current in his lifetime. It has him born in Kings Co., Ireland, the son of a soldier, May 4, 1832, and being taken to Quebec as an infant before going to Beardstown. The facts of his early life seem impossible to verify at this late date.

51. The quotation is from the deposition of Frederick B. Hargreaves, in the manuscript records of "Leslie E. Keeley Co. vs. The Memphis Keeley Institute," Equity No. 623, U.S. Circuit Court, Western Division, Western District of Tennessee (1906), cited hereafter as Keeley Case. Numerous depositions in this case refer to Keeley's background and work. Hargreaves was among Keeley's early associates. In this deposition he left the strong impression that Keeley was a fraud and that the Bichloride of Gold remedy contained no gold and was similar to many nostrums of the time. He was, however, clearly a vengeful witness, as the court noted in its judgment, even though it agreed with some of his views. Keeley, of course, was dead when the case came to trial. Hargreaves'

own life said volumes about drug treatment history, whatever the facts of the matter. He started life as a preacher in the Wesleyan Methodist Church in England, then became a Presbyterian minister in the United States. He practiced law, was a temperance lecturer, and in 1904 at the time of the deposition was a salesman for a bankrupt book publisher. When he left Keeley he started a regimen styled "Dipsocura," and a "Hargreaves Cure" in Chicago. The Chicago *Tribune*, August 13, 1891, has more information on him. As so often in the Keeley story, it is impossible to know when Hargreaves is truthful or merely vengeful. He claimed to know the formula of Bichloride of Gold, but refused categorically to reveal its contents, saying it would break faith with Keeley's memory, even though his testimony against Keeley in this case was exceedingly harsh.

52. Chicago *Tribune*, February 22, 1900.

53. Ibid.; deposition of E. B., and J. S., Keeley Case. Keeley Co. to O. K. T., March 31, 1914, Letterbook 77, p. 31, Leslie E. Keeley Collection, Illinois State Historical Library, Springfield, returns part of a fee in a case they found incurable.

54. The basic obituary articles are in the Chicago *Tribune*, February 22, 1900, and Los Angeles *Times*, February 22, 1900.

55. Keeley, *Drunkenness and Heredity*, pp. 4–5; and his *Popular Treatise*, p. 6; and his speech in Keeley League, *Proceedings . . . 1892*, pp. 29–37.

56. Keeley, "Inebriety and Insanity," p. 336. See also his *Drunkenness and Heredity*, p. 7, and the report of his speech to a huge and enthusiastic Chicago audience in Chicago *Tribune*, December 18, 1891. Keeley Co. to G. A. S., March 6, 1914, Letterbook 77, p. 3, Keeley Collection, is typical of the organization's later view that addiction involved psychology and was characteristic of weak personalities.

57. Keeley, *Popular Treatise*, p. 103. This work is dated April 20, 1880. Hargreaves deposition, Keeley Case repeats similar stories about the origins of Keeley's interest in inebriety.

58. Keeley, *Inebriety as a Disease*, pp. 5–6, says he canvassed the profession about gold. The Chicago *Tribune*, February 22, 1900, repeats the story of his experimenting with gold preparations on local alcoholics, as does the Hargreaves deposition, Keeley Case. The book *The Morphine Eater: or, From Bondage to Freedom* (Dwight: C. L. Palmer Co., 1881), bears Keeley's name as author, but is clearly a cooperative work with others, and mentions the substances useful in drug treatment. The deposition of C. R., Keeley Case, recounts seeing the mixture made about 1882.

59. Dwight was founded in 1854, the Keeley Institute there dated from 1879, and the Keeley Company was formed in 1880, according to J. H. Oughton, Jr., in an interview with the author, May 17, 1977. Hargreaves, *Gold as a Cure For Drunkenness*, p. 4, contains a letter dated 1880, referring to Keeley's experience of about fifteen years in studying inebriety. The deposition of John R. Oughton, Keeley Case, says he had no part in discovering the formula, which Keeley had made when he started working with him in 1880. Keeley Co. to G. C. H., March 4, 1914, Letterbook 77, p. 2, Keeley Collection refers to their "thirty-four years experience" with opiate addiction. The Dwight *Star and Herald*, September 29, 1939, has a general account of the Keeley Institute and partners.

60. Hargreaves deposition, Keeley Case. Hargreaves, *Gold as a Cure for Drunkenness*, describes how the bottle developed. Keeley, *Popular Treatise*, front and back covers, list costs and instructions. The folders in the Keeley Collection relating to patents, copyrights, and trademarks contain no information on the formula.

61. For early summaries on gold see: Henry Hollenbaek, "Chloride of Gold," *Eclectic Medical Journal of Pennsylvania* 3 (March–April 1865): 37–38; "Gold," ibid., 5 (September–October 1867): 228–29; Dr. Reed, "The Chloride of Gold," ibid., 6 (November 1868): 519; James I. Watson, "Gold as A Curative Agent in the Treatment of Diseases," *Medical Tribune* 3 (June 1881): 241–44.

62. "Gold," *Eclectic Medical Journal of Pennsylvania* 5 (September–October 1867): 228–29.

63. J. C. Burnett, *Gold as a Remedy in Disease* (London: Homeopathic Pub. Co., 1879), pp. 37, 48–50.

64. E. A. Wood, "Gold in Therapy," *New York Journal of Medicine* 58 (October 14, 1893): 435–37. Keeley's activities generated new interest in gold. See "Chloride of Gold," *Chicago Medical Times* 25 (April 1893): 147; E. Chancellor, "Two Years' Clinical Experiments With the Gold Solution," *New England Medical Monthly* 15 (October 1896): 455–62; W. H. Walling, "The Therapeutics of Gold and Combinations," *Medical and Surgical Reporter* 76 (February 13, 1897): 198–99; Daniel R. Brower, "Some Observations on the Auri et Sodii Chloridum U.S.P.," *JAMA* 31 (October 1, 1898): 754–55; Daniel R. Brower and Carl John Habhegger, "Further Observations on the Therapeutics of Gold and Sodium," ibid., 33 (November 25, 1899): 1334–37; J. P. Sheridan, "Gold in the Treatment of Anemia and Malnutrition," *New York Medical Journal* 69 (May 6, 1899): 634–35.

65. Keeley outlined the home reduction program, of which gold was only a part, in *The Morphine Eater*, pp. 128–41; *An Essay Upon the Morphine and Opium Habit*, pp. 13–15; and Chicago *Tribune*, December 19, 1891. John R. Oughton deposition, Keeley Case, says that as of 1904 they seldom used the home cure. Keeley Co. to H. W. M., March 9, 1914, Letterbook vol. 77, p. 7, Keeley Collection, says they still get letters asking for the old gold home remedy but have not sent it out in some time.

66. J. H. Oughton, Jr. interview with author, May 17, 1977; Mate Palmer, "Women and Narcotics," *Banner of Gold* 1 (March 5, 1892): 35–36; Keeley Co. to G. A. S., March 6, 1914, Letterbook vol. 77, p. 3, Keeley Collection.

67. Keeley, *Inebriety as a Disease*, pp. 10–11; Hargreaves deposition, and C. R. deposition, Keeley Case.

68. "Dr. Keeley and His Work," *Banner of Gold* 15 (March 1900): 37.

69. Chicago *Tribune*, June 4, 1891.

70. H. M. Bannister, "The Bichloride of Gold Cure for Inebriety," *American Journal of Insanity* 48 (April 1892): 470–75; and Henry Wood, "Does Bi-Chloride of Gold Cure Inebriety?" *Arena* 7 (January 1893): 149.

71. Richard Dewey, "Insanity Following the Keeley Treatment," *International Medical Magazine* (Philadelphia) 1 (December 1892): 1148.

72. C. S. Clark, *The Perfect Keeley Cure: Incidents at Dwight, and 'Through the Valley of the Shadow' Into the Perfect Light* (Chicago: n.p., 1898), p. 93.

73. W. A. S. B. deposition, Keeley Case. See also Chicago *Tribune*, February 18, December 19, 1891; Albert E. Hyde, "The Science of Inebriety," *Banner of Gold* 2 (August 20, 1892): 428–31; C. L. Hudgins, "A Physician's Experience," ibid., 14 (April 1899): 56–57.

74. Folder marked "Miscellaneous," Box 3, Keeley Collection.

75. Keeley, *Drunkenness and Inebriety*, pp. 13–16.

76. "History of the Bichloride of Gold Club," *Banner of Gold* 1 (February 10, 1892): 1–2. See also George A. Barclay, "The Keeley League," *Journal of the Illinois State Historical Society* 57 (Winter 1964): 341–65. Keeley, *Inebriety as a Disease*, pp. 18–19, has the story and a picture of the Keeley Baby.

77. F. F. Porter, "The Keeley Cure," *Memphis Medical Monthly* 13 (September 1893): 395; and F. E. Daniel, "The So-Called Bi-Chloride Treatment—Its Relation to the Medical Profession and to the People," *Texas Sanitarian* 2 (July 1893): 370.

78. Chicago *Tribune*, December 29, 1891; "Dr. Keeley and His Work," *Banner of Gold* 15 (March 1900): 37; depositions of E. D. and C. R., Keeley Case. Chauncey F. Chapman, "The Bichloride of Gold Treatment of Dipsomania," *Chicago Medical Recorder* 4 (February 1893): 104–111 is the highly critical account of one who posed as a staff member at an unnamed Keeley Institute in order to discredit the treatment. MacMartin, *Thirty Years in Hell*, pp. 122–24 recounts his failure to cooperate with the program at the Denver Institute. F. H. M. to Keeley Institute, Dwight, February 17, 814 (*sic*) in folder marked "Miscellaneous, 1899–1918," Keeley Collection, is a disgruntled patient's story of bad conditions and indifferent treatment at the Council Bluffs, Iowa, Institute. The muckraker Samuel Hopkins Adams, in *The Great American Fraud*, p. 121, thought the Keeley program, "which formerly made the most extravagant claims, is now conducted on a much sounder basis," though he thought claims of an 80 percent cure rate were absurd.

79. Chicago *Tribune*, February 23, 1920; Chicago *American*, May 7, 1967; Interview of J. H. Oughton, Jr., with the author, May 17, 1977.

80. See Keeley's interviews in Chicago *Tribune*, October 18, November 5, December 19, 1891.

81. Ibid., December 29, 1891.

82. "Dr. Keeley and His Work," *Banner of Gold* 15 (March 1900): 37.

83. Chicago *Tribune*, December 29, 1891.

84. Wood, "Does Bi-Chloride of Gold Cure Insanity?" p. 147. In his deposition, Keeley Case, John R. Oughton refused to reveal the formula and insisted that it was not written down. He alleged that Keeley repeated it to him orally. Opposing counsel held that it was written down and in a safe deposit box in Chicago, which Oughton denied. The deposition of one Dr. William Krauss in Keeley Case concerning composition of the formula is typical of the imprecision that dominated the entire debate about Keeley. This expert testimony in a federal court case is handwritten and illegible in places, but agrees with most other assays in finding substances such as strychnine, hyoscine, and pilocarpine that acted either as tonics or tranquilizers.

85. Chapman, "The Bichloride of Gold Treatment of Dipsomania," includes his assay of the formula.

86. See Keeley's articles and letters, "The Bichloride of Gold Treatment of

Dipsomania," *Chicago Medical Recorder* 4 (June 1893): 413; "Dr. Keeley and His Cure," *New Orleans Medical and Surgical Journal*, n.s. 21 (July 1893), p. 55; "Inebriety and Insanity," p. 329.

87. Chauncey F. Chapman, "Reply to Dr. Keeley," *Chicago Medical Recorder* 4 (June 1893): 415.

88. For various reactions see Thomas D. Crothers, "The Chloride of Gold Cure for Inebriety," *Medical Record* 40 (November 14, 1891): 613–14; Dewey, "Insanity Following the Keeley Treatment," p. 1148; "Editorial: Keeley's Cure," *New Orleans Medical and Surgical Journal*, n.s. 20 (April 1893), pp. 749–52; B. D. Evans, "Keeleyism and Keeley Methods, with Some Statistics," *Medical News* 62 (May 6, 1893): 477–85; J. W. Robertson, "The Keeley Cure of Alcoholism," Medical Society of the State of California, *Transactions* 23 (1893): 194–204; Thomas D. Crothers, "Gold Cures in Inebriety," *JAMA* 31 (October 1, 1898): 756.

89. See David Musto, "The American Anti-narcotic Movement: Clinical Research and Public Policy," *Clinical Research* 19 (1971): 601–605.

90. C. L. Seeger, "Opium Eating," *Boston Medical and Surgical Journal* 9 (October 2, 1833): 117–20.

91. William F. Waugh, "The Morphine Habit—Home Treatment," *Medical Brief* 23 (October 1895): 1187; and J. Thomas Wright, "Drug Using: Morphine Habituation," *Alkaloidal Clinic* 11 (January 1904): 32–40; G. F. Butler, "Treatment of the Opium Habit," *Illinois Medical Journal* 10 (November 1906): 474–80; C. W. Carter, "What Is the Morphine Disease?" *Journal of Inebriety* 30 (Spring 1908): 28–33.

92. George E. Pettey, "The Pathology of Morphinism," *Memphis Medical Monthly* 33 (February 1913): 53–60. Pettey wrote many other articles but summarized his views in *The Narcotic Drug Diseases and Allied Ailments* (Philadephia: F. A. Davis, 1913).

93. Pettey, *Narcotic Drug Diseases*, p. 6.

94. Ernest S. Bishop, "An Analysis of Narcotic Drug Addiction," *New York Medical Journal* 101 (February 27, 1915): 399; and his "Morphinism and Its Treatment," *JAMA* 58 (May 18, 1912): 1499–504, and *Narcotic Drug Problems*, p. 42.

95. Christian F. J. Laase, "Practical Application of the Facts of Narcotic Drug Addiction Disease," *Medical Record* 96 (August 9, 1919): 227.

96. David F. Musto, "Social and Political Influences on Addiction Research," in Seymour Fisher and Alfred M. Freedman, eds., *Opiate Addiction: Origins and Treatment* (New York: John Wiley and Sons, 1974).

97. A. J. Pressy, "Morphinism and Its Treatment," *Cleveland Journal of Medicine* 4 (January 1899): 20–25, 54; Crothers, *Morphinism and Narcomanias*, p. 138; Pettey, *Narcotic Drug Diseases*, pp. 275–76; R. E. Bering, "The Rational Treatment of Morphin Habituation," *Northwest Medicine* 5 (September 1913): 244; Bishop, *Narcotic Drug Problem*, p. 16; Williams, *Opiate Addiction*, pp. 3–4, 9.

98. A. J. Pressy, "Suggestions for Lessening the Frequency of Relapse After Treatment of Morphinism," *American Medicine* 1 (June 15, 1901): 498; J. Inglis, "Morphinism," *Denver Medical Times* 22 (February 1903): 391–95; Samuel Bell, "The Rational Treatment of the Opium Habit," *Detroit Medical Journal* 3

(August 1903): 147–49; R. V. Pearce, "How the Morphine Habit is Cured," *Medical Era* 15 (February 1906): 151–54; W. F. Waugh, "After the Morphine is Stopped," *Medical Standards* 30 (February 1907): 68; W. S. Robinson, "Drug Addiction and Its Treatment," *Memphis Medical Monthly* 29 (February 1909): 77–79; R. C. Cabot, "The Towns-Lambert Treatment for Morphinism and Alcoholism," *Boston Medical and Surgical Journal* 164 (May 11, 1911): 676–77; C. F. Hunter, "The Reclamation of Drug Addicts," *Medical Times* 46 (May 1918): 125–27.

99. A. M. Rogers, "Some Observations During Eighteen Years Experience With Drug and Liquor Habitues," *Wisconsin Medical Journal* 12 (July 1913): 40–43.

100. "Opium Eating," *Boston Medical and Surgical Journal* 9 (September 4, 1833): 66–67.

101. *Opium Eating: An Autobiographical Sketch*, p. 65.

102. Pope, "The Treatment of the Morphine Habit," pp. 563–64; and J. W. Robertson, "The Morphine Habit: Its Causation, Treatment, and the Possibility of Its Cure," *Pacific Medical Journal* 40 (May 1897): 270–78.

103. W. Xavier Sudduth, "The Psychology of Narcotism," *JAMA* 27 (October 10, 1896): 798.

6—REGULATION

1. See "Opium and Alcohol—Their Comparative Effects on the System, Described by One Who Experienced Them in His Own Case," *Boston Medical and Surgical Journal* 49 (November 23, 1854): 341–48; Wood, *Treatise on Therapeutics*, 1:732–33; "Use of Opium in This Country," *Medical and Surgical Reporter* 12 (April 15, 1865): 438; Kane, *Opium Smoking in America and China*, pp. 74–75; New York *Times*, November 19, 1882; J. B. Mattison, "The Curability of Opium Addiction," *Quarterly Journal of Inebriety* 5 (October 1883): 254; Hughes, "The Opium Psycho-Neurosis," p. 127; John W. Robertson, "The Morphin Habit: Its Treatment and the Possibility of Its Cure," *Medical News* 73 (August 27, 1898): 258.

2. "Effects of Opium Eating," *Western Journal of Medical and Physical Sciences* 5 (January, February, March 1832): 628.

3. Walter Colton, "Turkish Sketches: Effects of Opium," *Knickerbocker* 7 (April 1836): 421.

4. "The Opium Habit," *Toledo Medical and Surgical Journal* 4 (March 1880): 99–100; and Calkins, "Opium and Its Victims," pp. 35–36; Oliver, "The Use and Abuse of Opium," p. 169; Joseph Parrish, "Opium Intoxication," *Medical and Surgical Reporter* 39 (November 22, 1873): 363; Nolan, "The Opium Habit," p. 828.

5. New York *Times*, January 6, 1878; and Calkins, *Opium and the Opium Appetite*, pp. 277–78; Kane, *Opium and the Opium Appetite*, pp. 153–54; Hubbard, *The Opium Habit and Alcoholism*, p. 3; New York *Tribune*, April 13, 1890; Cole, *Confessions of an American Opium Eater*, pp. 187–88.

6. New York *Tribune*, October 8, 1893.

7. L. B. Edwards, "Opium Habit," *Virginia Medical Monthly* 4 (March 1878): 882; J. R. Black, "Advantages of Substituting the Morphia Habit for the Uncurably Alcoholic," *Cincinnati Lancet-Clinic,* n.s. 22 (May 11, 1889), pp. 537–41; Lathrop, "Sorcery of the Madjoon," p. 421; Brecher, *Licit and Illicit Drugs,* p. 9; Van Slyke, *The Wail of an Addict,* p. 29.

8. "Use of Opium in the United States," *Boston Medical and Surgical Journal* 72 (July 6, 1865): 476; Calkins, *Opium and the Opium Appetite,* pp. 278–85; New York *Tribune,* December 26, 1878; "Opium Mania," *Quarterly Journal of Inebriety* 3 (December 1878): 49; Hubbard, *The Opium Habit and Alcoholism,* p. 6; Nolan, "The Opium Habit," p. 832; "Editorial: On the Treatment of the Morphine Habit," *Medical Age* 7 (April 10, 1889): 157–58; Erlenmeyer, *On the Treatment of the Morphine Habit,* p. xii; Wilson, "The Indiscriminate Use of Opium," pp. 9–13; Cobbe, *Doctor Judas,* p. 50; Happel, "The Opium Curse, p. 727; Hynson, "Report of the Committee on the Acquirement of the Drug Habit," pp. 552–53; New York *Times,* April 13, 1919; C. B. Pearson, "The Psychology of Morphinism," *Medical Review of Reviews* 26 (May 1920): 260.

9. Cobbe, *Doctor Judas,* pp. 47–48, 176–77; see also New York *Tribune,* April 13, 1890; C. B. Pearson, "Has There Been an Increase of Suicide Among the Opium Addicts Since the Passage of the Harrison Act, and if so, Why?" *Alienist and Neurologist* 36 (November 1915): 349–56.

10. As late as 1931, a New Orleans physician concerned about marihuana use repeated this view: "The dominant race and most enlightened countries are alcoholic, whilst the races and nations addicted to hemp and opium, some of which once attained to great heights of culture and civilization, have deteriorated both mentally and physically." See A. Fossier, "The Marihuana Menace," *New Orleans Medical and Surgical Journal* 84 (May 1931): 247–52. The anonymous addict who wrote *Opium Eating: An Autobiographical Sketch,* p. 113, feared that opium would replace alcohol. "It will be a time of general effeminacy, sickness, and misery,—*should it come.*"

11. J. B. Mattison, "Cocainism," *Medical Record* 42 (October 22, 1892): 476; Cobbe, *Doctor Judas,* p. 95; John H. Billings, "A Unique Case of the Cocaine Habit," *Medical Record* 54 (July 30, 1898): 173; Frank F. Hutchins, "The Psychological Aspect of the Drug Habit," *Medical and Surgical Monitor* 8 (May 1905): 131–32; Thomas D. Crothers, "Cocainism," *Medical Record* 77 (April 30, 1910): 744–45; Alexander Lambert, "The Underlying Causes of the Narcotic Habit," *Modern Medicine* 2 (January 1920): 5–9; MacMartin, *Thirty Years in Hell,* p. 108.

12. W. A. Hammond, "Cocaine and the So-called Cocaine Habit," *New York Medical Journal* 44 (December 4, 1886): 638–39; P. Zenner, "The Cocaine Habit," *Cincinnati Lancet-Clinic,* n.s. 24 (January 11, 1890), pp. 35–41; W. F. Waugh, "Cocaine Addiction," *Quarterly Journal of Inebriety* 20 (April 1898): 192–97.

13. Waugh, "Cocaine Addiction," pp. 192–97; Foster Kennedy, "The Effects of Narcotic Drug Addiction," *New York Medical Journal* 100 (July 4, 1914): 21; Wilbert, "The Number and Kind of Drug Addicts," p. 419; Thomas S. Blair, "The Treatment of Narcotic Drug Addiction in Private Practice," *Therapeutic Gazette,* ser. 3, 35 (August 15, 1919): 540; Bishop, *The Narcotic Drug Problem,* p. 115; C. E. Sandoz, "Report on Morphinism to the Municipal Court of Bos-

ton," *Journal of Criminal Law* 13 (May 1922): 10–55; Williams, *Opiate Addiction*, p. 176.

14. Frank W. Ring, "Cocaine and Its Fascinations, From a Personal Experience," *Medical Record* 32 (September 3, 1887): 274–76; Cobbe, *Doctor Judas*, p. 141; Thomas D. Crothers, "Cocaine-Inebriety," *Quarterly Journal of Inebriety* 20 (October 1898): 369–76, and his *Drug Habits and Their Treatment*, p. 81.

15. New York *Times*, January 8, 1907, has a story about cocaine use among young toughs. Hamilton Wright said in an interview, ibid., March 12, 1911, that cocaine was part of the prostitution problem. For its identification with crime and the lower classes see J. Leonard Corning, "The Growing Menace of the Use of Cocaine," ibid., August 2, 1908; William Jay Schieffelin, "Safeguarding the Sale of Narcotics," National Conference of Charities and Correction, *Proceedings* 36 (1909): 208–212; House of Representatives, Ways and Means Committee, 61st Congress, 3rd Session, *Importation and Use of Opium* (Washington: GPO, 1910), p. 14; Edwin W. Knowles, "Narcotic Addiction and Its Treatment," *Colorado Medicine* 8 (August 1911): 287; G. C. Biondi, "A Few Remarks on Cocainism," *American Medicine,* n.s. 6 (September 1911): 465–68; G. D. Swain, "Regarding the Luminal Treatment of Morphine Addiction," *American Journal of Clinical Medicine* 25 (August 1918): 611; A Government Official, "The Government and the Narcotic Drug Problem," *American Medicine* 23 (December 1917): 806–807; Bishop, *The Narcotic Drug Problem,* p. 115; Hutchins Hapgood, *A Victorian in the Modern World* (New York: Harcourt, Brace, 1939), p. 167.

16. Thomas G. Simonton, "The Increase of the Use of Cocaine Among the Laity of Pittsburgh," *Philadelphia Medical Journal* 11 (March 28, 1903): 556; Eberle, "Report of the Committee on the Acquirement of the Drug Habit," p. 477; Harvey W. Wiley, "Soft Drinks and Dopes," *Good Housekeeping* 55 (August 1912): 242–50.

17. W. Scheppegrell, "The Abuse and Dangers of Cocaine," *Quarterly Journal of Inebriety* 20 (October 1898): 367–68.

18. Eberle, "Report of the Committee on the Acquirement of the Drug Habit," p. 480.

19. New York *Times*, March 12, 1911; and Pettey, *The Narcotic Drug Diseases*, p. 426; Towns, "Perils of the Drug Habit," p. 586.

20. Hynson, "Report of the Committee on the Acquirement of the Drug Habit," p. 551; New York *Times*, August 2, 1908; Harvey W. Wiley and A. L. Pierce, "Cocaine Habit," *Good Housekeeping* 58 (March 1914): 393–98.

21. New York *Times*, February 8, 1914; Williams, "Prohibition From the Medical Viewpoint," p. 277; Brown, "Enforcement of the Tennessee Anti-Narcotic Law."

22. New York *Times,* December 6, 1907.

23. Williams, "Prohibition of Cocaine From the Medical Viewpoint," p. 277.

24. Edward Huntington Williams, "The Drug-Habit Menace in the South," *Medical Record* 85 (February 7, 1914): 247–49 is typical.

25. Ways and Means Committee, *Importation and Use of Opium,* pp. 12–13.

26. See *The Oxford English Dictionary, Supplement and Bibliography* (Oxford University Press, 1933), p. 458; Horace Freeland Judson, *Heroin Addiction*

in Britain (New York: Random House, 1975), p. 4; David F. Musto, "Early History of Heroin in the United States," in Peter G. Bourne, ed., *Addiction* (New York: Academic Press, 1974), pp. 175–85.

27. See "[Heroine]," *American Druggist and Pharmaceutical Record* 33 (October 1898): 257; "New Remedies," ibid., 35 (August 10, 1899): 70; "[Preparations of Heroine]," ibid., 35 (July 10, 1899): 11; Wood and Bache, *Dispensatory of the United States*, 18th ed. (1899): 1683; "New Remedies," *Bulletin of Pharmacy* 14 (September 1900): 391.

28. "Incompatibilities of Heroin," *Practical Druggist* 9 (March 1901): 35; "[Heroin]," *Bulletin of Pharmacy* 18 (March 1904): 131, and ibid., 18 (May 1904): 216, and ibid., 18 (August 1904): 391; John Phillips, "The Prevalence of the Heroin Habit," *JAMA* 59 (December 14, 1912): 2146; Towns, "Perils of the Drug Habit," p. 586; Lindesmith, *Opiate Addiction*, pp. 67–68; Ashley, *Heroin*, pp. 5–6.

29. Terry and Pellens, *The Opium Problem*, pp. 76–82.

30. George E. Pettey, "The Heroin Habit Another Curse," *Alabama Medical Journal* 15 (1902–1903): 174–80.

31. Charles E. Atwood, "A Case of the Heroine Habit," *Medical Record* 67 (June 3, 1905): 856–57.

32. C. M. Fauntleroy, "A Case of Morphinism," *New York Medical Journal* 86 (November 16, 1907): 930; "Progress in Pharmacy," *American Journal of Pharmacy* 79 (December 1907): 576; W. C. Rountree, "Opium and Its Bad Effects, Gathered From Ten Years' Experience and Treatment of Its Subjects," *Texas Courier-Record of Medicine* 28 (June 1911): 11–17.

33. Charles F. Stokes, "The Problem of Narcotic Addiction of Today," *Medical Record* 93 (May 4, 1918): 755; Musto, "The Early History of Heroin in the United States," pp. 176–78; Ashley, *Heroin*, p. 6.

34. New York *Times*, December 5, 1913. An army doctor at Fort Strong, Massachusetts, reported the use of heroin among soldiers there, and that heroin use "was not uncommon in Boston among the habitues." See R. M. Blanchard, "Heroin and Soldiers," *Military Surgeon* 33 (August 1913): 140–43.

35. Wiley and Pierce, "The Cocaine Habit," p. 395; see also Courtwright, "Opiate Addiction in America, 1800–1940," pp. 150, 188.

36. *Bulletin of Pharmacy* 28 (August 1914): 394, and ibid., 29 (January 1, 1915): 47.

37. "Heroin Dangers," ibid., 28 (January 1, 1914): 3; Clifford B. Farr, "The Relative Frequency of the Morphine and Heroine Habits," *New York Medical Journal* 101 (May 1, 1915): 894–95.

38. New York *Times*, June 3, 1913, and December 5, 1916; Perry M. Lichtenstein, "Narcotic Addiction," *New York Medical Journal* 100 (November 14, 1914): 962–66; Farr, "The Relative Frequency of the Morphine and Heroin Habits," pp. 894–95; F. F. Kane, "Drugs and Crime," *Journal of Criminal Law* 9 (November 1918): 341–53; Charles F. Stokes, "The Military, Industrial and Public Health Features of Narcotic Addiction," *JAMA* 70 (March 16, 1918): 766–68; Cornelius F. Collins, "The Drug Evil and the Drug Law," New York City, Department of Health, *Monthly Bulletin* 9 (January 1919): 1–24; Sandoz, "Report on Morphinism to the Municipal Court of Boston," p. 20; Graham-Mulhall, *Opium, The Demon Flower*, chaps. 4, 5.

39. See Courtwright, "Opiate Addiction in the United States, 1800–1940," p. 170.

40. Brown, "Enforcement of the Tennessee Anti-Narcotic Law," pp. 323–33; and Pearce Bailey, "The Heroin Habit," *New Republic* 6 (April 22, 1916): 314–16.

41. Stokes, "The Problem of Narcotic Addiction of Today," p. 757.

42. Graham-Mulhall, "Experiences in Narcotic Drug Control in the State of New York," p. 110, and her *Opium, the Demon Flower,* p. 47; see also S. Dana Hubbard, "Some Fallacies Regarding Drug Addiction," *JAMA* 74 (May 22, 1920): 1439; Bishop, *The Narcotic Drug Problem,* p. 17; E. N. LaMotte, *The Ethics of Opium* (New York: Century Co., 1924), pp. 3–5.

43. Alexander Lambert, "Alcohol, Opium, Codeine, Heroin, Morphine, Cocaine," in William Osler, ed., *Modern Medicine: Its Theory and Practice,* 5 vols., 3rd ed. (Philadelphia: Lea and Febiger, 1925), 2:746; and Lawrence Kolb. "Drug Addiction In Its Relation to Crime," *Mental Hygiene* 9 (January 1925): 88; Graham-Mulhall, *Opium, the Demon Flower,* p. 13.

44. Hubbard, "Some Fallacies Regarding Drug Addiction," p. 1439.

45. Cornelius F. Collins, "The Law and the Narcotic Addict," *Long Island Medical Journal* 13 (August 1919): 272; and Eberle, "Report of the Committee on the Acquirement of Drug Habits," p. 488; B. R. Corbus, "Some Factors in the Causation of Drug Habits," *Medical Standard* 27 (January 1904): 14–17; Pettey, *Narcotic Drug Diseases,* p. 319; Lichtenstein, "Narcotic Addiction," p. 965. Jaffe, "Addiction Reform in the Progressive Age," p. 120, shows the peaks of popular writing on drug use as 1911–15, 1919, and 1923–25, as gleaned from a survey of the *Reader's Guide.*

46. Charles H. Brent to William Howard Taft, February 6, 1904, Brent papers, Library of Congress.

47. See Musto, *The American Disease,* pp. 25–28.

48. Hamilton Wright to Charles H. Brent, November 29, 1909, cited in Musto, *The American Disease,* p. 39.

49. For details of Wright's life, see *Dictionary of American Biography* 20:552–53; *National Cyclopedia of American Biography* 22:430–31; and also David F. Musto, "American Reactions to International Narcotic Traffic," *Pharmacy in History* 16 (1974): 115–22.

50. Merck and Co. to Wright, August 7, 1908, filed under New York entries, Box 29, Records of the United States Delegations to the International Opium Commission and Conferences, 1909–1913, Record Group 43, National Archives. The voluminous records of Wright's survey are in boxes 29 and 30 of this collection, filed by state. Wright summarized his findings and opinions on domestic drug use in "Report on the International Opium Commission and Opium Problem as Seen in the United States and Its Possessions," in *Opium Problem: Message From the President of the United States,* Senate Document no. 377, 61st Congress, 2nd Session (Washington: GPO, 1910).

51. Edmond Sharkey, "Case of Poisoning by Opium," *Medical Examiner,* n.s. 2 (May 1846), pp. 316–18, is a strongly worded early demand for such regulation.

52. Cole, *Confessions of an American Opium Eater,* pp. 49–50; Cobbe, *Doctor Judas,* pp. 127–28.

53. "Remarks on the Opium Habit," *Medical and Surgical Reporter* 37 (December 1, 1877): 436–37.

54. New York *Times,* December 30, 1877.

55. Marshall, "The Opium Habit in Michigan," pp. 63–73.

56. T. J. Happel, "The Opium Curse and Its Prevention," *Medical and Surgical Reporter* 72 (May 25, 1895): 730.

57. New York *Times,* March 15, 1911.

58. Martin I. Wilbert and Murray N. Galt, "Digest of Laws and Regulations in Force in the United States Relating to the Possession, Use, Sale, and Manufacture of Poisons and Habit-Forming Drugs," U.S. Public Health Service, *Bulletin,* no. 56 (November 1912), p. 15; and Martin I. Wilbert, "The Need for Greater Uniformity in Laws Relating to the Manufacture, Sale and Use of Poisons and Habit-Forming Drugs," *Journal of the American Pharmaceutical Association* 3 (August 1914): 1168–72. The story of state and local regulation is well told in Musto, *The American Disease,* pp. 91–120.

59. New York *Times,* February 9, 1913.

60. "Cocaine Alley," *American Druggist and Pharmaceutical Record* 37 (December 10, 1900): 337–38, reports the indiscriminate sale of cocaine to southern negroes, and hopes this does not give pharmacists a bad name. "Stop This Vile Traffic!" ibid., 45 (August 22, 1904): 105, makes a similar point about sales to criminal elements in Chicago. Referring to that city, a note in *American Pharmaceutical Association Bulletin* 1 (April 1, 1906), says that only about 5 percent of druggists are dispensing too much cocaine and opiates but wants them stopped to avoid restrictive laws. Hamilton Wright suggested in an interview in the New York *Times,* March 12, 1911, that about 10 percent of druggists were doing shady drug business. Several New York City pharmacists in 1915 condemned the ease with which drugs came into their city from neighboring states, often resulting in public blame against them, and wanted national legislation to stop the traffic; see New York *Times,* January 6, 1915. Hamilton Wright wrote Charles H. Brent, August 22, 1908, that: "Both by letter and by personal experience, I have found that the law against selling opiates is violated by the lower class pharmacists in all our large cities and that smoking opium can be obtained quite readily by white and negro smokers from the Chinese dealers, except in New York, where, under Inspector Russell, Chinatown has been reformed." Brent papers.

61. "Another Opium Conference," *Bulletin of Pharmacy* 23 (August 1909): 357; House of Representatives, Ways and Means Committee, *Importation and Use of Opium* (1910), p. 505; Philander C. Knox to President William Howard Taft, October 2, 1912, copy in Brent papers; "Symposium on the Proposed Harrison Bill," *Journal of the American Pharmaceutical Association* 3 (June 1914): 880–85; *Bulletin of Pharmacy* 29 (April 4, 1915): 167–72.

62. Oscar C. Young, "On the Use of Opiates, Especially Morphine," *Medical News* 80 (January 25, 1902): 154–56. An earlier article, P. C. Remondino, "The Hypodermic Syringe and Our Morphine Habitues," *Medical Sentinel* 4 (January 1896): 4–7, makes the same point: "We have seen the relatives of cases of hopeless cancer, consumption, or of some other soon fatal affection, argue most urgently against the use of morphia hypodermically, *for fear the patient would form the habit,* and that, when the poor suffering patient had at the most only a few days or weeks of painful existence before him."

63. Hamilton Wright to Charles H. Brent, August 22, 1908, Brent papers.

64. Towns, "Perils of the Drug Habit," p. 585.

65. "A New Cocaine Law for the State of New York," *New York Medical Journal* 97 (May 24, 1913): 1093.

66. A. E. Sterne, "When Should the Drug Neurotic be Regarded as Cured?" *Journal of Inebriety* 29 (Autumn 1907): 203–209; Musto, "American Anti-narcotic Movement," pp. 604–605.

67. Wright to Mahlon N. Kline, December 4, 1909, entry 51, box 46, Opium Commission Records; and Wright to William J. Schiefflin, July 8, 1909, entry 51, box 46, ibid.

68. Committee on Ways and Means, 61st Congress, 2nd session, *Importation and Use of Opium, Hearings,* (May 31, 1910) (Washington: GPO).

69. For this story see David T. Courtwright, "Opiate Addiction as a Consequence of the Civil War," *Civil War History* 24 (June 1978): 101–111.

70. L. L. Stanley, "Drug Addictions," *Journal of the American Institute of Criminal Law and Criminology* 10 (May 1919): 62–70; Eberle, "Report of the Committee on the Acquirement of Drug Habits," p. 484.

71. Farr, "The Relative Frequency of the Morphine and Heroine Habits," p. 894; Captain Edgar King, "The Use of Habit-Forming Drugs (Cocaine, Opium and Its Derivatives) by Enlisted Men," *Military Surgeon* 39 (September 1916): 273–81, and ibid., 39 (October 1916): 380–84; "The Problem of the Drug Addict," *American Medicine* 23 (December 1917): 794; G. E. McPherson and J. Cohen, "A Survey of 100 Cases of Drug Addiction Entering Camp Upton via Draft, 1918," *Boston Medical and Surgical Journal* 180 (June 5, 1919): 636–41; Bishop, *The Narcotic Drug Problem,* p. 118; Knopf, "The One Million Drug Addicts in the United States," p. 137; Pearce Bailey, "Nervous and Mental Diseases in United States Troops," *Medical Progress* 36 (September 1920): 193–97; "The Nightmare of Cocaine," *North American Review* 227 (April 1929): 418–22.

72. New York *Times,* April 15, 1915.

73. Ibid., April 16, 1915; and H. A. Sharpe, "Morphinism: Its Treatment at Home; the Harrison Law," *Journal of the Michigan Medical Society* 14 (June 1915): 316–18.

74. The clinic story is told in Terry and Pellens, *The Opium Problem,* pp. 849–76, and in Musto, *The American Disease,* pp. 151–82.

75. For the New York City clinic see New York *Times,* April 10, 1919; Williams, *Opiate Addiction,* pp. xx–xxii; Graham-Mulhall, "Experiences in Narcotic Drug Control in the State of New York," pp. 106–111, and the same author's "After-care for the Narcotic Drug Addict," *Mental Hygiene* 4 (July 1920): 605–610; Royal S. Copeland, "The Narcotic Drug Evil and the New York City Health Department," *American Medicine* 26 (January 1920): 17–23; AMA, Department of Mental Health, *Narcotics Addiction* (New York: AMA, 1963).

76. Clyde Langston Eddy, "One Million Drug Addicts in the United States," *Current History* 18 (July 1923): 637–43 describes the human conditions at the clinic. Alexander Lambert, "The Underlying Causes of the Narcotic Habit," *Modern Medicine* 2 (January 1920): 9, has some photographs of the addicts and facilities. Graham-Mulhall, "Experiences in Narcotic Drug Control in the State of New York," p. 109, describes the events in the adjacent neighborhood.

77. Hubbard, "Some Fallacies Regarding Narcotic Drug Addiction," p. 1441.

78. "Report of the Special Committee on the Narcotic Drug Situation," *JAMA* 74 (May 8, 1920): 1959; and AMA, *Narcotics Addiction*, p. 4.

79. "Mental Sequellae of the Harrison Law," *New York Medical Journal* 102 (May 15, 1915): 1014.

80. See the remarks of an anonymous "honest addict," a prominent New York lawyer who sets himself apart from "the degenerate who has become addicted," in *American Medicine* 23 (December 1917): 808–809.

81. "Editorial," ibid., 21 (November 1915), pp. 799–800. Earlier in the year, Dr. Alexander Lambert apologized for discussing the general drug question, "a subject with which I think most of the profession has grown weary." See his "The Intoxication Impulse," *Medical Record* 87 (February 13, 1915): 253.

82. J. C. Densten, "Drug Addiction and the Harrison Anti-Narcotic Law," *New York Medical Journal* 105 (April 21, 1917): 747.

83. Oscar Dowling, "Observations of the Drug Addict," *New Orleans Medical and Surgical Journal* 72 (October 1919): 192–93.

84. New York *Times*, December 7, 1916; A. Gordon, "The Relation of Legislative Acts to the Problem of Drug Addiction," *Virginia Medical Semi-Monthly* 22 (May 11, 1917): 57–59; "A Government Official," "The Government and the Narcotic Drug Problem," *American Medicine* 23 (December 1917): 804–807.

85. S. H. Rubin, "Drug Addiction and Modern Methods for Its Control," *Boston Medical and Surgical Journal* 175 (November 30, 1916): 792–94; C. Scheffel, "The Victims of Habit Forming Drugs From a Medical-Sociological and Legal Point of View," *Medico-Legal Journal* 35 (March–April 1918): 17–20. Oscar Dowling wrote in "Observations of the Drug Addict," p. 194, that "Even with the enforcement of the Federal Law and those of the several states (including new laws in states which have not yet acted) it will take a generation at least to cure the evil."

7—SOCIETY WITHDRAWS: THE 1920s TO THE 1950s

1. "Drug Addicts in America," *Outlook* 122 (June 25, 1919): 315.

2. See Jaffe, "Addiction Reform in the Progressive Age," p. 165

3. A. C. Prentice, "The Problem of the Narcotic Drug Addict," *JAMA* 76 (June 4, 1921): 1552; Musto, *The American Disease*, pp. 184–85.

4. See Musto, *The American Disease*, pp. 210–15; Rufus King, *The Drug Hang-up: America's Fifty Year Folly* (New York: Norton, 1972), pp. 69–71.

5. The Bureau profited from a great deal of rather breathless journalism on drug smuggling throughout this entire period. For a typical article see George Lee Dowd, "Seek Drug to Save Dope Fiends," *Popular Science* 118 (May 1931): 21–22, 134.

6. S. T. Moore, "Smashing the Dope Rings," *Forum* 85 (June 1931): 379–84.

7. See Harry J. Anslinger to Howland Shaw, (U.S. Embassy in Constantinople), August 28, 1931, and the reports of field agents to Anslinger, from Harry D. Smith (San Francisco), October 17, 1931, Harry V. Williamson (Kansas City), October 19, 1931, and to George Z. Medalie, (New York City District Attorney's Office), October 22, 1931, all in the correspondence files of the Harry J. Anslinger papers, Pennsylvania State University Library.

8. Hughes, "The American Medical Profession and the Narcotics Policy Controversy," pp. 48–52; King, *The Drug Hang-up,* pp. 44–45, and the same author's "The Narcotics Bureau and the Harrison Act: Jailing the Healers and the Sick," *Yale Law Journal* 62 (April 1953): 736–49, and "Narcotic Drug Laws and Enforcement Policies," *Law and Contemporary Problems* 22 (Winter 1957): 113–31; Lindesmith, *Addict and the Law,* pp. 99–134.

9. Bonnie and Whitebread, *The Marihuana Conviction,* pp. 20–21.

10. Mallincrodt Chemical Works (St. Louis), to Ernest Berger (Tampa), November 24, 1933, copy in correspondence files, Anslinger papers.

11. Jaffee, "Addiction Reform in the Progressive Age," p. 93.

12. Carleton Simon to Lawrence Kolb, December 3, 1924; Lawrence Kolb to J. A. French, March 8, 1927; Alexander Lambert to Alma E. Shimer, December 6, 1924, with covering letter to Kolb of December 20, 1924, all in Lawrence Kolb papers, History of Medicine Division, National Library of Medicine, Bethesda, Maryland.

13. New York *Times,* November 9, 1924.

14. Ellen La Motte, *The Ethics of Opium* (New York: Century, 1924), p. 3.

15. Jaffe, "Addiction Reform in the Progressive Age," pp. 255–56.

16. Anslinger to Isaac B. Ball, undated in 1936 correspondence files, Anslinger papers; and Maurice Helbrant, *Narcotic Agent* (New York: Vanguard Press, 1941), p. 4. Quotations from this book by permission of the publisher, Vanguard Press, Inc., Copyright 1941; Copyright © renewed 1969 by Maurice Helbrant.

17. Typical reports on surveillance of suspect doctors are T. W. Middlebrooks to Anslinger, December 12, 1930, and Joseph A. Manning to Anslinger, January 10, 1935, both in correspondence files, Anslinger papers.

18. Lawrence Kolb, "Let's Stop This Narcotics Hysteria!" *Saturday Evening Post* 229 (July 28, 1956): 19, 50–55; see also "Stripping the Medical Profession of Its Powers and Giving Them to a Body of Lawmakers," *Illinois Medical Journal* 49 (June 1926): 447; Williams, *Drug Addicts Are Human Beings,* p. 113; Kolb, *Drug Addiction,* pp. 146–47; King, "Narcotic Drug Laws and Enforcement Policies," pp. 113–31; Hughes, "The American Medical Profession and the Narcotics Policy Controversy," pp. 36–40; Jaffe, "Addiction Reform in the Progressive Age," pp. 134–35.

19. Kolb and DuMez, "The Prevalence and Trend of Drug Addiction in the United States," pp. 1197–98; and Carleton Simon, "Survey of the Narcotic Problem," *JAMA* 82 (March 1, 1924): 675–79; Carleton Simon to Anslinger, November 7, 1939, correspondence files, Anslinger papers.

20. See Terry and Pellens, *The Opium Problem,* pp. 482. There is a rough survey of 1,044 male addicts and 519 female addicts by the New York Narcotic Survey Committee in New York *Times,* August 12, 1929, that confirms the rising median age and lack of young beginning users. Anslinger to George Barton

[November 1930], copy in correspondence files, Anslinger papers, held that "the average age of addiction has increased of late years to 35 years, indicating that very few of the younger generation are being recruited to the unfortunate ranks." Harry D. Smith (Minneapolis) to Anslinger, September 5, 1940, ibid., holds that young users have declined in number since the early 1920s.

21. Terry and Pellens, *The Opium Problem*, pp. 479–81. Anslinger wrote in 1930 that, "It is believed that there is no foundation whatever for certain statements which have been circulated from time to time relative to narcotic drug addiction among school children." Anslinger to George Barton, [November 1930], correspondence files, Anslinger papers.

22. See Lindesmith, *The Addict and the Law*, pp. 99–122, for an analysis of statistics. Helbrant, *Narcotic Agent,* p. 85, believed the number was much higher than reports indicated.

23. Brecher, *Licit and Illicit Drugs,* pp. 128–32.

24. See the correspondence to the Keeley Company from W.E.G. March 19, 1929, R.E.C., December 13, 1930, J.J.B., January 4, 1934, O.L.D., April 11, 1934, and S.B., May 28, 1935, boxes 25–26, Keeley Collection.

25. Helbrant, *Narcotic Agent,* p. 47.

26. Hawkins, *Opium Addicts and Addictions,* pp. 62–63.

27. Walter L. Treadway, "Drug Addiction and Measures For Its Prevention in the United States," *JAMA* 99 (July 30, 1932): 372–79.

28. See folder labeled "Marihuana Users—Musicians, 1933–1937," in Box 8, Anslinger papers. Mrs. Gertrude McCord to Eleanor Roosevelt, January 25, 1937, typed copy unsigned in correspondence files, ibid., asks the first lady's help for the writer's son who was associating with marihuana-using musicians in Kansas City. The resulting report, Herbert S. Forcer, L. W. Gunnison, J. N. Surrell, to T. W. McGeever, acting district supervisor of the Bureau for Kansas City, February 19, 1937, ibid., shows how rapidly and thoroughly the Bureau agents followed up such leads and requests. E. A. Crews to James J. Higgins, copy, ibid., also concerns black musicians in Indianapolis who were using drugs. For the general question of drug use among musicians, see Charles Winick, "Narcotics Addiction and Its Treatment," *Law and Contemporary Problems* 22 (Winter 1957): 15, and the same author's "The Use of Drugs by Jazz Musicians," *Social Problems* 7 (Winter 1959–60): 240–53.

29. New York *Times,* September 14, 1930, reports a raid on opium smokers in a fashionable apartment house, with twenty-five resulting arrests, including twelve women. Ralph H. Oyler to Anslinger, February 13, 1931, correspondence files, Anslinger papers, reports on a Chinese opium den for upper-class people in Detroit. N. S. Yawger, "Marihuana: Our New Addiction," *American Journal of the Medical Sciences* 195 (1938): 351–57 notes the longstanding existence of "tea-pads" and similar operations in nearly every city.

30. Raymond Chandler, *The Lady in the Lake* (New York: Alfred A. Knopf, Inc., 1943), pp. 144–45, by permission of Alfred Knopf, Inc. See also J. A. O'Donnell, "The Rise and Decline of a Sub-Culture," *Social Problems* 15 (Summer 1967): 73–84.

31. Helbrant, *Narcotic Agent,* p. 72.

32. Unsigned to James A. Farley, and Farley to Stephen B. Gibbons, Assistant Secretary of the Treasury, December 19, 1934, in correspondence files,

Anslinger papers. Alfred B. Rollins, *Roosevelt and Howe* (New York: Knopf, 1962), p. 415, notes Roosevelt's harshness toward drug peddlers.

33. Pettey, *Narcotic Drug Diseases,* pp. 20–21.

34. Charles B. Pearson, "The Psychology of Morphinism and Alcoholism," *Alienist and Neurologist* 39 (January 1918), p. 1.

35. H. S. Cummings, "Control of Drug Addiction Mainly a Police Problem," *American City* 33 (November 1925): 509–513.

36. Charles F. Stokes, "The Problem of Narcotic Addiction of Today," *Medical Record* 93 (May 4, 1918): 757, is a shrewd early assessment of some psychological aspects of the problem: "While the psychoanalysts find homosexuality an underlying factor in addiction, we have noted but few such cases. It has seemed to me more in the nature of a forceful drive that has failed to find expression in proper outlets, has failed to sublimate, a kind of hybrid intoxication impulse that must be gratified." The well-known Dr. Alexander Lambert saw similar processes at work equally early: "In youth it is for the inflation of personality and the endeavor to feel and enjoy life more abundantly. In later years of life it is usually to forget things that one is unwilling to face or cannot face in consciousness, and something must be found to benumb the suffering"; see "The Underlying Causes of the Narcotic Habit," *Journal of the Medical Society of New Jersey* 17 (January 1920): ·1. A decade later, two more authors summarized this emerging view: "Drug addiction is always an evidence of defeat; the patient is unable to master his own problems by accepting them and making the best of them. So in their inability to adjust themselves they feel more 'normal' when using a drug"; see R. B. Richardson and T. H. Weisenburg, "The Indispensable Uses of Narcotics, Psychotherapy as a Substitute for Narcotics," *JAMA* 96 (May 9, 1931): 1574.

37. Williams, *Opiate Addiction,* pp. 56–57.

38. Oscar Dowling, "Three Great National Health Problems," *JAMA* 85 (August 15, 1925): 484–88; and Wholey, "Psychopathologic Phases Observable in Individuals Using Narcotic Drugs in Excess," pp. 721–25; Hughes, "The American Medical Profession and the Narcotics Policy Controversy," pp. 19–20.

39. Lawrence Kolb, "Pleasure and Deterioration from Narcotic Addiction," *Mental Hygiene* 9 (October 1925), pp. 699–724, and the same author's "Types and Characteristics of Drug Addicts," ibid., 9 (April 1925): 300–313, and his book *Drug Addiction,* passim; Musto, *The American Disease,* p. 288, n44; Jaffe, "Addiction Reform in the Progressive Age," pp. 240–45. One of the first students of the subject, the German Edouard Levinstein, held similar views, believing that no normal person would become addicted, especially if the physician administered opiates without explaining their actions and dangers, and did not allow the patient to employ the drugs unsupervised. See Levinstein, "On Morphiomania," *London Medical Record* 4 (February 15, 1876): 55–58.

40. Lawrence Kolb, "Drug Addiction in Its Relation to Crime," *Mental Hygiene* 9 (January 1925): 74–89.

41. Kolb, "Let's Stop This Narcotics Hysteria!" p. 19.

42. J. D. Reichard, "Narcotic Drug Addiction, a Symptom of Human Maladjustment," *Diseases of the Nervous System* 4 (1943): 275–81, and his "Addiction: Some Theoretical Considerations as to the Nature, Cause, Prevention and Treatment," *American Journal of Psychiatry* 103 (May 1947): 721–30.

43. Alfred R. Lindesmith, "The Drug Addict as a Psychopath," *American Sociological Review* 5 (December 1940): 914–20. Lindesmith's views are summarized in his two books, *The Addict and the Law* (Bloomington: Indiana University Press, 1965), and *Opiate Addiction* (Bloomington, Ind.: Principia Press, 1947). For a typical rebuttal of his views see David P. Ausubel, *Drug Addiction: Physiological, Psychological, Sociological Aspects* (New York: Random House, 1958).

44. The quotation is from the typescript autobiography of A. V., "The Drug Problem," May 18, 1939, correspondence files, Anslinger papers.

45. Van Slyke, *The Wail of an Addict*, p. 30.

46. "Confessions of an English Opium-Eater," *North American Review* 18 (January 1824): 91.

47. American Medical Association, Department of Mental Health, *Narcotics Addiction* (New York: AMA, 1963).

48. Anslinger to Isaac B. Ball, undated in 1936 correspondence files, Anslinger papers.

49. Anslinger to Joseph Willicombe, September 29, 1941, ibid.

50. Harry J. Anslinger and William F. Tompkins, *The Traffic in Narcotics* (New York: Funk and Wagnalls, 1953): 186–206.

51. Edward Huntington Williams, "Some Observations on the Narcotic Situation," *Medical Record* 100 (July 23, 1921): 140–43; Cummings, "Control of Drug Addiction Mainly a Police Problem," p. 512.

52. The narcotic facilities deserve a full-scale study. For various aspects of their work see Thomas Parran, "The Problem of Drug Addiction," *Public Health Reports* 53 (December 16, 1938): 2193–97; H. Whitman, "One Up On Narcotics: Addiction Can be Cured," *Collier's* 116 (December 15, 1945): 82, 85–90; S. J. Corey, "A Chaplain Looks at Drug Addiction," *Federal Probation* 15 (September 1951): 17–24; J. A. O'Donnell, "The Lexington Program for Narcotic Addicts," ibid., 26 (March 1962): 55–60; Kolb, *Drug Addiction*, pp. 127–40; Robert W. Rasor, "The United States Public Health Service Institutional Treatment Program for Narcotics Addicts in Lexington, Kentucky," in Brill and Lieberman, *Major Modalities in the Treatment of Drug Abuse*, pp. 3–4; Musto, *The American Disease*, pp. 85, 204–206.

53. Lindesmith, *The Addict and the Law*, pp. 265–66; Louis A. Cancellaro, "New Treatment Concepts at the NIMH Clinical Research Center, Lexington, Kentucky," in Wolfram Keup, ed., *Drug Abuse: Current Concepts and Research* (Springfield, Ill.: Charles C. Thomas, 1972), pp. 355–67; Lewis Yablonsky, *The Tunnel Back* (New York: Macmillan, 1965).

54. Coverage here of the marihuana problem is condensed; for the full story see David Musto, "The Marihuana Tax Act of 1937," *Archives of General Psychiatry* 26 (February 1972): 101–108, and the same author's *The American Disease*, pp. 210–29; and Bonnie and Whitebread, *The Marihuana Conviction*.

55. Henry Corbin Fuller, *The Story of Drugs* (New York: Century, 1922); Marty Sasman, "Cannabis Indica in Pharmaceuticals," *Journal of the Medical Society of New Jersey* 34 (January 1938): 51–52.

56. Wright to Brent, June 9, 1909, Brent papers.

57. New York *Times*, July 30, 1914.

58. "A Year of the Harrison Narcotic Law," *Survey* 36 (April 8, 1916): 58.

59. Fuller, *The Story of Drugs*, p. 220; Thomas S. Blair, "Economic, Social and Political Obstacles in the Way of Meeting the Drug Menace," *American Physician* 26 (November 1921): 886; Robert P. Walton, *Marihuana: America's New Drug Menace* (Philadelphia: Lippincott, 1938), pp. v, 29–30; Bonnie and Whitebread, *The Marihuana Conviction*, pp. 42–44.

60. M. H. Hayes and L. E. Bowery, "Marihuana," *Journal of Criminal Law* 23 (March 1933): 1086–98; New York *Times*, September 16, 1934; John P. Logan, U.S. Marshal, Northern District of Oklahoma to Anslinger, December 18, 1934, copy in folder marked "Marihuana," Box 8, Anslinger papers; and Anslinger's letter to the Editor of *Playboy Magazine*, September 29, 1969, copy ibid.

61. Musto, "The Marihuana Tax Act," p. 104.

62. See R. W. Wilcox, "Habit Forming Drugs and Crime," American Academy of Medicine, Easton, Pa., *Bulletin* 15 (June 1914): 149–55; New York *Times*, September 15, 1935; George Randall McCormack, "What Is Marihuana?" *Hygeia* 15 (October 1937): 898–99; Walton, *Marihuana* 1:25; William D. Armstrong and John Parascandola, "American Concern Over Marihuana in the 1930s," *Pharmacy in History* 14 (1972): 25–35; Bonnie and Whitebread, *The Marihuana Conviction*, pp. 32–40.

63. Earle Albert Rowell and Robert Rowell, *On the Trail of Marihuana, the Weed of Madness* (Mountain View, Calif.: Pacific Press Publishers Assn., 1939), p. 20; Helbrant, *Narcotic Agent*, pp. 34–36.

64. Walter Bromberg, "Marihuana Intoxication," *American Journal of Psychiatry* 91 (September 1934): 303–330; "Facts and Fancies About Marihuana," *Literary Digest* 122 (October 24, 1936): 7–8; Garland Williams (New York City) to Bureau of Narcotics, June 16, 1938, correspondence files, Anslinger papers; J. D. Reichard, "The Marihuana Problem," *JAMA* 125 (June 24, 1944): 594; Walton, *Marihuana*, p. 32.

65. Hugh A. Drum, Acting Secretary of War, to Secretary of War, June 13, 1933, signed cover letter for report, copy in Anslinger papers; J. F. Siler, "Mariajuana Smoking in Panama," *Military Surgeon* 73 (November 1933): 269–80. J.G. to Chief, Bureau of Narcotics, June 30, 1937, and G.A., Jr., to Dear Sir, April 14, 1938, both in correspondence files, Anslinger papers are from former soldiers who smoked marihuana while on duty in the Canal Zone and who thought it dangerous.

66. New York *Times*, September 16, 1934.

67. Ibid., June 6, 1937. The correspondence files for 1936 and 1937, Anslinger papers, have a great deal of material linking marihuana with crime and degeneration. George Randall McCormack, "Marihuana," *Hygeia* 15 (October 1937): 898–99, is typical of reports that saw marihuana as "an Old World drug with a record from crime, brutality and insanity as old as history." Frederick T. Merrill, *Marihuana, the New Dangerous Drug* (Washington: Opium Research Committee, Foreign Policy Association, 1938), is typical of the pamphleteering against marihuana, most of which reflected information and views gained from the Bureau of Narcotics. Rowell, *On The Trail of Marihuana*, p. 33, summarizes all the popular stereotypes about marihuana's effects. See also Armstrong and Parascondola, "American Concern Over Marihuana in the 1930s," pp. 30–31; Barry Charles Wukasch, "Marijuana and the Law: An Analysis of Evolving Federal Drug Policy," (Ph.D. diss., University of Arizona, 1972), p. 50; David F.

Musto, "Social and Political Influences on Addiction Research," in Seymour Fisher and Alfred M. Freedman, eds., *Opiate Addiction: Origins and Treatment* (New York: Wiley, 1974), p. 94.

68. A. Fossier, "The Marihuana Menace," *New Orleans Medical and Surgical Journal* 84 (May 1931): 247–52; "Marihuana Menaces Youth," *Scientific American* 154 (March 1936): 150–51; "Marihuana: New Federal Tax Hits Dealing in Potent Weed," *News-Week* 10 (August 14, 1937): 22; Walton, *Marihuana,* p. 122; "Vice in New York," *Fortune* 20 (July 1939): 60; Roger Adams, "Marihuana," *Bulletin of the New York Academy of Medicine* 18 (November 1942): 723.

69. H. J. Anslinger, "Marihuana, Assassin of Youth," *American Magazine* 124 (July 1937): 18–19, 150–53; S. P. Reznick, "Marihuana Addiction," *Social Work Techniques* 2 (1937): 173–77; "Santa Barbara Police Investigate and Report on Marihuana," *Western City* 25 (May 1938): 19; Rowell, *On the Trail of Marihuana,* p. 28; S. R. Winters, "Marihuana," *Hygeia* 18 (October 1940): 885–87.

70. H. A. Waite, "The Menace of the Drug Traffic," *Michigan Municipal Review* 2 (February 1929): 22–23.

71. Louise Berg, "Drug Addiction in School Children," *Public Health Nursing* 24 (December 1932): 667–70.

72. Stanley Hartnoll Bailey, *The Anti-Drug Campaign: An Experiment in International Control* (London: R. S. King and Son, 1935), p. 8, cites the southwestern United States as a major potential trouble spot in marihuana production and use. William Wolf, "Uncle Sam Fights a New Drug Menace ... Marihuana," *Popular Science Monthly* 128 (May 1936): 14–15, 119–20, is typical of articles that see marihuana use spreading rapidly, as is R. R. Spencer, "Marijuana," *Health Officer* 1 (December 1936): 299–305.

73. H. S. Becker, *Outsiders: Studies in the Sociology of Deviance* (New York: Free Press, 1963), pp. 141–42; Bonnie and Whitebread, *The Marihuana Conviction,* pp. 61–63, 94, 97; Musto, "The Marihuana Tax Act," pp. 104–105; Michael Schaller, "The Federal Prohibition of Marihuana," *Journal of Social History* 4 (Fall 1970): 61–74.

74. "Federal Regulation of the Medicinal Use of Cannabis," *JAMA* 108 (May 1, 1937): 1543–44.

75. See Lester Grinspoon, *Marihuana Reconsidered* (Cambridge: Harvard University Press, 1971), pp. 26–30; Armstrong and Parascandola, "American Concern Over Marihuana in the 1930s," pp. 29–30; Musto, "The Marihuana Tax Act," p. 101; Bonnie and Whitebread, *The Marihuana Conviction,* pp. 164–70.

76. Spencer, "Marihuana," pp. 299–305; Walton, *Marihuana,* p. 39; Rowell, *On the Trail of Marihuana,* p. 66.

77. Bromberg, "Marihuana Intoxication," pp. 303–330.

78. Walter Bromberg, "Marihuana: A Psychiatric Study," *JAMA* 113 (July 1, 1939): 4–12.

79. See for example, Adams, "Marihuana," p. 117; Samuel Allentuck and Karl M. Bowman, "The Psychiatric Aspects of Marihuana Intoxication," *American Journal of Psychiatry* 99 (September 1942): 248–51; Sol Charen and Luis Perleman, "Personality Studies of Marihuana Addicts," ibid., 102 (March 1946): 674–82. J. M. Pholen, "The Marihuana Bugaboo," *Military Surgeon* 93

(1943): 94–95. J. Bouquet, a well-known Tunis physician, friend of Anslinger, and leading figure in the effort for international control, disputed many of these findings and suggested that cannabis use in the Near East remained a major reason for its lack of development, in "Marihuana Intoxication," *JAMA* 124 (April 1, 1944): 1010–11.

80. Anslinger to Dr. Michael V. Ball, Warren, Pa., October 13, 1937, correspondence files, Anslinger papers.

81. Helbrant, *Narcotic Agent,* pp. 316–17.

82. Ibid., p. 318.

83. Copies of memos explaining these plans are in the correspondence files, Anslinger papers, directed to Assistant Secretary of the Treasury Gaston, January 14, 1942, and May 2, 1942. The correspondence files for 1942–45 contain many letters from physicians maintaining addicts, often family members, who were apprehensive that there would not be enough supplies of opiates during the war.

84. W. T. McCarthy, "A Prosecutor's Viewpoint on Narcotic Addiction," *Federal Probation* 7 (October 1943): 23–27.

85. Wallace Werble, "Waco Was a Barbiturate Hot Spot," *Hygeia* 23 (June 1945): 432–33; New York *Times,* February 13, 1943.

86. "Shortages of Narcotics Decreases Addiction," *Science News Letter* 42 (August 8, 1942): 83; "Dupe Cure for Dopes," *Time* 40 (August 24, 1942): 52; "What's Cooking," *Newsweek* 25 (April 9, 1945): 99.

87. New York *Times,* January 27, 1942. See also his remarks in "The Japanese and Illicit Opium Traffic," *JAMA* 118 (February 28, 1942): 736, and his article, "Opium After the War," *Prison World* 6 (May 1944): 10, 28–29, and *The Traffic in Narcotics,* pp. 54–55.

88. New York *Times,* November 8, 1944.

89. Ibid., June 24, 1946.

90. Ibid., October 19, 1945.

91. Gerard Piel, "Narcotics: War Has Brought Illicit Traffic to All-time Low," *Life* 15 (July 19, 1943): 82–94; I.B. Levitch, "Drug Addiction," *American Druggist* 112 (January 1945): 66–67; Harris Isbell, "The Changing Face of Drug Dependence," *Problems of Drug Dependence* (Washington: National Academy of Sciences, 1975), pp. 21–29.

92. Anslinger to Charles B. Dyar, April 1, 1947, correspondence files, Anslinger papers.

93. Anslinger to Francis X. DiLucia, October 7, 1947, ibid., says "Traffic from the Far East has not opened but you can be sure it will develop very soon." Bureau agents in Iran and Turkey wrote reports on the opium situation there and in Marseilles; see George H. White to Anslinger, June 10, 1948, and Garland Williams to Anslinger, February 1, 1949, with travel diary enclosed dating from January 21, 1949 to February 20, 1949, all ibid.

94. Edward J. Mowery, "The Dope Menace and Our Children," *Catholic Digest* 16 (October 1952): 44–48 is by a New York City reporter who began writing on drugs and adolescents in early 1950. James R. Dumpson, et al., "Gangs and Narcotic Problems of Teen-age Youth," *American Journal of Psychotherapy* 6 (April 1952): 312–46 notes that work with adolescent gangs and the drug problem began in the summer of 1950 in New York City.

95. The reporting in *Newsweek* gives a good sense of the scare's development; see, "Dopers' Decline," ibid., 32 (December 20, 1948): 42, which thinks the problem dead, to "Narcotics and Youth," ibid., 36 (November 20, 1950): 57–58; "New York Wakes Up to Find 15,000 Teen-age Addicts," ibid., 37 (January 29, 1951): 23–24, "Heroin and Hot Shots," ibid., 38 (July 9, 1951): 23, "Heroin and Adolescents," ibid., 38 (August 13, 1951): 50–51, and "Narcotics and Youth," ibid., 38 (November 20, 1951): 57–58, which has the quotation. See also Herbert Brean, "Children in Peril," *Life* 30 (June 11, 1951): 116–26.

96. Anslinger to Edward Norton, August 7, 1951, correspondence files, Anslinger papers.

97. See Kolb, *Drug Addiction*, p. 6; Oakley S. Ray, ed., *Drugs, Society and Human Behavior* (St. Louis: C. V. Mosby, 1972), p. 192; Hughes, "The American Medical Profession and the Narcotics Policy Controversy," pp. 79–81; Robert W. Rasor, "The USPHS Institutional Treatment Program for Narcotics Addicts in Lexington, Kentucky," in Brill and Lieberman, *Major Modalities in the Treatment of Drug Abuse*, pp. 10–15.

98. See R. K. McNickle, "Drug Addiction," *Editorial Research Reports* (March 28, 1951), pp. 221–37; "New York's Children Accuse," *Life* 30 (June 25, 1951): 21–25; "Teacher's Nightmare," *Time* 58 (December 3, 1951): 23; L. Higgins, "The Menace of Narcotics," *Catholic Mind* 50 (July 1952): 429–36; David P. Ausubel, "An Evaluation of Recent Adolescent Drug Addiction," *Mental Hygiene* 36 (July 1952): 373–82; W. McClain, "It's Quite a Problem," *Extension* 47 (November 1952): 55; Elizabeth L. Wheeler, "Facts About Drug Addiction," *National Education Association Journal* 42 (March 1953): 142–43; Isidor Chein and Eva Rosenfield, "Juvenile Narcotic Use," *Law and Contemporary Problems* 22 (Winter 1957): 52–68.

99. New York *Times*, February 15, 1951.

100. McNickle, "Drug Addiction," pp. 221–37, quoting the district attorney of New York City.

101. "True Drug Addicts," *Science Digest* (November 1952): 33–34.

102. Anslinger to Louis B. Mayer, August 25, 1948, October 12, 1948, with memoranda, correspondence files, Anslinger papers, indicate that the bureau monitored movie stars, and feared that as examples to the young they might make drug use popular. "Marines and Marihuana," *Newsweek* 38 (December 21, 1951): 17, discusses the availability of drugs at Camp Pendleton, a Marine base in southern California, and allies them with illicit sex, and Mexicans, since the base is near Tijuana. Lila Leeds and Bill Fay, "Narcotics Ruined Me," *Colliers* 130 (July 26, 1952): 22–24, recounts part of the story around the arrest of the actor Robert Mitchum for possessing marihuana, a celebrated scandal of the early 1950s. Allen Geller and Maxwell Boas, *The Drug Beat* (New York: Cowles Books, 1971), pp. 28–30, and Michael Harrington, *Fragments of the Century* (New York: Dutton, 1973), are typical reports of marihuana use among intellectuals and bohemians. Ann Charters, *Kerouac: A Biography* (San Francisco: Straight Arrow Books, 1973), gives a good sense of the Beat community, as does James A. Inciardi, "Patterns of Drug Use Among Village 'Beats': A Research Note," *International Journal of the Addictions* 7 (Winter 1972): 649–53.

103. Rowell, *On the Trail of Marihuana*, pp. 69–73, suggested in 1939 that marihuana use would rise as cigarette smoking became more acceptable, and even glamorous. He also suggested that the underworld organization would take

over distribution, and that marihuana could not be controlled if it ever did become popular. There are similar views in Williams, *Drug Addicts Are Human Beings*, p. 214, written in 1938.

104. The report is reprinted conveniently in David Solomon, ed., *The Marihuana Papers* (New York: Bobbs, Merrill, 1966).

105. The AMA views are in "Marihuana Problems," *JAMA* 127 (April 28, 1945): 1129. The Anslinger quotation is from *The Traffic in Narcotics*, p. 19. See also Victor H. Vogel, "Our Youth and Narcotics," *Today's Health* 29 (October 1951): 24–25, 68–71, an expert who held that "Most youthful addicts start by smoking marihuana cigarettes, which causes a form of intoxication popular among maladjusted or idle adolescents." A popular journal noted for its sense of sophistication reported much the same: "Most dope addicts begin on marihuana, which, though rarely habit-forming, is very apt to lure users of it on to deadlier drugs." "Saw-Toothed," *New Yorker* 27 (August 11, 1951): 18–19. "'High and Light,'" *Time* 57 (February 26, 1951): 24–25 holds that users graduate to heroin. Wukasch, "Marijuana and the Law," p. 77, notes the firm identification of marihuana with street crime, delinquency, and opiates.

106. See William Butler Eldridge, *Narcotics and the Law*, 2nd ed. (Chicago: University of Chicago Press, 1967), pp. 49–103; King, *The Drug Hang-up*, pp. 89–90, 146–48.

107. For early changes in this viewpoint, see John J. McLaughlin and William H. Haines, "Drug Addiction in Chicago," *Illinois Medical Journal* 101 (February 1952): 77, and Howard S. Becker, "Becoming a Marihuana User," *American Journal of Sociology* 59 (November 1953): 235–42.

108. Albert B. Southwick, "Treating Narcotics Addiction," *Christian Century* 76 (December 16, 1959): 1467–68.

109. Kolb, "Let's Stop This Narcotics Hysteria!" p. 55.

8 – A NEW PROBLEM

1. Hughes, "The American Medical Profession and the Narcotics Policy Controversy," pp. 233–34.

2. See Dan Rosen, "Britain Gives a Fix to Its Addict," *National Observer* 11 (January 22, 1972): 1, 18; Horace Freeland Judson, *Heroin Addiction in Britain* (New York: Random House, 1975), p. 13.

3. See for example, "Writing-Off Narcotics Addicts," *Social Justice Review* 48, (October 1955): 241.

4. "Council on Mental Health, Narcotics and Medical Practice," *JAMA* 185 (September 21, 1963): 976–82, and the editorial comment, "Medical Ethics, Narcotics, and Addicts," ibid., 185 (September 21, 1963): 962–63.

5. For the methadone story see Harris Isbell and Victor H. Vogel, "The Addiction Liability of Methadone," *American Journal of Psychiatry* 105 (June 1949): 909–914; Kolb, *Drug Addiction*, pp. 132–33; Nathan B. Eddy, "The History of the Development of Narcotics," *Law and Contemporary Problems* 22 (Winter 1957): 6–7; Marie Nyswander, *The Drug Addict as a Patient* (New York: Grune and Stratton, 1956); Platt and Labate, *Heroin Addiction*, pp.

260–307; the articles in *International Journal of the Addictions* 5 (September 1970); King, *The Drug Hang-up*, pp. 257–260; Musto, *The American Disease*, pp. 237–40; Dorothy Nelkin, *Methadone Maintenance* (New York: Braziller, 1973).

6. See William Burroughs, "Kicking Drugs: A Very Personal Story," *Harper's Magazine* 235 (July 1967): 39–42; Ashley, *Heroin*, pp. 39, 170, 185–201; James V. De Long, "The Methadone Habit," *New York Times Magazine*, March 16, 1975, pp. 16–17, 78–79, 86–87, 90–91; "The Methadone Jones," *Newsweek* 89 (February 7, 1977): 29.

7. See "Synanon House, Where Drug Addicts Join to Salvage Their Lives," *Life* 52 (March 9, 1962): 52–65; Lewis Yablonsky, *The Tunnel Back* (New York: Macmillan, 1965): Daniel Casriel and Grover Amen, *Daytop: Three Addicts and Their Cure* (New York: Hill and Wang, 1971): Richard E. Hardy and John G. Cull, eds., *Drug Dependence and Rehabilitation Approaches* (Springfield, Ill.: Charles C. Thomas, 1973); Barry Sugarman, *Daytop Village: A Therapeutic Community* (New York: Holt, Rinehart, 1974); Robert H. Coombs, ed., *Junkies and Straights: The Camarillo Experience* (Lexington, Mass.: D. C. Heath, 1975); Grover Sales, *John Maher of Delancey Street* (New York: Norton, 1976).

8. See the chart depicting public opinion and its view of the relation of heroin and marihuana use to crime in National Commission on Marihuana and Drug Abuse, *Drug Use in America: A Problem in Perspective* (Washington: GPO, 1973), pp. 154–55.

9. New York *Times*, March 29, 1970.

10. Ibid., May 16 and September 12, 1971.

11. Platt and Labate, *Heroin*, p. 327.

12. See "Heroin Crisis Ending? Signs Point That Way," *Medical World News*, April 13, 1973; and Robert L. DuPont, "The Rise and Fall of Heroin Addiction," *Natural History* 83 (June–July 1974): 66–71.

13. National Commission on Marihuana and Drug Abuse, *Drug Use in America*, pp. 218–19.

14. Lester Grinspoon and James Bakalar, *Cocaine* (New York: Basic Books, 1976); and Ann Crittenden and Michael Ruby, "Cocaine: The Champagne of Drugs," *New York Times Magazine*, September 1, 1974, pp. 14–17. For two rather glossy accounts of the use of cocaine among swingers see Richard Rhodes, "A Very Expensive High," *Playboy* 22 (January 1975): 131, 170–72, 262–70, and Thomas Thompson, "Cocaine," *Playgirl* 3 (February 1976): 52, 112–14; and "The Cocaine Scene," *Newsweek* 89 (May 30, 1977): 20–25.

15. Brecher, *Licit and Illicit Drugs*, pp. 291–92.

16. See "Resolutions Against Promiscuous Use of Barbituric Acid and Derivative Drugs," *JAMA* 108 (June 26, 1937): 2215, 2225; W. E. Hambourger, "The Promiscuous Use of Barbiturates," ibid., 114 (May 18, 1940): 2015–19; S. W. Goldstein, "Barbiturates: A Blessing and a Menace," *Journal of the American Pharmaceutical Association* 36 (January 1947): 5–14; Robert W. Rasor, "The USPHS Institutional Treatment for Narcotics Addicts in Lexington, Kentucky," in Brill and Liberman, *Major Modalities in the Treatment of Drug Abuse*, p. 5. For the story of an unusual example of abuse see Charles E. Jackson, "The Amphetamine Inhaler: A Case of Medical Abuse," *Journal of the History of Medicine* 26 (April 1971): 187–96. In 1973 the National

Commission on Marihuana and Drug Abuse noted: "The Commission believes that barbiturate dependence may be the modern equivalent of the hidden opiate dependence of the late 19th Century." See their *Drug Use in America,* p. 144.

17. Ibid., p. 109.

18. "Happiness by Prescription," *Time* 69 (March 11, 1957): 59; and Ian Stevenson, "Tranquilizers and the Mind," *Harper's Magazine* 215 (June 1957): 21–27; R. W. Gerard, "Drugs for the Soul: The Rise of Psychopharmacology," *Science* 125 (February 1, 1957): 201–203; David L. Cowen, "The Role of the Pharmaceutical Industry," in John B. Blake, ed., *Safeguarding the Public: Historical Aspects of Medicinal Drug Control* (Baltimore: Johns Hopkins University Press, 1970), pp. 76–77; Ray, *Drugs, Society and Human Behavior,* p. 3; Charles E. Goshen, *Drinks, Drugs and Do-Gooders* (New York: Free Press, 1973), pp. 133–35, 164–65.

19. Walter Bromberg to Lawrence Kolb, May 11, 1945, Kolb papers. Ausubel, *Drug Addiction,* pp. 92–98, repeats the conventional wisdom as of 1958. Kolb, *Drug Addiction,* p. 5, sees marihuana as nonaddictive but as affecting will and volition. Betsy M. Silverman, "The Menace of Dope," *Parents Magazine and Better Housekeeping* 37 (October 1962): 82–83, 126–34 is a typical popular account that notes that young people seem increasingly bewildered and alienated and likely to turn to marihuana for release of tension, but does not see marihuana as causing severe emotional problems. Lindesmith, *The Addict and the Law,* pp. 241–42, suggests that marihuana smoking will increase markedly at the end of the Sixties.

20. National Commission on Marihuana and Drug Abuse, *Marihuana: A Signal of Misunderstanding* (Washington: GPO, 1972), pp. 8–9.

21. Ibid., pp. 16–22.

22. *Wall Street Journal,* August 20, 1969.

23. Norman E. Zinberg and John A. Robertson, *Drugs and the Public* (New York: Simon and Schuster, 1972), pp. 29–30.

24. National Commission on Marihuana and Drug Abuse, *Marihuana: A Signal of Misunderstanding,* pp. 103, 124–25.

25. Brecher, *Licit and Illicit Drugs,* p. 421.

26. National Commission on Marihuana and Drug Abuse, *Marihuana: A Signal of Misunderstanding,* pp. 128–77.

27. Aldous Huxley, *The Doors of Perception* (New York: Harper, 1954); Walter Bromberg, "More on Mescalin," *Saturday Review of Literature* 37 (March 6, 1954): 24; and also Edward Anderson, *Peyote: The Sacred Cactus* (Tucson: University of Arizona Press, 1980).

28. See the interesting comments in Martin Lawley, *The Private Future* (New York: Random House, 1974), p. 200.

29. "Artificial Psychoses," *Time* 66 (December 19, 1955): 60–63; Brecher, *Licit and Illicit Drugs,* pp. 346–48.

30. Arnold M. Ludwig and Jerome Levine," Patterns of Hallucinogenic Drug Abuse," *JAMA* 191 (January 11, 1965): 93.

31. National Commission on Marihuana and Drug Abuse, *Drug Use in America,* pp. 79, 176.

32. Surely the most bizarre substance experimented with was plastic explo-

sives, whose ingestion gave a few soldiers a high, but with the risk of death from overdose; see James H. Knepshield and William J. Stone, "Toxic Effects Following Ingestion of C-4 Plastic Explosive," in Wolfram Keup, ed., *Drug Abuse: Current Concepts and Research* (Springfield, Ill.: Charles C. Thomas, 1972), pp. 296–301.

33. See Carl D. Chambers and Richard D. Heckman, *Employee Drug Abuse: A Manager's Guide for Action* (Boston: Cahner's, 1972); Susan Halpern, *Drug Abuse and Your Company* (n.p.: American Management Assn., 1972); Harrison M. Trice, and Paul M. Roman, *Spirits and Demons at Work: Alcohol and Other Drugs on the Job* (Ithaca: Cornell University Press, 1972); Jordan M. Scher, *Drug Abuse in Industry: Growing Corporate Dilemma* (Springfield, Ill.: Charles C. Thomas, 1973); Studs Terkel, *Working* (New York: Pantheon, 1974), pp. 172, 193, 210.

34. Richard H. Blum et al., *The Dream Sellers* (San Francisco: Jossey-Blass, 1972), p. 264; Goshen, *Drinks, Drugs and Do-Gooders*, p. 128; Peter Joseph, *Good Times: An Oral History of America in the 1960s* (New York: Morrow, 1974), pp. 76–77, 138.

35. E. V. Taylor, "Heroin and the Black Community," *American Scholar* 40 (August 1971): 691–94.

36. Ronald Bayer, "Liberal Opinion and the Problem of Heroin Addiction: 1960–1973," *Contemporary Drug Problems* 4 (Spring 1975): 93–112.

BIBLIOGRAPHICAL ESSAY

HE NOTES reveal my principal sources, and although voluminous they are only a sample of the material I studied. They complement the text, since I have arranged citations within each note chronologically to show the development of various opinions on the subject noted. I also use material from different regions to show how widely information spread through the medical and popular literature, especially in the nineteenth century. The information in many of these citations is much broader in its social implications than the titles may suggest. This is especially true of medical literature in the nineteenth century, which was less technical and specialized than its counterpart in the twentieth century. Many authors, for instance, in medical articles report on informal surveys of patients, families, and communities, which give some insight into social attitudes.

The medical literature is a mine of information for the social historian. Medicine is a social enterprise, susceptible to public opinion and the climate of its time. The theories about disease origins, and methods of treatment have social as well as scientific implications. In the last hundred years at least, every major social problem has produced a body of expertise that involves medicine, psychology, the social sciences, and public health. No student of women's history, communicable diseases, sexual attitudes and practices, drug use, alcoholism, and many other social issues can ignore the medical literature. Gerald N. Grob, "The Social History of Medicine and Disease in America: Problems and Possibilities," *Journal of Social History* 10 (June 1977): 391–401, is a good introduction to the possible uses of this material outside of formal medical history.

The views of the medical profession about both drug use and its social role are important. Rosemary Stevens, *American Medicine and the Public Interest* (New Haven: Yale University Press, 1971), focuses on medicine's general relationship to society and is helpful for understanding social problems.

William G. Rothstein, *American Physicians in the Nineteenth Century: From Sects to Science* (Baltimore: Johns Hopkins University Press, 1973), is an insightful study of internal changes in the medical profession that had social results. Morris J. Vogel and Charles E. Rosenberg, eds., *The Therapeutic Revolution: Essays in the Social History of American Medicine* (Philadelphia: University of Pennsylvania Press, 1979), is a collection of original essays devoted to changing therapies and ideas within the medical professions. Arnold Jaffe, "Addiction Reform in the Progressive Age: Scientific and Social Responses to Drug Dependence in the United States, 1870–1930," (Ph.D. diss., University of Kentucky, 1976), has information on treatment, the medical profession's roles and attitudes, and the development of scientific knowledge about drug use in that period. James Walker Hughes, "The American Medical Profession and the Narcotics Policy Controversy," (Ph.D. diss., Indiana University, 1967), deals mainly with the 1950s and 1960s, and focuses on the effort to alter the medical profession's attitude toward drug use while changing the law enforcement system. The outlines of the attitudes of the medical and scientific communities toward drug use are clear, but a general interpretative study based on a fresh reading of primary sources for the entire period since 1800 is in order.

The medical profession's relation to cure and treatment programs also needs careful study. Figures such as J. B. Mattison, Thomas D. Crothers, George E. Pettey, and Lawrence Kolb, to mention only a few, merit study. The role of the federal health bureaucracy in shaping both attitudes and procedures through research and theory is important. A study of the U.S. Public Health Service Narcotic Farms in Lexington and Fort Worth would be useful.

There is no really comprehensive history of drug use in America. Brian Inglis, *The Forbidden Game: A Social History of Drugs* (New York: Scribner's, 1975), is worldwide in scope, and though general, has many insights that apply to the American situation. John Rublowsky, *The Stoned Age: A History of Drugs in America* (New York: Putnam's, 1975), is superficial but has some useful information.

Drug use and social responses to it are ideal subjects for comparative studies. It would be interesting to know the similarities and differences in the history of the subjects in industrializing countries such as Austria, Germany, France, and Italy. There are some suggestive studies of the opium problem in Great Britain. Elizabeth Lomax, "The Uses and Abuses of Opiates in Nineteenth Century England," *Bulletin of the History of Medicine* 47 (March–April 1973): 167–76, deals chiefly with the substances used and their perceived impact on public health. Virginia Berridge, "Victorian Opium Eating: Responses to Opiate Use in Nineteenth-Century England," *Victorian Studies* 21 (Summer 1978): 25–36, is broader and focuses on users and the role of social pressures and medical professionalization in shaping broader public attitudes against opiate use. The same author's "Opium in the Fens in Nineteenth-Century England," *Journal of the History of Medicine* 34 (July 1979): 293–313, is a case study of opium use in a marshy, rural area that was prey to fevers, and of the kinds of users and the responses to them. Studies of drug use in nations such as Egypt, Turkey, or Mexico would doubtless illuminate many contrasting patterns of social approval and disapproval based on ideals of traditionalism or modernism.

Some of these points are covered tangentially in studies of efforts to control the international narcotics traffic. Jack Bruce Thomas, "An Introduction to Some Socio-cultural Factors Influencing the Role of the United States in International Narcotics Control, 1833–1920," (Ph.D. diss., Indiana University, 1959), is useful. Arnold H. Taylor, *American Diplomacy and the Narcotics Traffic, 1900–1939* (Durham: Duke University Press, 1969), is a magisterial survey that focuses on formal diplomacy but has many insights applicable to the social aspects of the issue. Kettil Bruun et al., *The Gentlemen's Club: International Control of Drugs and Alcohol* (Chicago: University of Chicago Press, 1976), continues the story for the 1950s and 1960s. William O. Walker, "The Politics of Drug Control: The United States and Latin America, 1900–1945," (Ph.D. diss., University of California, Santa Barbara, 1974), is a good survey.

Domestic efforts at narcotic control are covered exhaustively in David F. Musto, *The American Disease: Origins of Narcotic Control* (New Haven: Yale University Press, 1973). Musto's book details far more, however, than the story of regulation at state and federal levels. It touches on most aspects of the drug question, even though its focus remains on regulation, and is an outstanding work. Rufus King, *The Drug Hang-up: America's Fifty Year Folly* (New York: Norton, 1972), is a sustained and often shrill attack on law enforcement but contains useful information relating to law-making, medical attitudes, and the process of enforcement. William Butler Eldridge, *Narcotics and the Law: A Critique of the American Experiment in Narcotic Drug Control,* 2nd ed. (Chicago: University of Chicago Press, 1967), is a historical source for the effort to replace law and punishment with medical and psychiatric therapies that is still valuable. James A. Inciardi and Carl D. Chambers, eds., *Drugs and the Criminal Justice System* (Beverly Hills: Sage, 1974), offers a good cross section of opinion and analysis. In some ways, as is so often the case in history, the most interesting account of law enforcement is from an insider, Maurice Helbrant, *Narcotic Agent* (New York: Vanguard Press, 1941).

The story of regulation is fairly well known, but case studies of its development on the local level are needed. Once again, the comparative approach would be interesting. Comparing drug use in various rural areas, such as upstate New York or New England with parts of the South or Midwest would enhance the national story. The same is true of urban studies. It would be interesting to know if the pattern of drugs used and of users varied in Boston, Atlanta, Kansas City, and Los Angeles in a given period of time. Studies of New York City and Chicago may have overemphasized certain kinds of users. This inevitably would involve more than the use of statistics, since they accumulated only after regulation made drug sales and use illegal.

The efforts to devise theoretical explanations for the origins of drug use deserve a careful study. Nineteenth-century observers tended to seek explanations rooted in physiology, but they always allowed for the play of individual psychology and temperament. In the twentieth century, most explanations have focused on psychological or sociological factors. None is fully satisfactory. All are inevitably open-ended and tend to become flexible when they result in therapeutic practice. The psychological model that identified drug use with delinquency and crime was attractive because delinquents and criminals seemed to use drugs, a circular problem that no theory ever really overcomes. The sociological view so popular in the 1950s and after that drug use resulted from racism, poverty, and thwarted ambitions among marginal groups failed to explain why all members of these groups did not employ drugs, and why affluent members of society did so. The root causes clearly vary in individuals and are not dependent solely on external environmental factors. These theories are not properly predictive; at most they suggest tendencies and likelihoods.

Hamilton Cravens and John C. Burnham, "Psychology and Evolutionary Naturalism in American Thought, 1890–1940," *American Quarterly* 23 (December 1971): 635–57, offers good general background. Arnold Jaffe, "Reform in American Medical Science: The Inebriety Movement and the Origins of the Psychological Disease Theory of Addiction, 1870–1920," *British Journal of Addiction* 73 (June 1978): 139–47 is a basic source for the subject. Joseph R. Gusfield, "The Futility of Knowledge? The Relation of Social Science to Public Policy Toward Drugs," *Annals of the American Academy of Political and Social Sciences* 417 (January 1975): 1–15, is also helpful. Chaman Nahal, ed., *Drugs and the Other Self* (New York: Harper and Row, 1971), gives some varied insights into psychology and drug use. The Group for the Advancement of Psychiatry, *Drug Misuse: A Psychiatric View of a Modern Dilemma* (New York: Scribner's, 1971), remains important. Leon Wurmser, "Drug Abuse: Nemesis of Psychiatry," *American Scholar* 41 (Summer 1972): 393–407, is an elegant, persuasive and clearly written statement of the psychoanalytical approach to drug use. I could cite many other sources, but the student of this complex subject, and of the varied therapies the theories produced, must return to the primary materials with a fresh eye for irony, the vagaries of social change, and the limits of expertise to do the subject justice. One other source merits notice, though it is not purely psychological in its approach. Alethea Hayter, *Opium and the Romantic Imagination* (Berkeley: University of California Press, 1968), treats the use of opium among writers of the eighteenth and nineteenth centuries. It is evocative, brilliantly written, and studded with striking insights for the social historian.

There are numerous studies of the specific substances employed in drug use. Why society changes its views of them periodically, and why the states they produce are attractive at one time and not another are questions related to social change, demography, and communication. Opiates have aroused the most controversy for the longest period of time. In many ways, Charles E. Terry and Mildred Pellens, *The Opium Problem* (New York: Bureau of Social Hygiene, 1928), remains a classic study. This impressive work attempted to survey the literature relating to opium as of the mid-1920s, and its abstracts remain invaluable. The authors' comments on causes and treatments of addiction, the limits of social policies, and the nature of legal regulation are also important. David F.

Musto, "Early History of Heroin in the United States," in Peter G. Bourne, ed., *Addiction* (New York: Academic Press, 1974), pp. 175–85, is invaluable, as are the portions of his book *The American Disease* that deal with heroin. Jerome J. Platt and Christina Labate, *Heroin Addiction: Theory, Research, and Treatment* (New York: Wiley, 1976), is a comprehensive study of current knowledge and theory about heroin. Richard Ashley, *Heroin: The Myths and the Facts* (New York: St. Martin's, 1972), is an assault on legal controls and social punishment of addicts and is often shrill or naive, but contains interesting information.

David T. Courtwright, "Opiate Addiction in America, 1800–1940," (Ph.D. diss., Rice University, 1979), is a valuable study in demography and epidemiology. It is also useful for attitudes in the medical profession, treatment, and the drive for and against law enforcement. In addition, several technical works contain a good deal of information useful to the social historian. Wolfram Keup, ed, *Drug Abuse: Current Concepts and Research* (Springfield, Ill.: Charles C. Thomas, 1972), has articles on comparative aspects of drug abuse in several countries, information on epidemiology, treatment and causes, as well as more technical subjects. John G. Cull and Richard E. Hardy, eds, *Types of Drug Abusers and Their Abuses* (Springfield, Ill.: Charles C. Thomas, 1970), is valuable for the focus on the people involved in drug use.

Cocaine is dealt with in several books. Lester Grinspoon and James B. Bakalar, *Cocaine* (New York: Basic, 1976), is a good survey of cocaine's history, therapeutic uses, and role in the drug abuse controversy. Richard Ashley, *Cocaine: Its History, Uses and Effects* (New York: St. Martin's, 1975), argues against legal control and social disapproval. Robert Byck, ed., *Cocaine Papers by Sigmund Freud* (New York: Stonehill, 1974), and George Andrews and David Solomon, eds., *The Coca Leaf and Cocaine Papers* (New York: Harcourt, Brace, 1975), are both valuable collections of primary materials relating to the controversy over cocaine, especially for the nineteenth century. Dennis J. Helms et al., "Cocaine: Some Observations on Its History, Legal Classification and Pharmacology," *Contemporary Drug Problems* 4 (Summer 1975): 195–216, is important.

The controversy over marihuana has produced a large literature. The most important book for the historian is Richard J. Bonnie and Charles H. Whitebread II, *The Marihuana Conviction: A History of Marihuana Prohibition in the United States* (Charlottesville: University of Virginia Press, 1974). This work focuses on the movement to control marihuana but summarizes very well other aspects of its history in the American drug debate. David Solomon, ed., *The Marihuana Papers* (New York: Bobbs-Merrill, 1966), is an excellent collection of materials relating to marihuana in history. Vera Rubin, ed., *Cannabis and Culture* (The Hague: Mouton, 1975), surveys its history, use, and social impacts in numerous countries. John Kaplan, *Marihuana–The New Prohibition* (New York: World, 1970), and Lester Grinspoon, *Marihuana Reconsidered* (Cambridge: Harvard University Press, 1971), summarize much existing knowledge and generally favor relaxing restrictions against marihuana use. William Novak, *High Culture: Marihuana and the Lives of Americans* (New York: Knopf, 1980), details the controversy over marihuana's effects and the expectations people have of its use, and contains other useful material. M. D. Merlon, *Man and Marihuana* (Rutherford, N.J.: Fairleigh Dickinson University Press, 1972), and Jack H. Mendelson, *The Use of Marihuana: A Psychological and Physiological Inquiry* (New York: Plenum, 1974), are significant. Robert G. Shepherd, "Science, Social Issues, and the Popular Press: An Investigation of the Marijuana Controversy," (Ph.D. diss., State University of New York, Stony Brook, 1976), contains information on professional and public opinion. Gabriel Nahas, *Marihuana, Deceptive Weed* (New York: Raven Press, 1973), is typical of the experts who remain skeptical about marihuana's alleged harmlessness.

Studies of amphetamines tend to be very technical, but the following are useful to the social historian: Chauncey Leake, *The Amphetamines* (Springfield, Ill.: Charles C. Thomas, 1959); Robert J. Russo, *Amphetamine Abuse* (Springfield, Ill.: Charles C. Thomas, 1972); and Lester Grinspoon and Peter Hedbloom, *The Speed Culture: Amphetamine Use and Abuse in America* (Cambridge: Harvard University Press, 1975), which is a basic work.

The so-called hallucinogens, especially LSD, created very sharp controversy both among users and critics in the 1960s and 1970s. Users seemed certain that these substances offered alternate life styles and insights to the ones they rejected in the material world. Critics took an equally strong stand that the substances posed great psychological threats, especially to young and immature minds, and were merely escapist rather than creative. John Cashman, *The LSD Story* (Greenwich, Ct.: Fawcett, 1966), A. Hoffer and H. Osmond, *The Hallucinogens* (New York: Academic Press, 1967), Maurice S. Tarshis, *The LSD Controversy: An Overview* (Springfield, Ill.: Charles C. Thomas, 1972), and Brian Wells, *Psychedelic Drugs* (New York: Jason Aronson, 1974), all offer some kind of perspective on these substances. W. V. Caldwell, *LSD Psychotherapy* (New York: Grove, 1968), discusses the use of LSD in psychiatry. David Solomon, ed., *LSD: The Consciousness Expanding Drug* (New York: Putnam's, 1964), Charles T. Tart, *Altered States of Consciousness* (New York: Doubleday, 1972), and R. C. Zaehner, *Zen, Drugs and Mysticism* (New York: Pantheon, 1973), all focus on the alleged mystical or mind-expanding aspects of the substances involved. Lester Grinspoon and James B. Bakalar, *Psychedelic Drugs Reconsidered* (New York: Basic, 1979), surveys the literature and discusses most aspects of the problem.

There is a wealth of sociological inquiry on drug users. A classic study that focuses on why society treats drug users as outsiders is Howard S. Becker, *The Outsiders: Studies in the Sociology of Deviance* (New York: Free Press, 1963). The same author's "History, Culture and Subjective Experience: An Exploration of the Social Bases of Drug-Induced Experience," *Journal of Health and Social Behavior* 8 (September 1967): 163–76 is also important. It is impossible to remain current in gauging social attitudes, but the following works take some kind of overview of the relationships of the drug user and the larger society: Richard H. Blum et al., *Society and Drugs* (San Francisco: Jossey-Blass, 1969); Nils Bejerot, *Addiction and Society* (Springfield, Ill.: Charles C. Thomas, 1970); Erich Goode, *Drugs in American Society* (New York: Knopf, 1972); Oakley S. Ray, *Drugs, Society and Human Behavior* (St. Louis: C. V.

Mosby, 1972); Norman E. Zinberg and John A. Robertson, *Drugs and the Public* (New York: Simon and Schuster, 1972); Richard H. Blum et al., *The Dream Sellers* (San Francisco: Jossey-Blass, 1972); Erich Goode, *The Drug Phenomenon: Social Aspects of Drug Taking* (New York: Bobbs-Merrill, 1973); and Philip Bean, *The Social Control of Drugs* (New York: Wiley, 1974). Troy Duster, *The Legislation of Morality: Law, Drugs and Moral Judgement* (New York: Free Press, 1970), discusses some important questions about social and individual rights. John Helmer, *Drugs and Minority Oppression* (New York: Seabury, 1975), is a good summary of the idea that the majority's antidrug bias is rooted in racism and hostility to minorities.

The writing on drugs and young people has been extensive. College students naturally figured in many accounts, such as James T. Carey, *The College Drug Scene* (Englewood Cliffs, N.J.: Prentice-Hall, 1968), Richard H. Blum et al., *Students and Drugs* (San Francisco: Jossey-Bass, 1969), and Helen H. Nowlis, *Drugs on the College Campus* (New York: Doubleday, 1969). Other elements of the youth population are discussed in Joseph H. Brenner et al., *Drugs and Youth* (New York: Liveright, 1970); John H. McGrath and Frank R. Scarpitti, *Youth and Drugs* (Glenview, Ill.: Scott, Foresman, 1970); Richard H. Blum et al., *Horatio Alger's Children* (San Francisco: Jossey-Bass, 1972); and Ernest Harms, *Drugs and Youth* (New York: Pergamon, 1973). Walter Cusket et al., *Drug-Trip Abroad: American Drug Refugees in Amsterdam and London* (Philadelphia: University of Pennsylvania Press, 1972), is an interesting account of the international ramifications of drug use, and of the view some Europeans had of the "American Problem." Nat Hentoff, *A Doctor Among the Addicts* (New York: Grove Press, 1968), and Alan Geller and Maxwell Boas, *The Drug Beat* (New York: Cowles, 1971), are interesting accounts of life inside the drug world, especially relating to heroin. Drug Abuse Council, *The Facts About "Drug Abuse"* (New York: Free Press, 1980), is a good summary of most aspects of the drug debate at the present moment.

The controversy over drug use and misuse will continue, and attitudes and tastes will undergo cyclical changes as they have for a hundred years. A wealth of writing and comment continues at present but has begun to resemble that of the postprogressive years earlier in this century. The special pleading one way or another becomes ever more strident and overstated, and the scientific and theoretical literature becomes ever more narrow and obscure. Both the citizen and scholar trying to understand the question need a better sense of history in order to see why emphases change cyclically, what the issue represents in American life, and why it seems so intractable.

INDEX

DRUGS IN AMERICA

was composed in 10-point VIP Times Roman and leaded two points, with display type in Egyptian Bold and Egyptian Bold Condensed, by Partners Composition; printed on 55-pound, acid-free Glatfelter Antique Cream, Smythe-sewn and bound over boards in Joanna Arrestox C, by Maple-Vail Book Manufacturing Group, Inc.; and published by

SYRACUSE UNIVERSITY PRESS
SYRACUSE, NEW YORK 13210